I0126448

A Civil Society Deferred

University Press of Florida

Florida A&M University, Tallahassee
Florida Atlantic University, Boca Raton
Florida Gulf Coast University, Ft. Myers
Florida International University, Miami
Florida State University, Tallahassee
New College of Florida, Sarasota
University of Central Florida, Orlando
University of Florida, Gainesville
University of North Florida, Jacksonville
University of South Florida, Tampa
University of West Florida, Pensacola

A Civil Society Deferred

The Tertiary Grip of Violence in the Sudan

Abdullahi A. Gallab

University Press of Florida
Gainesville · Tallahassee · Tampa · Boca Raton
Pensacola · Orlando · Miami · Jacksonville · Ft. Myers · Sarasota

Printed in the United States of America. This book is printed on Glatfelter Natures Book, a paper certified under the standards of the Forestry Stewardship Council (FSC). It is a recycled stock that contains 30 percent post-consumer waste and is acid-free.

First cloth printing, 2011
First paperback printing, 2013

Library of Congress Cataloging-in-Publication Data
Gallab, Abdullahi A.
A civil society deferred : the tertiary grip of violence in the Sudan / Abdullahi A. Gallab.
p. cm.
Includes bibliographical references and index.
ISBN 978-0-8130-3688-5 (cloth: alk. paper)
ISBN 978-0-8130-4446-0 (pbk.)
1. Violence—Sudan. 2. Sudan—Politics and government. I. Title.
HM886.G35 2011
303.6'40962409045—dc22 2011011181

The University Press of Florida is the scholarly publishing agency for the State University System of Florida, comprising Florida A&M University, Florida Atlantic University, Florida Gulf Coast University, Florida International University, Florida State University, New College of Florida, University of Central Florida, University of Florida, University of North Florida, University of South Florida, and University of West Florida.

University Press of Florida
15 Northwest 15th Street
Gainesville, FL 32611-2079
http://www.upf.com

To my wife, Souad, and our children, Ahmed, Azza, and Shiraz,
the best life can give.

Contents

Preface

I know, of course, the Sudanese state. As a citizen, a journalist, a government employee, and a scholar, I have written extensively and shared ideas, criticism, and images with readers, scholars, other Sudanese, and non-Sudanese intellectuals and friends.

Yet perhaps we should first pose the question, how might one define the state? It is true that the language and the terminology that describes the state has changed over time and it is also true that past and different writers and scholars often used the word *state* in different ways. Both the historical and contemporary narratives and body of literature in the field are rich with details. Thinkers, philosophers, and scholars—from al-Farabi to al-Mawardi to Ibn Khaldun, Machiavelli, Hobbes, Locke, Rousseau, Karl Marx, Emile Durkheim, Max Weber, Antonio Gramsci, Michel Foucault, Anthony Giddens, Theda Skocpol, and others—have defined the state in different terms. But they all saw, with some variations, the state simply as a governing organization, an instrument, a tool or apparatus for the purpose of control, claiming formal political sovereignty over territories and exercising power and sometimes violence over the people inhabiting them. The state is a human-made creature manufactured as institutions of discipline and welfare; extraction and coercion; maker or breaker of social change. The state could be, as characterized by Max Weber, a legal-rational, or an illegal-irrational, or a benign entity assigned to serve the values, the needs, and the public norms of those who mandated it an authority. This authority is expected to be exercised within the public interest and the welfare of the communities upon whom that authority is to be exercised. Without oversimplifying the functioning of the state as a human construction and a governing organization for the purpose of control, or for the public good in terms of the improvement of public life and the advancement of social arrangements, the state originated independently in a number of times and places. In many places and in different times states were thrust at certain people only to make them suffer ferocious and unwelcome afflictions. The Sudan is one of these places, endowed with a rich history of all types and different experiences in this field that goes back to antiquity.

Some of these experiences have molded the Sudanese perceptions of the state more than others. Two experiences of invasion and expansion, dissimilar in their nature, means of violence, and consequences, left behind an enduring effect: the Turko-Egyptian and the British imperial systems of colonization, which can be traced back to the nineteenth century. In each one of these two experiences, the Sudanese resisted the colonial designs and tried "to carve out spheres of autonomy of their own."[1] Hence, the division of the Sudanese private sphere, which resisted those who hold power over them, versus the colonial public sphere, which used the state through different strategies of oppression and control, became a rudimentary factor to the limits of success, failure, and influence exercised by an emerging Sudanese civil society. But in all these experiences the relationship between the state and civil society remained an enigma. Civil society here is taken to mean "the social space large or constrained, as it is shaped by social forces,"[2] where diverse social movements "attempt to constitute themselves in an ensemble of arrangements so that they can express themselves and advance their interests."[3] The civil society can be, and through time has been, a source of the production of a self-regulating power. The Sudan has its history and experiences of such production of civil power. This civil power influenced the dynamics and conditions of peaceful and violent practices. Similarly, out of this civil power emerged regulatory institutions such as political parties and different associations. As the state in the Sudan during this era (precolonial, colonial, and postcolonial developments and their chains of events) was not differentiated from Sudanese society, violence and conflict between that state and civil society continued to create its different formations.

* * *

During my four years in London as a diplomat at the Sudanese embassy, I met with some of the surviving members of the Sudan's colonial civil service. Most were already old. We had long discussions and they were eager to share their memories. In London, I tried to capture the Sudanese experience within the visible, the recorded, and the remnants of the historical saga of imperialism. It was a heart of darkness in reverse. The best part of that journey was the encounter with diverse groups of intellectuals; the effects and aftereffects of the imperial experience had brought them together from different parts of the world into the heart of the former empire. It is true, as Edward Said has remarked, that "one of imperialism's achievements was to bring the world closer together, and although in the process the separation between Europeans and natives was an insidious and fundamentally unjust one, most of us should now regard the historical experience as a common one."[4] Common or not, however, the congregations of those intellectuals, which local and "overseas" institutions of learning produced, represent an important aspect of the postimperial experiences in one of the world's developing civil spheres. In terms of perspective, and within the most important intellectual endeavors of such an encounter, that discourse built on, contested, and sometimes went far beyond the arguments by John Atkinson Hobson about imperialism as "the most powerful movement in the current politics of the Western world."[5] It was the discourse set by a new breed of postcolonial intellectuals, chief among whom were Jean-Paul Sartre, Albert Memmi, Basil Davidson, Andre Gunder Frank, Samir Amin, Frantz Fanon, Anouar 'Abdel-Malek, Hamza Alavi, Walter Rodney, Fernando Henrique Cardoso, and Edward Said. In addition to all that, a new body of social science theories such as the Singer–Prebisch thesis, the dependency (or dependencia) theory, theories of development, world-systems theory, and neo-Marxist scholarship opened new ways of investigation and fields of enquiry for postcolonial scholarship, discourse, and studies. These trends and discourses also had to do with the Islamists and Arab and African socialist practices and theories of the state. Because of the complex and sometimes passionate feelings relating to the defeat of and the liberation from a number of isms—such as Nazism, fascism, and imperialism—and the fierce competition that followed between what, as a matter of generalization, was then called the East, the West, and the South, a diversified international discourse gained a distinctive tone. Within that discourse, the history and the development of the different modes of imperialism were not only acknowledged as a peculiar human experience but were also thoroughly debated within the course of the arguments of academic, intellectual, political, and journalistic discussions.

First, the economic impact of imperialism was as "profoundly unequal . . . [as] the relationship between metropoles and dependencies was highly asymmetrical."[6] Accordingly, "the impact of the first on the second was dramatic and decisive, even without actual occupation, whereas the impact of the second on the first might be negligible, and was hardly a matter of life or death."[7]

Second, as emerging postcolonial studies have investigated and argued the significance and the impact of the relationships among knowledge, power, and distance, along with the modes and manners of transmission of the colonial experience, the essence and condition of colonialism as a hegemonic, violent, and exploitive project became even clearer. Within that particular situation, knowledge relates to the creation of the concept and the imagined reality of the imperial core state, or "the 'Center' as the heartland of social and religious models of organized cosmic space and social and ideological life, and as the focal point for communication with the sacred."[8] At the same time, all that evolves into a dark side of imperialism that relates to the creation of the imagined and real periphery. In addition, modes of differentiation, the production of racism, and the construction of what Immanuel Wallerstein describes as peoplehood (belonging to a people: which is more than an ethnicity but less than a nation), through different forms and the exercise of violent means of control and exploitation, contributed to the colonial experience.

Third, through that experience, the comprehensions of the meanings of the geographical distance, and knowledge created and controlled by that experience, were removed from the field of the discourse. They were all appropriated and placed into the hands of the colonial-state workers where knowledge, the exercise of power, and violence were deeply connected.

Fourth, because the colonized could not accept the mode of colonization and its system of exploitation, resistance presented itself in different forms and representations, framing the discourse about a civic community as well as cultural and religious resources.

Fifth, as resistance continued to be the main response of the colonized people's social world, violence became the main stimulus of the colonizers' social world.

Finally, the colonial state was the legitimate child of that imperial experience. If Marx perceived that state within the capitalist system as the executive committee of the ruling class, the colonial state was the agent of that system. It was an instrument by which that system dominated, disciplined, and colonized the lifeworld of a group of people to exploit and manipulate their material factors of production.

It is true that the end of imperialism loosened the ties that bound the center to the periphery within the imperial system. Violence has persistently signaled different forms of dissatisfaction on the part of the "national" state and how its Sudanese surrogate mother, the community of the state—which was supposed to embody its citizens' hopes—manipulated that state system and power apparatus. Every now and then we have been reminded of what most Sudanese people and observers describe as *the Sudanese dilemma*. Alexis de Tocqueville would have explained the Sudanese dilemma as a reflection of the sharp contradictions between on the one hand the spontaneous vitality of Sudanese social life, the pleasant and gentler side of the Sudanese personality, the tendency to create associations that lies at the heart of civil society, and on the other hand the different forms of violence that compose the Sudanese experience.

* * *

The purpose of this study is to situate this deeply rooted and historical trail of violence within a wider context. In this respect, many characteristics of Sudanese life and experiences deserve careful scrutiny. Especially with regard to the state, a thorough investigation into the way it grew as a powerful centralized entity with a total monopoly on all the means of physical, hegemonic, and symbolic violence merits more attention. Also, the growth of the state in the Sudan with that brand of authority by which the conduct of the population is governed and disciplined—sometimes without any moral control to restrict its coercive desire to force people to take this direction or that—mandates even more thoughtful consideration. The result is likely to be the continuation of an oppressive governing system, the evolution of a state that Jean François Bayart describes as the "major manufacturer of inequality," racial engineering, and a subsequent embrace of a form of division of labor that produced a structure of social stratification on a grandiose scale: the development of underdevelopment.

At the same time, the state sustained and maintained itself as an economic enterprise, with a hegemonic system of domination and exploitation and with the capacity to organize all aspects and forms of labor. It processed and reproduced, as well, all the constitutions of a dominant ideology that bestowed upon it the social status and entitlements of the ambition to control. Simultaneously, it produced in its citizens feelings of trepidation and stimulated discontent. On the whole, the production of the social character and the creation of that state as an objective and objectified entity with all the attributes and the dynamics of a dominant, all-embracing power placed it as a distinct sociopolitical and economic field.

Most important, during its colonial and postcolonial development, the Sudanese state emerged and continued to cast itself as a fetish or new deity. On the one hand, and in both colonial and postcolonial phases, the myth of the state produced and reproduced worshippers, priests, and prophets who preached its qualities and range of power and presented their gospels among the population but especially among the community of the state. On the other hand, that myth of the state is produced by "numerous encounters, everyday forms of defiance and obedience . . . [which] represent widespread, popular, and highly interesting points of access to how the state is mythologized, externalized, and abstracted from ordinary existence yet is believed to be omnipresent."[9]

Many would agree with Crawford Young that the colonial state was not a full-fledged state. It had no sovereignty, no autonomy, no embedding in society, and it remained a mere appendage to powerful European core states and their administrative complexes. It might be difficult, however, to find many who agree with the World Bank economists who describe the postcolonial state as an entity "devoid of distinct characteristics."[10]

The Sudan is an old country, as evidenced by its mention in ancient Greek texts and the Bible and confirmed by archeological evidence. Within its territorial borders, the Sudan has historically included many states and a unique human experience. Norman O'Neill argues, "Sudanese history has witnessed a process of class formation and state-building for more than four thousand years." He adds, "Lineal antecedents of important elements of Sudan's contemporary classes can be traced back at least to [the] Funj and Keria sultanates—particularly to the struggles between rising merchant classes and royal authorities in the eighteenth century."[11] Many different issues have emerged from the experiences that have characterized the rise and fall of these states and the ups and downs of that human experience. These issues have enriched our intellectual and academic ideas about the place and its population.

Earlier than most African countries, the Sudan first gained its independence, in 1881, from "a colonial occupation that was both Muslim (Turko-Egyptian) and non-Muslim (British)."[12] In 1899, Britain and Egypt recolonized the Sudan, and with them they brought what they called the Anglo-Egyptian condominium.[13] The Sudanese regained their independence in 1956 and then had to come to terms with the reality of building a new state.

The complex past experiences of the place and its people were expected to induce the essential conditions—economic, cultural, and political—for a promising state. But, in its more than half century of order-building exploration, the country's governing system has never been liberated from the grip of the inherited colonial-state design, nor has its population been fully independent. They have struggled with the constant hazards of reproductions of the sociopolitical realities and imagined and real communities and spheres constructed out of the precondominium (Turkiyya and Mahdiyya), condominium (British colonialism), and postcondominium (the postcolonial state) regimes and experiences. Taken together, all these experiences point to the complexity of the relations and limitations that alternately prohibited and facilitated for different regimes of power to turn the imagined into realities full of sound and fury. Within these realities of sound and fury there is something special about the condominium colonial state and its relationship to the creation of institutional procedures, specialized structures, and regimes of power, control, and violence that later the postcolonial nation-state expanded and used arrogantly against its citizens. From its first day and through the experimentations of its military founding fathers—Kitchener (1898–99),[14] Wingate (1899–1916),[15] Cromer (1879–1907 as British controller and consul general in Egypt),[16] and Slatin (1899–1916)[17]—the condominium regime established an oppressive state that bred, incubated, and nurtured difference and conflict-ridden stratification through the most violent means of coercion. The condominium experience left behind an oppressive state, whose manufactured sets of elites and dissenters, whom I call the community of the state, maintained and added to its coercive systems and their plausibility structures ever after.

This community of the state—including white-, blue-, and khaki-collar workers in addition to white-*'arrāqi*[18] (peasant) workers—inherited the colonial state and became its surrogate mother. For the last more than fifty years of this state's lifetime, the Sudanese people could not talk to each other with their own voices because the state always looked on them not as citizens but as invisible beings. For the most part, these invisible beings have become visible only when their prominent shadows were made out and typified as *mutamerideen* (rebels), *ṭaifiyeen* (sectarians), and *'unsiriyeen* (racists). Most of the time, the state labeled them as being plagued by systemic strangulations of *al-jahl, wa al-jū'*, and *wa al-marad* (ignorance, hunger, and pestilence) by their own choice. The current regime (1989-present) has upgraded the cast of characters to include *'ilmaniyeen* (secularists) and almost everyone in the country who could be targeted by *al-d'awa al-shamila* (the comprehensive call) and *al-mashrou' al-hadari* (the civilization project), which, like its colonial predecessor, the civilization mission, lacks civility.

Therefore, it is surprising that the generations of state-manufactured elites and dissenters did not make a social contract based on "citizenship" and "citizenship rights" encompassing the nature, structure, and functions of the state and mandating how to rule. This flies in the face of the Sudanese tendency to spontaneously create bonds of togetherness. Instead, the Sudanese—as groups and individuals—have continued to enlist the military to resolve their political conflicts, through either a coup or more violent means. Behind every military coup in the Sudan—successful or abortive—a civilian political party or a group of conspirators has been operating, while within every military regime were groups of civilian as well as military collaborators.

Since the military action of staging a coup is, in essence, an exercise of violence, the transformation of the coup into a regime is a progressive programming of violence into oppressive practices. In turn, each regime ends up failing to achieve legitimacy in the eyes of the citizens, who have to pay a terrible price as the system turns oppressive, politically violent, and morally bankrupt. Thus, the many consequences of the coup come to resemble an intellectual, political, and civil genocide at its highest level. Such violence reached its climax under the current regime through different manifestations of its terror machine. The regime deployed its brutal parallel army of the *mujahideen* of the Popular Defense Forces (PDF) and their subcontractors from the militias of the *murahileen, fursan*, and *jinjaweed*. Together, they pillaged property and human life in different parts of the country, in an attempt to repress dissent, resistance, and tribulations that they, the Islamists, and other regimes have planted. No wonder that some relate the term *jinjaweed* to the term *jinn* (demon).

It is shameful that the last fifty-something years in the life of the Sudan have been exhausted in violence and counterviolence. It is shameful that the Sudan has the largest displaced population in the world. It is even more shameful that in order for any group of the population to be heard, they have to take up arms against the government. The state has nothing for its grieved citizens but brute force. And, indeed, the insurgencies in the south, Darfur, and the east themselves demonstrate that the state understands nothing but violence. All these different types of violence, which set about to undermine the great promise of citizenship, have continued in the most frightening ways.

In the prevailing Sudanese discourse, violence and nonviolence have never been expressed in a language that could adequately convey the depth and breadth of the country's human experience in conflict, peacebuilding processes, and everyday life. Even before independence, the Sudanese people held peace conferences, beginning with the 1947 Juba Conference. Other conferences have included the Round Table Conference, in Khartoum in 1965; the Addis Ababa Conference, in 1972; the Koka Dam Conference, in 1986; the DUP-SPLM accord, in 1987; the Bergen (Norway) Forum, in 1989; the SPLM-RCC negotiations, in 1989; the Abuja I negotiations, in 1992; the Abuja II negotiations, in 1993; the IGAD initiative, in 1993; peace talks in Naivasha, Kenya, in 2002; and the ongoing Abuja talks between Sudanese government envoys and the leaders of a rebellion in the western province of Darfur, which in October 2004 opened formal peace negotiations at the African Union–sponsored conference. Not only that, but every capital in the Sudan's vicinity—including Cairo, Tripoli, N'Djamena, Asmara, Djibouti, and Doha—hosted at least one or more rounds of talks between the Sudanese government and an opposing Sudanese group in the last ten years. Many would agree with 'Abdel Ghaffar M. Ahmed that "had we [the Sudanese] for once read our recent history seriously, we could have learned a lesson rather than continue the process of re-living this history every few years."[19]

Yet more than a century after the country's first independence and more than half a century after its second independence, the Sudanese experience in the field of developing a system of governance and state building by default or design has been marred by episodes of violence, which have drained the intrinsic worth of public life and almost destroyed the country. The gentler side of Sudanese life and the people's propensities for "spontaneously creating the bonds of friendship, trust, and cooperation that lie at the heart of civil society," once again have been severely weakened.[20]

The Sudan's internal wars—which are only one part of the larger problem—could reveal much about the formation of different power groups in the country, their competition for power, their recognition or lack thereof, and each one's approach to state and nation building. The propensity toward internal violence might be seen as a significant part of an even larger sociopolitical development in the country and the numerous reproductions of conflict closely linked to state building. This does not mean that the Sudanese people are violent by nature. Ted Robert Gurr's catalogs and studies of violence inflicted by governmental and nongovernmental agents show that neither the degree of involvement nor the scope of violence is confined to a specific group, country, or time. However, different types of violence have emerged in the Sudan as an outcome of complex factors—one of which, the state, was designed and redesigned during two colonial eras as a centralized oppressive apparatus—and have continued to grow stronger over time. This violence represents the distinctive character of these internal wars. Needless to say, the violence, which started even before the self-government of 1953–55 and continued through the independence of the country from 1956 until the present, has persisted through the intermittent successions of civilian rule and during the military regimes that have played an oppressive and burdensome role in the course of the Sudanese life.

The Sudanese state is a product of a unique and complicated encounter between imperial designs of exploitation, hegemony, ideology, and control that acted violently as an anathema to civil society, inhibiting its discourse and repressing its liberating forces. However, even in the dark oppressive moment the communicative institutions of civil society "have influence but not power in the more instrumental sense." As Jeffery Alexander says, civil society "is a project. It cannot be fully achieved, even in the fullest flush of success. Nor, despite tragedy and defeat, can it ever be completely suppressed."[21] Nevertheless, civil society can be deferred.

Acknowledgments

This study has taken decades of exploration and inquiries, extensive visits to villages and cities in the Sudan, field research, a very close look at the state structure, interviews with scholars, politicians, and state workers, and long visits to the metropolis of the center, periphery, and semiperiphery of the old colonial system that connected Cairo and Khartoum to London. This lifelong journey has profoundly influenced my research, deepened my reflections, widened the scope of my deliberations, and suggested and informed new paths for my writings. Throughout this period and the development of the project, many friends, colleagues, and media and academic institutions were of great help. I am privileged to know a number of scholars, politicians, journalists, civil servants, and knowledge workers from the three countries: the Sudan, Egypt, and England. I continue to discuss with some of them a shared interest in Sudanese issues, and I am grateful to them all as my work has been enhanced by their intellectual assistance, encouragement, support, criticism, comments, and suggestions.

I will always cherish the friendship and continuous support of my colleagues Peter Woodward, Mark Duffield, and Carolyn Fluehr-Lobban, who, in addition to the careful reading of all of the manuscript's chapters, have provided insightful comments and helpful suggestions and have discussed with me in detail many of the ideas of my work. I am immensely grateful to el-Tag Fadalla, Mohamed A. Mahmoud, Abdullahi Ali Ibrahim, Souad T. Ali, and al-Sir Sidahmed for our ongoing conversations on issues and developments in the Sudan and for their insightful ideas and critical skills through the years. I also thank Dr. Mohammed Bamyeh, Bushra al-Tayeb, Abdel Magid Ali Bob, Richard Lobban, Noah Solomon, and David Kader for reading one or more chapters and for their invaluable comments and suggestions. I thank in particular Jane R. Hogan, senior assistant keeper of archives and special collections at Durham University Library, who helped me access the university's archival system.

I am obliged to the Department of Religious Studies, the Center for the Study of Religion and Conflict (CSRC), the School of Social Transformation, and the Department of African and African American Studies at Arizona State University for their continuous support. Special thanks are also due to my graduate and undergraduate research students who were assigned to me by the Department of Religious Studies and the CSRC. I am very grateful to Brookes Schedneck, Semiha Topal, Cole Wirpel, and Rachel Stewart, whose help has been greatly appreciated. Gratitude is due to Timothy Swanger, my research assistant for two semesters, for his efficiency and meticulous editorial support. I am particularly grateful to Nicole Grinstead, my research assistant, for her tireless devotion and the skill she exhibited while diligently participating in the editing of the first and second drafts, checking the accuracy of every quotation, and creating the bibliography.

My thanks go to assistant director and editor-in-chief Amy Gorelick, project editor Marthe Walters, director of sales and marketing Dennis Lloyd and his team, of the University Press of Florida, who made this process easy. My thanks go to the copy editor, Bob Furnish, for his careful attention.

As always, my warmest appreciation is reserved for my wife, Souad T. Ali, and our children, Ahmed, Azza, and Shiraz, and our families in the Sudan for their unfailing love and unrelenting support, forbearance, and encouragement.

While all these colleagues and friends have been helpful in different ways, any remaining deficiencies or inaccuracies are solely my responsibility.

For this study I used several resources in the field of Sudanese studies both written in English and Arabic and translated into these two languages. It is gratifying to notice how this corpus of knowledge has grown through time. In addition, there is a similar corpus of Sudanese expressive culture. Tapping into and synthesizing these two gigantic bodies of knowledge is both intellectually edifying and rewarding. I thank all those who have contributed to that body of knowledge. In particular I thank

Cambridge University Press for granting me permission to quote extensively from M. W. Daly's *Empire on the Nile: The Anglo-Egyptian Sudan, 1898–1934*. I am also grateful to Princeton University Press for permission to quote from Janice Boddy's *Civilizing Women: British Crusades in Colonial Sudan*. And I thank Peter Woodward, who kindly granted me permission to quote extensively from his works.

A Note on Transliteration

For the transliteration of Arabic and Sudanese terms and names of people, places, and institutions I have followed a simple style based on *The Chicago Manual Style* and the *International Journal of Middle East Studies.* However, Arabic words and names that appear frequently in English, such as *sheikh, jihad, Islam, Sudan,* and *Khartoum,* are used as they usually appear in English and with no diacritics. Less familiar Arabic and Sudanese words are italicized, followed by a translation of the word or concept. However, some of those words that I use often, such as *jallaba,* are not italicized after their first appearance. I have tried to be consistent in my transliteration of given names, especially for commonly cited historical names, for which I have followed the most usual spellings. For the names of many contemporary Sudanese and Egyptian authors, I have followed the spellings used by the authors themselves. Finally, unless specified, all translations from Sudanese and Arabic sources, poetry, proverbs, and other expressive culture are mine.

1

The Sociopolitical Construction of a Country

The assumption that the name *Sudan* is an expression of its people's identity, color, or racial construction is a crucial misconception. There is more to the Sudanese experience in its complexity than meets the eye or what color alone can capture. The multiple names others have applied to the country, however, raise a difficult sociopolitical and intellectual question.[1] Unlike many countries of the world, the names others have applied to the Sudan have always connoted the color of its population. These names have turned the Sudan's human landscape into a sightseeing vista perceived by others as leaving behind multiple hierarchies and proliferations of stigma and few legacies of privilege. The semiotic systems and the history of articulations in this long descriptive narrative emphasize stigma more than privilege in this respect. Such a phenomenon has produced evolving essentialist orientations and claims of difference with implications that go far beyond labeling different groups of people who have lived in the place.

On different levels and at different times, such objective reality has remained, in certain ways, an integral part of constructing the Other. They have continued to be sources of constraints and power enforcements, as well as sources of hegemonic impulses, that colonial powers inspired and that internal Sudanese culture and its ongoing discourses in part reflected. That is not to say that the Sudanese construct their collective self through what the Other stipulates. On these two different levels and in these two different times, the Sudanese defined themselves by many identifiers other than color. Their referential declarations to themselves range from relation to a sultanate or region (*al-ṣulṭana al-Zarqa*, also known as Funj and Sinnār, Taqali, Musaba'at and Darfur, Dar Hamid, Dar

Hamar, or Dar Zaqaua), an ethnic group (Danagla, Kababish, Beja, Nuba, or Dinka, Fur, or Fallata), a city (Shandi, Ḥalfa, or Kassala), or a village.

As early as the fourteenth and fifteenth centuries, multiple economic, cultural, and religious transactions helped form growing networks across local geographies. They formed urban and semiurban centers that facilitated and strengthened the emergence of social classes of holy men (*fuqarā'*; sing., *faqīh*, or *faki*, in colloquial Sudanese) and merchants (*jallaba* and *khawajat*); the latter "appropriated the surplus of its subordinate producers through diverse means unknown or unacceptable to ancient custom, but characteristic of commercial capitalism."[2] More than that, the "making" of this new middle class helped create and fashion "institutions which defined the identity of middle class itself, its relations with the subjects, and with the ruling establishment."[3] This institutional differentiation is important because it affected long-standing patterns of reproduction of social relationships, civic discourse, and corresponding transformations that all gave meaning to the organized mode of living.

Jay Spaulding explains that organized modes of living from that time comprised three inner and outer acts of power relations. First, "the new middle class claimed Arab identity, practiced patrilineal descent, employed coin currencies, and bound itself in its dealings by the standards of Islamic law." Second, "it elicited alms, purchased slaves, monopolized exchange relationships, and imposed perpetual indebtedness upon its free subjects." Finally, "it imposed its own legal and ideological concepts upon the government, demanded exemption from all obligations to the state, and took up a variety of duties hitherto exercised by the state or the nobility, such as the administration of justice and the collection of taxes."[4] The end of the Funj kingdom, in 1821, was the beginning of a complex relationship between different actors within the model of centralized government.

Different types of resistance to the Turkish occupation of the Sudan generated diverse processes of exercising centralized violence over a defined territory, its population, and their organized mode of living. The Turkiyya colonial regime (1821–84), a period in which Muḥammad 'Ali's Egypt[5] "experienced an exercise in imperial imagination . . . that proved to be highly influential on successive generations," is one such example.[6] This imperial imagination found its fulfillment when Muḥammad 'Ali "followed the practice of early European mercantile countries like England and France, who sought to build colonies in the New World, and for the same reasons. That is why he regarded military expansion and imperialist designs as essential for independence."[7] Hence, invading the Sudan was part of a plan that gave Muḥammad 'Ali control over one of the largest empires in the history of Egypt—almost half the size of the European continent. The Turkiyya was followed by the Mahdiyya (1885–98), which started as an Islamic revolution, transformed into a nationalist liberation movement, and ended as an autocratic, oppressive regime. Finally, a strange condominium rule in which a European empire, Britain, with a semicolonized state, Egypt, imposed colonial rule over the country from 1898 until 1956.

Here, one would disagree with the Sudanese political scientist Muddathir 'Abdel-Raḥim, who argues, "Until at least the beginning of [the twentieth] century, the 'Sudanese' identified themselves as members of different tribes and sub-tribes, adherents to various *ṭuruq* (singular, *ṭarīqa*), religious fraternities, belonging to this or that religion of the country and (especially the Northern Sudanese, when thinking of wider affiliation) as Muslim and/or Arab people. But they never thought of themselves as 'Sudanese,' unless they happened to belong to the less sophisticated, non-Islamised and non-Arabised sections of the population."[8] What makes 'Abdel-Raḥim's last statement look inappropriate is that those "less sophisticated" have never labeled themselves as such. In fact, they initiated a sequence of interactions, reactions, and challenges for change that, in and of itself, put the entire society and its active forces in action. When we seek to identify the composition of the racial sonata and structural changes, which made the pedigree of contemporary Sudanese society, we cannot fail to see distinctive features and forces of Sudanese socialization in habitual negotiations, efforts to the tasks, growth, and construction of a civil society, and the success stories that nurtured the sultanates of Sinnār, Taqali, Darfur, and the Mahdiyya. Such propensity to form associations eventually succeeded in transforming the pejorative term *Sūdāni* (Sudanese) into one of pride.

One such "less sophisticated" person was 'Ali 'Abd al-Latif (1892–1948), a son of ex-slave parents of Nuba and Dinka backgrounds. He was an officer in the Sudanese army, as well as a leader and organizer of a movement and association known as the White Flag League. That propensity to associate, which represents a form of regenerating the self and resisting the colonial onslaught, made 'Abd al-Latif the first person to promote the term *Sūdāni* as the central theme of an emerging Sudanese nationalism, thus endowing his association with the dynamism and vigor to invent a new self-image.

'Abd al-Latif and his association stand as one example of the emerging civil societies that have characterized the Sudanese experience. But the effects and aftereffects of outside and sometimes inside encounters have worked—collectively and separately—within the people's own lived experiences. They have taken a deadly toll on most if not all of these experiences and their moral and sociopolitical sensibilities. In addition, they have buttressed violent and hegemonic countercultures to ravage and sometimes demolish these emerging societies. Further, they have created local geographical knowledge and the social construction of differentiated imagined entities and exclusionary territories in their place. These internal and external factors each emerged as significant, especially as they were not able to debilitate the Sudanese people's propensity to revitalize and regenerate themselves. What precisely these factors are, and the dialectical processes that acted to produce such a social construction of a society, a nation, a country, and their successive narrations, discourses, and shifting terrains is the subject of this chapter.

The Remnants of the Ethiopian Image

The ancient Greek and Roman sources called the people who lived south of Egypt *Aithiops* (Ethiopians), or "the people with burnt faces," an indication of their dark color. Such color distinctions "were noted and represented, but without the specific scientific or cultural concepts of 'race' as the West has used it, meaning phenotypic difference that is ranked."[9]

Homer described the Ethiopians as "at the world's end." The Greek god Poseidon "had gone [to them] to receive a great offering of bull and ram, and there he was taking his pleasure now, seated at the banquet."[10] In *The Iliad*, Homer reported that Zeus went to the "blameless Ethiopians," with whom the gods leave their abode frequently to visit and to feast, during the Trojan War. In that particular visit Zeus and his entourage of gods stayed for twenty-five days.[11] Other writers of the ancient world included the Greek historian Herodotus,[12] who, reporting from a distance in the fifth century BCE, described the Ethiopian capital of Meroe in detail. He also divided the Ethiopians into two groups: the Macrobians, who were thought to be the tallest and the most beautiful people in the world, and the cave-dwelling Ethiopians, the swiftest of men, who fed on snakes and lizards.[13] Another ancient historian, Diodorus the Sicilian, wrote in the first century BCE. He relied on interviews with Ethiopian ambassadors in Egypt and other secondhand sources. Diodorus divided the Ethiopians into many tribes, some dwelling on either bank of the Nile, others residing in the Libyan interior. According to his report, they had black skin, flat noses, and wooly hair. They were entirely savage and displayed the nature of wild beasts.[14] According to Diodorus, Ethiopians had been created by the sunlight. According to Pliny, the Ethiopians had no articulate voice, instead uttering a kind of squeaking noise. A king with one eye in his forehead ruled them.

The medieval Arab geographers, on the other hand, named the region from the Red Sea to modern Senegal *bilād al-Sudan*, literally "the land of the blacks." It included the Saharo-Sahelian sector of Africa, which stretches south of the Arabic-speaking north and includes modern Egypt, Libya, Tunisia, Algeria, and Morocco. Ibn Khaldun maintains, "The name 'Abyssinians,' however, is restricted to those Negroes who live opposite Mecca and the Yemen, and the name 'Zanj' is restricted to those who live along the Indian Sea."[15] He explains that these names "are not given to them because of an alleged descent from a black human being, be it Ham or anyone else."[16] Ibn Khaldun's description of the geographical location of these groups agrees with other Arab writers and geographers like Abu 'Uthman 'Amr ibn Baḥr al-Jaḥiz (776–869), Abu al-Ḥasan 'Ali ibn al-Ḥusayn al-Masūdi (896–956), who visited the *bilād al-Zanj*, and Yakut al-Ḥammawi, whose encyclopedia was completed in 1228. The geographical demarcation of *bilād al-Sudan*, according to Chambers's *Encyclopaedia*, includes an area "South of Latitude 20 bounded on the North East by the Sahara, on the West by Senegambia, on the South by Upper Guinea and on the East by Kordofan."[17]

According to the Sudanese political scientist 'Abdel-Raḥim, "the Firman granted to Muḥammad 'Ali Pasha by the Sublime Porte in 1841 did not refer to the Sudan but to 'the states of Nubia, Dar Fur, and Kordofan and Sinnār' as individual and separate entities: nor did the term 'Sudan' appear in the Firman of 1866 whereby the viceroyalty of Egypt and 'those territories and dependencies' which belonged to it were vested in Khedive Isma'il[,][18] and his descendents."[19] According to 'Abdel-Raḥim, "when the expression began to be habitually used in official and other statements, during the last third of the century, it signified a loosely defined area from the Great Lakes in Central Africa and included considerable areas of the Horn and the Somali Coast."[20] On the other hand, as all aspects of Muslim tradition indicate, Muslims highly regarded al-Ḥabasha, a region on the western coast of the Red Sea, and its inhabitants (al-Ḥabash). Prophet Muḥammad elucidated this in the Ḥadith several times. 'Abdullah el-Ṭayeb argues, "the term AL HABASHA was applied to all the lands which lay south of Egypt, whose coast was opposite to the Arabian Coast south of Mecca."[21]

Many scholars find in the label *Ethiopia* a clear distinction between blackness and other skin colors. In *Blacks in Antiquity*, Frank Snowden argues that the ancient Greeks and Romans in their different articulations were explaining differences between themselves and other races. Snowden emphasizes, "The Greeks and Romans attached no special stigma to color, regarding yellow hair or blue eyes a mere geographical accident, and developed no special racial theory about the inferiority of darker peoples qua darker peoples."[22] To support his argument, Snowden quotes H. L. Shapiro, who claims, "modern man is race conscious in a way and to a degree certainly not characteristic previously."[23] If Snowden's and Shapiro's approach are of particular significance here, it is equally important to give attention to the other view that perceives in their approach "a one-sided temptation by which the misty nobility of Homer's Ethiopians is taken for real. An ancient relationship with Black Africa based on admiration and respect has an obvious appeal in our times as a corrective to racism, especially if the interaction between black and white could be grounded in real referential 'reports,' not just 'an idealization of dark-skinned' people."[24] The other two labels, on the other hand, assert and acknowledge the difference between *al-Sudan* or *al-aḥbash* as black people within the intercolor relations within that geographical region. In other words, it distinguishes the Arabs as people who "might describe themselves as black in relation to the Persians who are red, while at other times they may describe themselves as red or white in contrast to the Africans who are black."[25] Such opposition, however, may have captured the Arabs' attention for reasons that have to do with colorism—discrimination within a related race because of the shade of the person's skin—rather than what W. E. B. Du Bois describes as the color line, which demarcates the relation of the darker to the lighter races.[26] Yet this form of colorism could turn into blatant racism within deferential power relations and modes of prejudice.

The way the *sīra* (allegory) of the legendary black pre-Islamic Arab poet-warrior 'Antara ibn Shaddād[27] of the sixth century CE has been told and retold in Arab societies for the last fourteen centuries or more reflects a sense of guilt that perpetuates and maintains a system of colorism. Of all the *aghribat al-'Arab*—black Arabs (lit., ravens of the Arabs)—'Antara was the proudest of his blackness; he confidently tried to reverse the association black-dark-night for a positive functional reasoning when he said, "Had it not been for the darkness of night, there would be no daybreak."[28] For the last fifteen centuries, Arab popular culture has lamented its failure to appreciate 'Antara's color in the same way it appreciated his other qualities: courage, love, eloquence, and poetic talent.

Islam came with an explicit message that celebrated the difference of color as one of God's signs of existence. The Qur'an reads: "And among His Signs is the creation of the heavens and the earth, and the variations in your languages and your colors: verily in that are Signs for those who know."[29] Certain prejudices have persisted throughout the Arab lived experience in expressive culture and daily practice despite the prominence of the Qur'an and the popularity of 'Antara's *mu'alaqa* (ode) (pl., *mu'allaqāt*) and sīra (allegory) in Arabic folk culture. The feeling of guilt within the Arab consciousness over their failure to fully appreciate 'Antara is, in a sense, similar to the sense of guilt felt by the Shī'a community for failing to support al-Ḥussein. Within the Shī'a collective mind, 'Ashoura[30] ritualizes the annual anniversary of the death of the Prophet Muḥammad's grandson Ḥussein, who was killed in the battle of Karbala, in 680 CE. The event reflects in essence a collective sense of guilt and atonement on the part of the Shī'a community. Similarly, the continued live performance of 'Antara's sīra by the *haqawati* (Arab folk storyteller) and the way his pre-Islamic poetry has been memorized by Arab generations since time immemorial reflects a moral dilemma entangled within public life that Islam has never omitted.

Such prejudice, which was primarily a way of thinking and an instrument of a cultural order, has placed extraordinary costs, role strain, and role conflict on both Sudanese and Arab sides. Role conflict is a situation in which incompatible role demands are placed on a person by two or more statuses held at the same time. Role strain is a condition that occurs when incompatible demands are built into a single status that a person occupies.

The highest cost, one would argue, are "the constructions of racial differentiation in the Arab world that trace back to the early medieval period, which imbued black Africans with certain unalterable characteristics that rendered them 'suitable' to enslavement."[31] Reconciling the gap between the Islamic ideal, which celebrates color as one of God's signs of existence, and such constructions as color, racial differentiation, and the practices of slavery remains one of the most damaging human experiences for both sides. What makes the situation even worse is that "until quite recently Arab scholars were reluctant to probe this aspect of their past."[32] For some Arabs, the moral cost not only lingers not only within this sense of guilt and moral dilemma, so often replayed in the sīra of 'Antara, but also lies deeper in the Arab psyche. It manifests itself whenever they define and see themselves in relation to a black fellow citizen, expatriate, or alien. This experience came with its political cost, which overshadowed the role of the Arabs as "purveyors of new ideas"[33]—including the introduction of Islam, the Arabic language, and Arabs of Arabia trading with the African continent in the past and as partners in the liberation battle against colonialism in the last century. It left an "extreme bitterness in the central parts of the [African] continent against Arab minorities which lived on the coast."[34]

To borrow Jean-Paul Sartre's analysis in *Anti-Semite and Jew*,[35] the dynamics of the phenomenon of anti-Arabism have created an "idea of the Arab" as a slave trader and provoked negative images and sentiments within different political spheres in Africa. Various political forces have, time and again, expanded this "idea of the Arab" to include negative impulses about Islam as well as the Arabs. Within this framework, one could easily see how this "idea of the Arab" has been played and overplayed through time to feed tension in Sudanese political and social life. Within the Sudanese discourse, this "idea of the Arab" defines an embedded impulse for conflict. Dustin M. Wai assumes that "Africans perceive Arabs as cunning, crafty, dishonest, untrustworthy, and racially as well as culturally arrogant. Many Africans do not feel at ease in dealing with Arabs: for educated and Westernized Africans, Arab culture is unattractive, and as for the masses of Africans, they are mystified in general by most foreigners."[36] The Sudanese scholar adds, "Although African Muslims feel a sense of religious solidarity with Arabs, many of them don't feel at ease with non-African Muslims."[37] From there, Wai highlights one of this ideology's internal problems by revealing the thread that ties it to another essentialist negative impulse toward Islam. For him, "Islam doesn't seem to provide the religious bond that would cement relations between African Muslims and Arabs."[38] What makes Wai's assertion a typical characterization of the "idea of the Arab" is that there is only one Arab who represents "an opposing race" and an incarnation of everything negative, as included in Wai's above-mentioned list. On the other hand, there is also one African who needs to be protected from the evil Arab. This unitary Arab is the Arab that Wai knows, whose essential qualities are frozen in time and place. Such an idea has become one of the assets used by different parties involved in the Sudanese conflict.

The Double Sources and Reproductions of Islam and Arabization

But even before this persisting dilemma, other developments wove the progression of events into multiple layered fabrics of lived experiences. Some of these were accepted and absorbed by Sudanese society, while others were resisted and rejected by all or some of the population. Both accepted and rejected developments have shaped all other dimensions of Sudanese society at large and its underlying structures. These developments have had a double source and a double set of reproductions. The first source was the long and slow process of Islamization of most of the northern Sudan, which includes the area above latitude 10° north. This process has undergone a parallel pattern of negotiation in accommodating aspects of indigenous cultural and linguistic traditions. Hence, when Islam became victorious in the country, both Islamic traditions and Arabic language were appropriated in some parts of the country, and, at the same time, selectively absorbed or partially dropped in other parts. The unevenness of the distribution, assimilation, and influence of Islam and the Arabic language are major factors behind the diverse, cultural, and ethnic territorial boundaries and associations in the country at large. In observing this phenomenon's historical development, one perceives this distinctive mode of cultural and ethnic augmentation.

This has been a source and driving component of a system of conflict and integration that has characterized and deeply affected Sudanese life for the last five centuries. Two of the main Sudanese sultanates, Sinnār and Darfur, ascertained new identities and religious ideals that prompted integrationist and expansionist policies. These new policies included part or all of the Sudanese territory in one. What Sulṭān Tirab of Darfur (1752–85)[39] and Sulṭān Bādi of Sinnār (1644–81)[40] failed to achieve, Muḥammad

'Ali of Egypt accomplished through invasion in 1821, and Muḥammad Aḥmed al-Mahdi[41] through revolution from 1881 through 1885.

The second source has been supported by the systemic distinction between Muslim communities and regimes of high status that grow and develop within the core Muslim states, and others with lower status within the periphery and semiperiphery of the Muslim world that grow away from that core. Through long processes of war, peace, trade, different patterns of immigration, and settlement and intermarriages, the uneven and slow processes of Islamization and Arabization encouraged the Sudanese to function freely in "the rooting of that faith"[42] and establish their national states in Sinnār, Taqali, Musabba'āt, and Darfur. These conditions have placed the idea of the Sudan both inside and outside the Muslim world from the very early start. Whereas the move toward Islamization and Arabization was perceived by the Sudanese states as their own way of walking into the abode of the Muslim *umma* (which included both Arabs and non-Arabs), the surrounding Muslim communities had never included them within their geographical and anthropological imagined communities. This unique situation, however, involved what Roland Robertson described as "invention of locality" or the ideology of home.[43] There are many aspects of this invention of locality or ideology of home, particularly in what Jay Spaulding describes as the creation of the precolonial independent states of the Sudan. He argues, "What was different about the new state form of government that emerged during the early modern age was not allegiance to Islam per se, but the finality of society's ideological commitment to the faith and the new uses it would now be expected to serve."[44] This reproduction of difference has continued to be a necessary structural element in the system that emerged within the region after the fifteenth century. That system reflected itself within parallel forms of exchange within the surrounding Muslim system organizing around mutatis mutandis encounters between easy and uneasy forms of relations. What emerged out of this experience has very important distinguishing features and continuing effects. The Sudanese self-representation, which continues to find its frame of reference in the invention of locality, has always resisted all forms of Muslim and non-Muslim intervention. According to Spaulding, "During the sixteenth century, Sinnār resisted Ottoman advances up the Nile and allied herself with Ethiopia to contain Turkish ambitions at their newly annexed Red

Sea city-states island outposts of Sawakin and Musaww'a. On the other hand, Sinnār was obligated to repel two major invasions (in 1618–1619 and 1744), and during the later seventeenth century she invaded and annexed the surviving Christian Alodian successor state of Fazughli that controlled important sources of gold near the upper Blue Nile."[45] Another example of Sudanese resistance to outside intervention flared in 1881 when Muḥammad Aḥmed al-Mahdi declared jihad against the Muslim Turkish rule of the Sudan, who according to him personified "illegitimate innovation and love of the things of this world."[46] This frame of reference has developed through time, inspiring this spirit of independence to remain alive as an idea of cultural and historical continuity in Sudanese life.

Yet to all this, two sets of reproduction have added other important traits to the making of the place, its location within the system, and its attached stratification position within the region. The first set of reproductions reflects the identity formation or the internal reproduction of the self in relation to the Sudan's close-yet-distant relationship with the surrounding Arabic-speaking Muslim world and its institutions of culture, learning, and different expressions of Islam. Since the early days of Sinnār, thousands of Sudanese students and knowledge seekers have headed to Islamic learning centers in the region (especially Egypt, Mecca, and al-Madinah al-Monawarah) only to appropriate and reproduce Islamic knowledge in a way that contributes greatly to the broad local identity and is as distinctive as their Sudanese garb. Many Sufi saints and their disciples came to the country and preached their *ṭuruq* only to usher in a new style incorporating a multitude of local rituals and symbols constituted and deeply soaked in the "enormous residue" of the local.

Even the new political parties and movements, such as the Communists and the Muslim Brotherhood, which came to the country from Egypt, eventually established themselves and proliferated within a system of meaning associated with the place, its traditions, and its national discourse.

The second set of reproductions is related to the way the Sudan's Arabic-speaking neighbors, like Egypt, drew a sharp distinction between themselves and the Sudanese. After the annexation of Egypt by the larger Muslim world, in 640, reinforcing this idea, the Sudan became a religiously and culturally landlocked space. The new regional system that emerged as a result of that development had cut the Sudan off from its Christian and commercial fields of interaction.

Accordingly, the insular Christian Sudan slowly started to dwindle in importance for its neighbors and no one, with the exception of Arab nomads and some adventurous slave traders, continued to travel there. For this reason, the Sudan's Arab Muslim neighbors perceived the Sudan and the Sudanese as different. Even after the founding of the Sinnār sultanate, in the fifteenth century, the Muslim world never considered the Sudanese relationship to Islam and Arabic culture as relevant. This cultural and ethnic difference, and the racialization of its people as different, gave Muḥammad 'Ali, the Ottoman viceroy (*wāli*) of Egypt, the pretext to invade the country in 1820–21. He separated its people from their rights as human beings by turning the country into a hunting ground for slaves and transferring its natural resources, such as gold, gum arabic, and ostrich feathers to his colonialist state. Under Muḥammad 'Ali and his family, slave hunting became an organized function of the state. Within the new regional system ('Ali's *nizam jadīd*), the Sudan was perceived by those neighbors as a frontier and as an abode of cheap labor—slaves, in the Turkiyya—and as a source of other valuable resources. During his invasion of the Sudan, Muḥammad 'Ali sent messages to his son Isma'il and his son-in-law Muḥammad Bey, the *daftardar* (finance officer), instructing them "to bring slaves in large numbers."[47] For Muḥammad 'Ali, the Sudanese, regardless of their relation to Islam, were fair game for slavery. The French traveler Pierre Trémaux, who visited the country from 1847 to 1854, maintained, "The only benefit he [Muḥammad 'Ali] made from these far regions was the selling of entire populations reduced to slaves and the commerce in gum Arabic, ivory, livestock, etc."[48]

The Enduring Factors of Class Differentiation: The *Jallaba* and Slavery

To come to grips with how the Sudan and its people have been socially constructed through time, it is necessary to look through an entanglement of developments that set that construction in motion. On top of these developments, one would argue that the Sudan experienced a trade economy—a mercantile capitalism—that stretched all the way across most of its existing geographical boundaries as early as the sultanate of Sinnār. In *The Heroic Age in Sinnār*, Jay Spaulding discusses how that major import and export network—administered trade—had been established in the Sudan under the control of Sinnār rulers from the beginning of the sixteenth century. European travelers such as the French doctor Jean-Baptiste Poncet gave a detailed description of Sinnār in 1699 as a city of one hundred thousand with extensive trade connections to India through the Red Sea port of Suakin. Poncet described some of the women about the sultan's court as wearing silk dresses and silver rings on their arms and ankles and lining their eyes with kohl.[49] At the same time, "it seems probable that the 16th and 17th centuries also saw some development in free domestic trading in subsistence commodities."[50] Niblock adds that, "the commercial system within the Sinnār sulṭanate was at this stage based on gold ounce as a 'currency.' Later, by the 17th century, the system of administered trade began to break down as profit-seeking traders started to take over and a new means of exchange—the Spanish dollar—replaced the old gold ounce currency."[51] Lidwein Kapeteijns and Spaulding argue, "lineal antecedents of important elements of Sudan's contemporary classes can be traced back at least to the Funj and Keira sulṭanates—particularly to the struggles between rising merchant classes and royal authority in the eighteenth century."[52]

Two classes grew out of these developments. The first was the merchant class, or *jallaba,* who were able to expand their activities in networks, trading communities, and stations that covered a significant part of the country. The second class was the underclass of slaves, which expanded as a by-product of these economic developments. Identifying the origin of these classes is beyond the scope of this study. Nevertheless, this book takes the position that the emergence and the growth of the trading class was the turning point in the Sudan's history. It constituted one of the main components of the local system in its connection with an international "subsystem that connected Egypt with the Indian Ocean via the Red Sea."[53]

William Adams maintains that trade between that part of the Sudan and the Mediterranean world had a long history.[54] Not only the traders but also the "rulers of this period took the initiative in opening and organizing trade between their lands and the Mediterranean world."[55]

In *Travels in Nubia,* John Lewis Burckhardt, who traveled in the Sudan in 1813–14, vividly described some of the major trading centers in the Sudan at that time, including Berber, Shendi, and Suakin. He also described the different types of goods traded across the country in places like Sinnār and Kordofan. In the Shendi market, where, according to Burckhardt, commerce was the very life of society, international trade activity had been taking place. He describes people of Hadramaut, for example, as residents of Shendi dealing in goods imported "from Madras and Surat; and coarse muslins from Bengal are partly wanted for the use of the Shendy and Sinnār inhabitants themselves; but the greater part is given in exchange to the Kordofan merchants for slaves."[56] He adds that "They bring also spices, especially cloves, ginger or *zanjabīl*, India sugar, Mokha beads, as they are called, though none are made at Mokha; sandal wood, which is an article of consequence, and finds its way from hence to the countries west of Darfour, as far as Bagermé."[57] This trading activity had gone beyond the region to reach "English and American traders."[58]

By the nineteenth century, "the *jallaba* of the Nile valley joined private traders of Mediterranean origin as agents in the conduct of the foreign trade of the western sultanates, and in the twentieth, men of western origin who aspired to the vocation of private trader often adopted their ethos and label of identity."[59] Whether they adopted the ethos of foreign traders or not, the jallaba class proved to be adaptable to local circumstances in the Sudan as well as larger regional developments, an ability that permitted considerable accumulation of capital. Even before the nineteenth century, three interrelated developments enhanced the growth of the merchant economy in the Sudanese daily life.[60]

In his detailed description of the Sinnār marketplace, Krump mentions among other goods "wheat and *dhurra* from which they bake bread and with which they also feed cattle."[61] The growing demand for agricultural products had a significant economic benefit that transformed farming from subsistence into production that could satisfy the needs of an expanding market. The demand was especially high for two products, *dhurra* (millet) and *dhukn* (sorghum), which, in addition to being used as dietary staples and for beverages, such as mariessa and other types of local beer, for a wide population across the Sudanic belt, were also used as fodder for animals, and as a medium of exchange for salt in some parts of the region. In his history of the Sudan, written in the seventeenth century, the Arab traveler 'Abderraḥman Al-Sa'dī describes the growth of cities in the region into warehouses of grain.[62] Richard Roberts maintains, "Millet and sorghum formed the base of the agrarian order. Grain provided both subsistence and the means to expand the economy through exchanges across ecological zones. Savanna agriculture could yield considerable surplus, often two to three times in excess of the producers' needs."[63]

The development of a system of communication and transportation based on caravans had connected the Sudan with western and eastern Africa. Krump states that caravans were continually arriving in Sinnār "from Cairo, Dongola, Nubia, from across the Red Sea, from India, Ethiopia, [Dar] Fur, Borno, the Fezzan, and other kingdoms. This is a free city, and men of any nationality or faith may live in it without a single hindrance."[64] The basis of this system, which connected the African savanna to the Red Sea and the Mediterranean, was the camel.

Finally, these processes necessitated a division of labor and justified its values of domination and exploitation. The form of social stratification and the mode of production that emerged out of this development helped the jallaba accrue superior power and use that power to avoid certain types of labor and transfer all service aspects of this economy to the slave.

Slaves were employed in farm production, armies, and homes, as well as to accompany caravans to load and unload goods, cook, and watch over the animals. They were trained for these jobs and they could be sold. According to Paul Lovejoy, "This helps distinguish slavery in sub-Saharan Africa from slavery in the Muslim heartlands, where the production function was not as important in the century or two before 1600."[65]

For some time, scholars disagreed on the status of slaves as a social class and their location within the mode of production. Neil Faulkner, for example, refutes the slave mode of production as a redundant concept for the following reasons: "1. Slaves did not produce the bulk of the surplus in classical antiquity. 2. Slaves were not a class and cannot therefore define a mode of production. 3. No mode of production can be defined simply in terms of the primary producers' formal status."[66] Ted Crawford disagrees with Faulkner: "The key question as far as a slave mode of production is concerned must be the proportions that were employed in the productive process, above all in plantation agriculture, and did such plantations provide the dynamic for that society, even if for a limited period."[67] In addition, most scholars would agree with the argument that within any society the production forces include labor, technology, and input. As production forces are established and maintained through division of labor, social relations between slaves and their owners, who use them as means of production—property relations—turns this ownership arrangement of the means of production into a mode of production and turns slaves into an underclass. The entire formulation of racism that grows with this system, economic deprivation, and the entire slave experience were the basic factors in the formation of such an underclass.

Different Modes of Entry

In effect, all the internal and external processes of this system of exchange and stratification, and its structures—within their own dynamics of gradual movement and profound internal changes—emerged over time in the cumulative Sudanese experience, and are central to the Sudanese buildup of states, classes, institutions, and their ideological identifications. These processes and their reproductions came packaged with several different elements.

One of these was an expanding core zone, which embraced the Arabic-speaking greater riverain part of the Sudan, including the north and a major part of the Gezira area, between the Blue and White Niles. The trading system that emerged in the sixteenth and seventeenth centuries, as explained earlier, facilitated major transformations that made that zone a primary seat of power and wealth. The most significant among these developments was the growth of urban trading centers running from Suakin in the Red Sea to Ed-Damer, Shendi, Arabaji, Wad Medani, and Sinnār.[68] European travelers like W. G. Browne (who visited Darfur in 1793)[69] and Ignatius Pallme (who visited Kordofan in the 1820s)[70] described other cities, such as al-Fashir and al-Obeid, as vibrant, important commercial outposts. Accompanying the growth of these urban centers was the emergence of the trading class (jallaba) that brought together different groups, among whom were many of the "nomadic groups, and among them the Beja were predominant by virtue of their strategic location between the Nile and the Red Sea and their long tradition of commercial expertise."[71] The entry of those groups into new systems and modes of production swelled the population of these urban trading centers. The dwellers of urbanized core zones, who were sometimes known as *awlad al-baḥr* (riverains), were the most mobile in the Sudan. They became well established in society, in part because of their strong class ideology, networks, and group solidarity as jallaba.

The emergence of this economic network and its modes of production acted in different ways, influencing the local spaces and their formal authorities through time. In this way, the direct or indirect involvement in politics has been an essential characteristic of the jallaba. As Ahmad Sikainga explains, "the Khartoumers undermined the position of the Fur Sultanate in the southern hinterlands. The old sultanate itself was finally conquered by Al-Zubair in 1874."[72] Another contributing factor to the development and strength of the core zone was that it remained the center of Sufi ṭuruq, their families, and the most prestigious *masseeds* (Qur'anic schools). Neil McHugh argues, "The historical consciousness of northern Sudanese Muslims is all but dominated by the Muslim holymen or Shyoukh, singular shaykh, also known as *faqīh* or *fakī* (pl., *fuqarā'*)."[73] In addition to the previously mentioned characteristics, O'Fahey and Spaulding argue that the spread of the Sufi ṭuruq and the influence of their leaders undermined the authority of the sultān of Sinnār. Moreover, within the Sudanese experience, those Sufi centers have remained places "that express most clearly a relation between cosmology and private experience."[74]

More significantly, the relationship between the place, its religious institutions, and different forms of rituals and practice "allows for negotiation, revision, and reinterpretation, signaled in the study of religion, by such terms as *conversion, syncretism,* or *reform*."[75] Put differently, the curriculum of the masseed—which included the Qur'an, Arabic, Islamic studies, and mathematics—was a significant tool in the "technology of the intellect" that effectively worked, in addition to other factors, as a mode of communication and attitude toward work that lent toward capitalist enterprise within an expanding system, which has taken numerous forms.

Accordingly, the jallaba, as disciples of different ṭuruq, continued to embody these forms, which shaped the history and the present of the country. As this class has occupied a growing central position in the fields of wealth and power distribution in the country through time, the mode of thought they have been using—including literacy, gained first through the masseed and later through the public school system—has made it possible for them to grow and develop their means of communication and to unify culture within their core and trading zones. The partial literacy the jallaba gained from the masseed and the brotherhood solidarity they developed through the ṭarīqa networks have empowered them to become the harbingers par excellence of an ideology that finds in the

Arabic language and Islam the most prominent substructure of a community, whose expansion coincides with their trading, power, and prestige interests while being continuously on the lookout for markets and the pursuit of profits.

Starting with the colonial period, the educational institutions and the certification of teachers and curricula—in other words, the control of knowledge—became a function of the state. The colonial state, its communities, missionaries, and some groups of the local elite not only contested but also despised the masseed education. Yet, followers of various orders brought about substantial forms of engagement to yield the most prominent change. After the end of the Mahdist state, they who brought with them new attitudes and ethics helped build what Weber describes as a "tremendous cosmos of the modern economic order" and accumulation of capital. These attitudes and work ethics evolved and organized around two principle figures and each one's ṭarīqa: Sayyid 'Ali al-Mirghani and his Khatmiyya, and 'Abd al-Raḥman al-Mahdi and his Ansār. With them came significant transformative potentials that influenced the entire religious, social, and political fields of power.

According to Neil McHugh, "The heroes of the Sudanese past include kings and warriors, yet their ranks are filled by a much greater number of religious figures, from Ghulām Allāh b. 'Â'id, who brought learning to a benighted Nubia in the fourteenth century, to Muḥammad Aḥmed, the Mahdi, who brought to it righteous government in the nineteenth."[76] Sayyid 'Ali al-Mirghani and 'Abdel Raḥman al-Mahdi could easily fit within the Sudanese orientation (see chapter 3). Each of these orientations converged to define the representations of a spirit of capitalism that had three major characteristics: the reproduction of the effects and aftereffects of the emergence of financial institutions; the new relations of production and markets sustaining a rural and urban capitalist economy; and the expansion of the jallaba class. These developments have cleared the way for a progressive system of stratification and identity management in the country.

The country's transformation from a pre-ṭarīqa and pre-trading gemeinschaft to a ṭarīqa and trading gesellschaft has partially shaped the different stages of the construction and reproductions of the Sudanese nation-entity as it has been evolving through time. The development of systems of modern communication, transportation, education, and agriculture in the country through the twentieth century has consolidated the power of the religious leadership of the Khatmiyya, the Ansār, and the jallaba. It forged different types of alliances between them and the emerging generations of the new elite who made up the community of the state. Finally, the core zone has remained the seat of power for the last five centuries, moving from Sinnār, Wad Medani, Khartoum, and Omdurman, finally returning to Khartoum. The emergence of this economic network and its modes of production have acted in different ways to influence the local spaces and their formal authorities. In this way, Ahmad Alawad Sikainga provided an analysis of exchange relationships between the core and other zones. This is reflected in the destruction of the Fur sultanate, which the Khartoumers undermined, and al-Zubair conquered in 1874. Presumably, al-Zubair's move was an attempt to establish an exchange relationship between the core and the zones by expanding his own empire, which he himself explained when Flora Shaw interviewed him. Al-Zubair made it very clear that his ambition was to expand his empire as a trader and not a slaver (see chapter 6).

The trade zone, which included greater Kordofan, parts of eastern Sudan, and Darfur, continued to expand to the south and continued to be a frontier and a major source of the jallaba wealth. For the last three centuries, different parts of this zone have competed with the core zone for power. In the eighteenth century, Darfur sultān 'Abdel Raḥman el-Rasheed and his powerful successors consolidated their dynasty's hold on the western part of the Sudan and established a capital at al-Fashir. They then started their push east against the Funj kingdom of Sinnār. Their goal was control of Kordofan and its millet, sorghum, camels, and slave-raiding regions. In 1881 Muḥammad Aḥmed al-Mahdi found in western Sudan and in particular the Kordofan region "a large following and won a series of major military victories."[77] Kordofan and western Sudan provided al-Mahdi with several advantages, including an abundant supply of food for his army, a transportation system, highly trained military leaders, and many *bazinger* (private slave armies well trained in the use of firearms). Ahmad Sikainga explains, "most Mahdist soldiers had served in the Turco-Egyptian Army and in the merchants' bazinger."[78] After the death of al-Mahdi, his successor, al-Khalifa 'Abdullahi and his west Sudanese relatives and supporters ruled the country until 1898.

In recent years, the issues of race and ethnicity have entered into the center of the politics of both the regime and the country. The regime's policies on regional, racial, and ethnic representations in the government and the party have opened the door for serious complications within the social and political fields. The growing perception of regional, racial, and ethnic group solidarity or affiliation as vehicles to political power has created a new kind of politics in which the path to power begins in belonging to the "right" group. What brought this development to the forefront as an irreconcilable political dispute between north *riverain* and western (*gharabi* or *gharbawi)* groups of Islamists were the deeply seated factors in the groups' formations of regional and ethnic entity in colonial and postcolonial Sudanese states.

The conflict that split the Islamist National Congress Party into two antagonistic groups is embedded in the revitalization and deconstruction of race and ethnicity questions within the Islamist groups and the country at large. The group of Islamists from western Sudan, in particular, who stood behind al-Turabi and constituted a substantial number in his party leadership represented more than an ordinary political association. They represented the project of a community with specific cultural and ethnic characteristics and "tactical necessity" and "common interest."[79] On the other hand, because al-Turabi himself is not a gharabi, his leadership might help break the closure practices enforced by the dominant northern groups. In this respect, it seems that the regional and race issue has brought two things within the ranks of the Islamists: on the one hand, cultural prejudice and ethnocentrism and, on the other, the creation of different techniques of breaking barriers and closure to move these groups into the Sudanese mainstream. When these two processes come together, an interesting phenomenon emerges that is worthy of exploration. It seems that the conflict between the two groups was rife before surfacing in 1999, and I think the *Black Book*, which was printed and widely distributed after the split, was one of the delayed bombs of their propaganda war.[80]

The third zone includes most of southern Sudan, western Ethiopia, and some parts of central Africa, as well as the Congo and northern Uganda. This zone was at one time the major source of the slaves who continued to make up the backbone of the periods' armies, including those of the Funj and Fur sultanates, the Turkiyya, and the Jihadiyya during the Mahdiyya. These groups constituted one-third of the colonial invading army. Slaves also formed the core of the private armies of the slave traders who emerged in the raid zone to hunt and export slaves to Egypt. They became especially common after Muḥammad 'Ali's conquest of the Sudan. Al-Zubair Raḥma, the most famous of those traders, was successful in building a private army of more than a thousand bazinger. After the departure of al-Zubair to Egypt, where he was detained, his son Sulayman grew his army to 6,400 men. He led his men against the Turkish government for two years. In 1879, Sulayman was defeated and later executed by the government commander Gessi Pasha. Before that, members of slave armies had played important roles in challenging the seat of power in Sinnār. They also played an important role in support of the Mahdiyya army and initiated the mutiny of the Eleventh and Fourteenth Sudanese battalions of the invading army in January 1899, while their descendants spearheaded the 1924 revolution during the colonial period.

On the other hand, until the turn of the last century, the Sudan was a slave-producing and a slave-using society. This strange situation has created an endless pattern of conflict that shaped the thought patterns and feelings of the Sudanese people. The incompatible nature of the Sudanese ethnic makeup has created a state or condition of status inconsistency. The shifting locations of Sudanese ethnicity, between an outside world that perceives the Sudan and the Sudanese as different and its internal world, which contested and resented this perceptual focus, together with the implications of both, have been at the heart of this inconsistency. This was not an easy matter to consider, for the experience gave the Sudanese inner soul a world organized around a complexity of denial and indifference on one side and anger and trepidation on the other. However, most northerners within their official and expressive culture hold positions on most openly debated issues far closer to the basic Islamic ideal. But the northern consciousness of its own blackness has not been able to develop these ideals to invite in and develop further a Sudanese identity within the country's own existential characteristics. In addition, as Mark Duffield observed in one of our correspondences, "South Sudan is always experienced as a zone of exception. First, as a slaving frontier; then as a colonial Closed District; then an area under martial law during the 1st civil war; then an area of initial UN/NGO involvement in the 1970s; then turned into a new form of Closed District under the OLS [Operation Lifeline Sudan] during the 2nd civil war; and now under the CPA [Comprehensive Peace Agreement] as part of a 'one country, two systems' approach."[81]

Ultimately, the colonial and postcolonial states have overplayed this gap within all aspects of marginalization, prospects of homoreferential impulses, and policies of identity management, and the gap has been negotiated among Sudanese society at large in the hardest way: through different forms of violence at the center and in the south, which later grew to include the west and the east, as each party continued to see in itself the repository of specific cultural values that enhance or constrain the entrance into the true zone of the Sudanese imagined community (see chapters 7 and 8).

This long saga, with its gaps and its peaceful and violent events, was thus a result of a complex reality leading to different pathways. On the one hand, the form of consolidation of movements and state building continues to disentangle and integrate the effects of growth, resurrection, and devastation of civil society, expansion of markets, religious institutions, and social interaction to build an imagination that has been leading the way. On the other hand, other forms, policies, and measures of organized material violence from home or coming from abroad continue to check such actions of development and hamper that imagination. Different social strata within locals' and outsiders' experiences have developed by merging the means of conduct that assert a way of life and by clashing with different local and colonial imperatives. But, first and foremost, all these developments and reproductions, in accordance with the vicissitudes of social, cultural, and political struggles, have been working together and separately to structure the space and form leading the social construction of a country and a nation.

2

Constructing New Identities

The sociopolitical construction of the newborn twentieth-century Sudan has been marked by a series of serious events as well as long and complex processes. These include violent forms of domination and subjugation, which, like a malignant brain tumor, provoked the immune responses of various forms of resistance and change. These patterns have worked together to create the social, cultural, and political structures of the colonial state and have influenced the postcolonial state to a great degree. At the same time, these patterns have systematically continued to reproduce ever-growing, conflict-charged effects in the fields of power, the state, its workers, and the nationalist community of the state, as well as in conditions that empower or suppress the existence and growth of a civil society and undergird the Sudanese lifestyle. Key to understanding the role of colonial and postcolonial experiences in the formation of the state in the Sudan are the similarities and differences between the developments and interactions of the dialectical opposites that characterize these experiences. At the same time, these experiences entail a series of peculiar historical relationships. By now, the forces that built the colonial state and influenced the ideological foundation of the postcolonial state are entirely, or almost entirely, exhausted. So, either things are falling apart, or a new identity of the nation and the country—as certain groups have been demanding a place in the national space and a share of power and wealth—will be built in an uneasy way.

The undercurrents of the emerging conflicts and violence since the early days of the colonial state are intimately connected to the construction of the different forms of totalitarian and semitotalitarian thought, regimes, and practices of the colonial and postcolonial states. This situation and its conflict with emerging Sudanese identities and different emerging power groups has produced an expansion and contraction of manifest and latent clashes of interest, creating conditions for each group's mode of existence, shifting positions within the civil and uncivil life (or what Tocqueville defines as the darker properties of associational life) and appropriating or choking modes, fields, and spheres of social change.

The Emergence of the Colonial State

The emergence and development of the colonial state, its various institutions, and the symbolic, as well as direct, forms of violence it exercised over Sudanese society came into being through peculiar and sometimes complicated relationships. These developments altered civic life in the Sudan and greatly influenced the way its different groups of people are defined and sectioned. After the second independence of the country, in 1956, the state's purpose and functions, ideas of development, and its thoughts of nation building became conjoined with totalitarian forms of militarism and violence at the expense of civil society for a considerable period of the life experience of the independent Sudan.

The colonial state in Africa, as Crawford Young rightly describes it, was a creature with a number of peculiar attributes, including ambiguous territoriality where sovereignty is emphatically denied. According to Young, the colonial state, alien to its core and to its own inner logic, was shaped by the vocation of domination, with no embedding in society or international representation,[1] and thus remained an appendage of powerful European military and administrative complexities.[2]

In addition, the Sudanese experience in this field added unique characteristics of naked power, violence, and odd relationships between the colonizer and the colonized. The first of these relationships was the British colonial powers' pretext for the invasion of the Sudan. As Britain's outright invasion and eventual occupation of the country "would have offended other European states, thus making the Egyptian façade desirable, any full return to Egypt would have involved the extension into the Sudan of the rights the other powers then enjoyed in Egypt under the capitulations."[3] According to Woodward these capitulations were "an annoyance to Lord Cromer, Britain's consul general in Egypt: [such was] the 'cumbersome paraphernalia of internationalism,' as he called it."[4]

The second peculiar element of these relationships was the composition of the invading army. It "contained 24,000 soldiers, of whom 8,200 were British and the rest Egyptian and Sudanese."[5] The Sudanese regiments, which represented one-third of the invading force, embody part of this peculiarity. They reflect how enslaved Sudanese were turned against their own people. This phenomenon can be traced back to 1821, when Muḥammad 'Ali, the viceroy of Egypt, invaded the Sudan and turned hunting slaves into an organized function of the state. That set a precedent, which held for some time, in which the enslaved Sudanese were forcibly incorporated into the Egyptian army.[6] The British general Horatio Herbert Kitchener was named *sirdar* (commander in chief) of the invading army, while the Egyptian treasury financed the entire campaign's expenses and later the operating expenses of the condominium government. After the invasion, the Sudanese members of the military units were reinserted into the Sudanese society through "a series of 'Colonization Schemes' in which soldiers were settled."[7] But the invasion went beyond the exploitation of the Egyptian human and material resources, extending to holdover impulses that devalued the people and the territory that the sirdar conquered. As Kitchener boasted to Lord Cromer one day, "he [Kitchener] conquered a country of approximately one million square miles and two million inhabitants at a cost of two pounds, six shillings and six pence a square mile and only one pound three shillings and three pence a head."[8] This kind of dehumanizing logic continued throughout the colonial period.

The third peculiar element was the combined forces of the colonial regime, its history, and the violence it perpetrated. These combined forces always led to the extermination of high numbers of the population. The invading army's brutal treatment of Sudanese soldiers is one example. Upon receiving the news of Sirdar Kitchener's victory over the Mahdists at Karari, Queen Victoria telegraphed him to express her joy. "Surely [General Gordon] is avenged," she exulted, and named Kitchener the baron of Khartoum in gratitude. Winston Churchill, an eyewitness who accompanied the colonial invading army as a journalist, explained in *The River War* precisely how this vengeance was exacted. According to Churchill, the idea of avenging Gordon circulated among the ranks of the army, "inflamed the soldiers' passions and 'led them to believe that it was quite correct to regard their enemies as vermin—unfit to live.'"[9] In his criticism of the sirdar's conduct at Karari, Churchill asserted, "there was a very general [mistaken] impression that the fewer the prisoners, the greater would be the satisfaction of the commander."[10] He went on to describe how after the battle the Sudanese wounded were divided into three groups. The first and largest of the groups consisted of those who were considered dangerous, and they were wiped out. The second group included those whose wounds were life threatening and painful. The sirdar decided to put them out of their pain by slaughtering them "out of compassion." The third group was composed of those who had surrendered. Though disarmed, they were killed nonetheless. Churchill maintained, "about the third class there can be no dispute, how many were dispatched I cannot tell, although they threw down their arms and appealed for quarter."[11] Churchill lamented that "the victory at Omdurman was disgraced by the inhuman slaughter of the wounded and that Lord Kitchener was responsible for this."[12] Moreover, the "killing of wounded soldiers on the day of battle pales in comparison with the horrific neglect, related by Churchill and others, of the wounded left on the battlefield. Three days after the battle, Churchill revisited the site: 'The scenes were pathetic,' he wrote. 'Where there was a shady bush four men had crawled to die. Someone had spread a rag on the thorns to increase the shade.' Legless and armless men had dragged themselves unaided for miles to the river. Even a week after the battle 'there were still a few wounded who had neither died nor crawled away, but continued to suffer.'"[13]

The slaughter in Karari that Churchill recounted was only one of the brutal suppressions that the colonial state carried out after the battle of 1898, in order to put down different forms of resistance to the occupation. These forms of violence represent open wars, conducted either against rebellious provinces in order to recover territory (Egypt, 1896–98; Darfur, part of the Sudan, 1917) or to pacify resistance led by rebels or others who combated the colonial expansion ('Abdel Gadir wad Ḥaboba, 1908; 'Ali wad Almi mek of the Miri Nuba, 1915; the Nuer, 1927–28 and Dinka, 1919–20 rebellions).

The Karari massacre set the tone for this long and violent trek, which marked the end of the conquest phase of colonialist involvement in the Sudan. Later followed an amplification of systematic and incorporated forms of violence, both overt and covert, on the part of the colonialist state. These forms of violence worked both together and separately, as patterns of domination that remained in place during the entire lifetime of the colonial state.

The fourth peculiar element was how the Sudan was defined within the 1899 Anglo-Egyptian Agreement (see appendix), which describes the country as certain provinces "which were in rebellion against the authority of His Highness the Khedive [and] have been reconquered by the joint military and financial efforts of her Britannic Majesty's Government and the Government of His Highness the Khedive."[14] Only Britain and Egypt had a claim, as "accrued to her Britannic Majesty's Government by right of conquest, to share in the present settlement and future working and development of the said system of administration and legislation."[15] According to that agreement, the Sudan was defined as territories south of the twenty-second parallel. These territories were split into three distinct groups: territories that Egyptians had previously administered and had now been reconquered; territories that Anglo-Egyptian forces might, in the future, reconquer; and territories that Egyptian troops had never evacuated. These terms diverged from Britain's stated goal of recapturing rebellious Egyptian territory. They included within the Sudan, Wadi Ḥalfa and Suakin, which the Mahdists had never captured, and excluded parts of the old Equatorial Province and other territories that Anglo-Egyptian forces had never conquered—and would never reconquer. This kept alive the possibility of purely British expansion northward from Uganda.

The fifth peculiar relationship reflects the nature of the condominium, the composition of those involved in it, and the structure of thought and type of rule that Britain and Egypt pursued. This was a unique arrangement in which a European superpower and a semicolonized African state entered into an unprecedented partnership to colonize another country. Article 3 of the condominium agreement specified that "the supreme military and civil command in Sudan shall be vested in one officer, termed the 'Governor-General of Sudan.' He shall be appointed by Khedival Decree on the recommendation of Her Britannic Majesty's Government and shall be removed only by Khedival Decree, with the consent of Her Britannic Majesty's Government."[16] To the disappointment and criticism of the Egyptians, an Egyptian had never filled the posts of sirdar (supreme military commander) and governor general (*al-hakim al-'amm*) of the Sudan. From the very first day of the condominium up through 1924, the governor general and the sirdar of the army of the Sudan continued to hold both positions at the same time. Not only that, but the upper echelons of the administration were to remain in the hands of the British. These offices included the governor general's financial, legal, and civil secretaries; the inspector general; and the governors of the provinces and inspectors of the regions. In the entire codominium period, the British never assigned, or even nominated, a single Egyptian for any of these positions.

Another aspect of this out-of-the-ordinary arrangement was that the governor general of the Sudan was to report to the Foreign Office in London through Lord Cromer in Cairo, not the Egyptian prime minister. The governor general continued to report to the Foreign Office after the office of consul general was changed into the office of the high commissioner for Egypt and the Sudan and had never reported to the Colonial Office in London. Francis M. Deng and M. W. Daly argue that the Sudan "was not a colony in either the specific or a general sense."[17] While Daly describes it as an *Empire on the Nile*, Peter Woodward has suggested in correspondence with the author that the Sudan "was an imperial state or a colonial-style state since 'colonial' might be seen as indicating a formal status."[18]

Lord Cromer and the Egyptian minister of foreign affairs, Boutros Ghali, who was later assassinated for his overt collaboration with the British,[19] signed and brought into effect the condominium agreement on January 19, 1899. The sirdar, Kitchener, was appointed the first *hakim 'amm* (governor general) of the Sudan under the new arrangements of the condominium agreement. According to Lord Cromer, "After this fashion, the new Soudan was born. It was endowed with sufficient strength to support its existence. Nevertheless, it was of necessity to some extent the child of opportunism. Should it eventually die and make place for some more robust, because more real political creation, its authors need not bewail its fate."[20] In essence, however, "the salient point was that Britain had gained control of the Sudan, and while her policies and plans there would often have to take account of Egypt, that control was maintained by force, not by the Condominium Agreement."[21]

The sixth peculiar aspect of this relationship is in the planning of Khartoum—the new seat of the colonial state (see chapter 4). The city's layout was intended to resemble the Union Jack, a flag whose design features the intersecting crosses of the patron saints of the United Kingdom: Saints Patrick, Andrew, and George. Khartoum's major streets were named after the patron saints of the colonial state: Kitchener, Cromer, Victoria, and Gordon. Invoking such a complex paradigm, which brought together all patrons in matrimony, Khartoum was turned into "a persuasive, evocative city, both a crusader fortress and an outpost of reason in a barbarous land. Defying it across the Nile lay Omdurman—the Mahdi's bastion, 'the Orient,' Islam" (see chapter 5).[22]

The "new" Sudan and its condominium state and rule were born with all sorts of latent and manifest functions, dysfunctions, and differences as its state continued to be a meeting point of conflicting internal and external developments. All these developments and their social and political tribulations were built within a series of different and intricate opposites that characterized the peculiar nature of that arrangement. These different and intricate opposites became clear from the first day and continued to breed and reproduce other forms of uncoordinated modes of conflict that gave rise to a differentiated structure imposing itself on the Sudanese people. This structure continued as a single unit of division of labor, multiple cultures, and profound problems within a miniversion of the British imperial system. Like all colonial structures, this British minisystem represents another model that could be described as "part of a system where everything is anomaly. It is the strangest of all governments; but it is designed for the strangest of all Empires."[23]

Within the internal and external structures of the new imperial system, most of the Nile Valley was incorporated as one unit, reinventing and then integrating its different labor forms within a functioning division of labor under the control of Britain's resource extraction power. The United Kingdom stood as the only dominant core zone of that unit, while Egypt—a de facto dominated country and de jure codominus with Britain—was considered and treated as part and parcel of the semiperiphery zone. Within the same arrangement, both partners perceived the Sudan as the periphery zone. Not only were the political cultures and state ideologies of the two codomini not congenial to each other, their relationship with regard to the stipulations of ruling the Sudan was far from amiable or reverential. For Egypt, from the first day to the end, it was clear that "the Condominium was little more than having her face rubbed in the dirt by her British oppressors."[24] Egypt's resources and manpower were critical during the invasion of the Sudan and some of its employees were recruited as cheap labor. Although the British perceived the Egyptians as not a wholly efficient way to staff the colonial administration, they nevertheless filled the lower strata of *ma'mur* (subordinate) and *na'ib ma'mur* (subordinate deputy). Within the administrative structure of the colonial state, the Egyptians occupied an intermediate position between the British and the Sudanese. Although this position is important, as it brought them closer to the Sudanese people than to the British, for the same reason it rendered them suspect in British eyes.

The Construction of the "New" Sudan

Of the essential attributes of the construction of the "new" Sudan and its colonial state, four crucial elements are prevalent. The first of these attributes could be related to the makers of this new colonial state. At the very core of this state making, a few personalities played a very important role. In a speech delivered at the House of Commons in 1833, Lord Thomas Babington Macaulay, arguing about the government of India, stated that the "Empire is itself the strangest of all political anomalies. That a handful of adventurers from an island in the Atlantic should have subjugated a vast country divided from the place of their birth by half the globe; a country which, at no very distant period, was merely the subject of fable to the nations of Europe." The Sudan, however, differs from India in that it was "a country violated before by the most renowned of Western Conquerors" such as General Charles Gordon (1833–85) and Colonel William Hicks Pasha (1830–85). Both were killed in battle in the Sudan and their troops badly defeated. Nevertheless, the British attempted to "govern a territory ten thousand miles from us [Britain] . . . a territory, inhabited by men differing from us in race, colour, language, manners, morals, religion; these are prodigies to which the world has seen nothing similar. Reason is confounded. We interrogate the past in vain."[25] It might be important to note that this "handful of adventurers," whether in India, the Sudan, or another colony, represented the managerial elite of a corporate institution that Edward Said rightly described. They were exercising a system of domination, restructuring, and power.[26] All those managerial elites shared what could be described as specialized knowledge and uncontested assumptions about the place and its people. Janice Boddy describes these managerial elites and their mission as "haunted yet authorized by history; imbued with Christian values; assured of the merits of industrial technology, scientific rationalism, discipline, hard work, and commercial enterprise; ideological, sometimes arrogant, and perpetually defensive, the British mission in the Sudan had about it the aura of a crusade."[27] The makers of the new Sudan may be, in that sense, the most thoroughly knowledgeable individuals about the country who ever lived within that corporate institution. Lord Cromer belonged to that breed of the top managerial elite of the corporate institution, who "had been especially well placed in positions of uncommon influence to follow the Afghan and Zulu wars, the British occupation of Egypt in

1882, the death of General Gordon in the Sudan, the Fashoda Incident, the battle of Omdurman, the Boer War, [and] the Russo-Japanese War."[28] In addition to all that, Sirdar Kitchener, the first governor general of the Sudan, was at the helm of the military establishment as the governor of the Red Sea Province before the invasion. After this, he was appointed sirdar of the Egyptian army that headed the invasion and was then assigned to deal with the French military expedition under Jean-Baptiste Marchand in what became known as the Fashoda Incident. As for Francis Reginald Wingate, he held the position of director of military intelligence from 1889 until he was appointed governor general of the Sudan, in 1899. Before the invasion and for a decade, Wingate's work "developed into four main spheres of activity: firstly, military intelligence regarding the Khalifa's forces in the Sudan; secondly, the political and economic position in the Sudan itself; thirdly, the relations of the Sudan with its neighbours; and finally, the fate of those Europeans who had fallen in the Mahdi's hands when the Dervishes were overrunning the Sudan."[29] Wingate's book *Mahdism and the Egyptian Sudan* was published in 1891 and was followed in 1892 by the translation and publication of Father Joseph Ohrwalder's *Ten Years' Captivity in the Mahdi's Camp*. Wingate facilitated the escape of Father Ohrwalder and Sisters Elizabeth Venturini and Catterina Chincarini, the three members of the Austrian Roman Catholic Mission who had been prisoners in the Sudan since 1882. In 1894 Wingate facilitated the escape of Rudolf Slatin from Omdurman and early in 1896 he translated into English and published Slatin's *Fire and Sword in the Sudan*. By all these concerted efforts Wingate was successful in reviving British interest in the reconquest of the Sudan. The association of Cromer, Kitchener, and Wingate "with Egypt and the Sudan covered a period of thirty-six years—Cromer for the first twenty-four; Kitchener the first seventeen and then, after an interval of ten years, three more; and Wingate the whole thirty-six years, during seventeen of which he was Governor-General of the Sudan."[30]

The colonial state in the Sudan, its system of government, and its institutions based on this shared specialized knowledge and on an "aura of a crusade" were militaristic and totalitarian. Within this ethos, Kitchener was "determined to inscribe the signature of power on the rebuilt capital," the "crusader fortress," "without delay by constructing a governor's palace projecting the force and majesty of the colonial state whose blueprint he was sketching. His instructions differ from many other administrative circulars in this first phase of building a colonial state only in their brutal candor; state agents everywhere were driven by the logic of constructing institutions of domination with improvised resources."[31] Kitchener's governor generalship in the Sudan, which lasted only eleven months, expressed "the broader drama of the colonial state in its initial period: simultaneously to create agencies of rule and to invent extractive devices imposing on the subordinated societies the cost of the unsolicited governance proposed for them" (see chapter 4).[32]

What was more unique about the Sudanese experience, however, in this respect was that the two main architects of its colonial state, Wingate and Slatin, were the proprietors of a rare experience and a highly specialized knowledge about the place and its people. Wingate had been carefully and closely following all the events and developments in the Sudan from outside for about a decade, while Slatin, the wild card among the colonial patron saints, had been part of, and a close associate with, the Sudanese authorities for more than a decade, watching events from inside. As a "servant" to the khalifa, 'Abdullahi, as he claimed, Slatin "had not only learned a great deal about the ways of the Sudan, he had also, naturally enough, acquired grievances and formed biases that, when he returned to office, he did not forget."[33] The two persons complemented each other's knowledge and experiences very well. Over such an exceptionally long period (December 1899–December 1916), as a governor general with "supreme civil and military power, he was made a dictator."[34] Wingate had conspicuously put in practice a military structure of the state based on the three financial, civil, and legal secretaries, and a few military aids in the regions supervised by Slatin (the only Mahdist in the colonial camp), who "administered a heavy rebuke to those silly people who wish[ed] to shove the English Bibles down the throats of the African blacks."[35] What began as a military dictatorial rule gradually consolidated and maintained itself as Wingate continued to militarize the government by increasing the number of "British officers in the civil administration[, which] rose from 50 in 1901 to 105 in 1913."[36] As Daly explains, "it was Wingate's determination to maintain the military character of the regime that gave rise to the term 'Sudan Political Service.'"[37]

The second attribute of the structure of the colonial state relates to the Sudan Political Service (SPS), which was the regime's civil administration under the supervision of one of the three primary aids of the governor general, the civil secretary. The SPS, which was entirely composed of British subjects, "had a small secretariat in Khartoum under the Civil Secretary with the remaining members (never more than 150) serving as Province Governors, District Commissioners, or in other similar functions."[38] The SPS was Lord Cromer's initial attempt to address a private worry: that the "youthful soldiers [who] are in many respects excellent. . . . will, through ignorance of the language, fall into the hands of scheming native subordinates."[39] Those scheming native subordinates always included "some Egyptian underling or Arab Shaykh," standing between the "natives" and the Englishman.[40] Thus, "Cromer concluded that 'The only remedy' was 'gradually to train up a number of young English civilians' who would 'be prepared to stay in the country and acquire a thorough knowledge of the language.'"[41] From the beginning of the early days of the colonial rule, it was Lord Cromer's plan to recruit and build such a stratum of government employees from only "'active young men, endowed with good health, high character and fair abilities'; he did not want 'the mediocre by-products of the race, but the flower of those who are turned out from our schools and colleges.' The first six civilians were recruited in 1901 from Oxford and Cambridge, and several others added annually."[42] This corps d'elite, sometimes called the "blues," although it was modeled after and had to perform functions similar to those of the Indian civil service, differed from its counterpart in several aspects.

For one, the Sudanese civil service "could never rank as an imperial service, with all that was implied in the term, in security and advancement."[43] Second, in addition to being small, "its members would not be able to look to any promotion beyond the governorship of a province—what would be called in India the headship of a District—or a secretarial post such as Chief Secretary."[44] Third, the SPS personnel were selected from British subjects who would be prepared to spend their best years and their entire careers in the Sudan, "but would not look to more than limited preferment in the Sudan, and retiring before they were fifty, would . . . be able to continue a useful existence elsewhere."[45] Wingate, the sirdar and the head of the military regime, "was not alone in seeing civilian recruits as possibly out of place, inferior substitutes for the soldiers he preferred."[46]

The British journalist, historian, and essayist Sir Sidney James Mark Low (1857–1932) reported similar views in his famous book *Egypt in Transition*, which was published with an introduction by Lord Cromer in 1914.[47] So, Wingate was adamantly determined to build, propagate, and maintain the power of his military regime by keeping a close relationship with his officers, "which, though it inevitably became less personal as the administration of the country increased, was nevertheless maintained during the seventeen years of his rule."[48] The SPS members, for whom "the romance of empire made colonial service highly desirable and prestigious,"[49] were mostly "devout Christians or had been raised in a Christian milieu. Over a third of all Sudan Political Service officers were clergymen's sons, and even the least pious held Islam to be a backward-looking faith that inspired fatalism, superstition, and indolence."[50] Furthermore, they were caught up in a clear status inconsistency with the military officers. In one dimension, as graduates of the British elite schools, they possessed a self-image that placed them at the highest rank within the power structure of the colonial state. However, Wingate and his military enthusiasts tended to respond to them as "inferior substitutes for soldiers." These discrepant statuses resulted in three important traits.

First, the SPS continued to develop a life of its own by emphasizing the highest to rank self-image of their educational, national and imperial self-pride that "translated into the self-image of the lone District Commissioner, who could 'single-handedly' run an area the size of Yorkshire or Switzerland, or a population as large as Denmark's."[51] Second, all the SPS team were forced into a form of secular celibacy, as marriage "during the first two-year probationary period was cause for dismissal, and permission to wed was routinely denied for a further two or three years after that. Even then, juniors were actively discouraged, and often prevented, from bringing their wives to Sudan."[52] Third, through this self-image of higher rank they showed no affinity with the local population, to whom they manifested a "racial arrogance that piqued early nationalists."[53]

Finally, the SPS members developed their own definition of their function as one of serving the Sudanese. Despite the apparent dislike of civil servants expressed in such pithy phrasings as "inferior substitutes for soldiers," the SPS politics fostered the goals of the colonial state. On the one hand, such defining attributes of the SPS, though helpful in building the foundation of the Sudanese civil service and its ethos of impartiality, did not set it apart from the agents of rule in the colonial state; they were all dependent on the colonial state, without which they would lose their definition and efficacy. On the other hand, both the latent and overt dynamics were built on the dispensation of the colonial state as an apparatus of subjugation, domination, and expansion of British hegemony and an instrument of "extraction and exploitation."[54]

The third attribute relates to the colonial state as a central organizer of the construction and order of the political space. Wingate introduced and diligently followed a policy that extended, strengthened, and maintained an imperial order meant to sustain British cultural and political power as superior and to separate and debase what was non-British as inferior. On one hand, "Wingate employed all means at his disposal to stem the infiltration of Egyptian nationalist and pan-Islamic ideas into the Sudan. A special system of intelligence was devised in order to deal with this subtle penetration. The intelligence department, whose headquarters were in Cairo, kept a close watch on developments in the Egyptian capital and warned its branch in Khartoum to take any necessary action."[55] On the other hand, the imperial order Wingate devised and the military rule he established developed into a total "disciplinary institution" (to borrow Foucault's phrase), which continued to deal firmly with Egyptian nationalist and pan-Islamic ideas as well as Sudanese Sufi Islam and its jihadist orientations, which was Wingate's main worry during the early period of his colonial state. Wingate's fear and the Victorian suspicion of Islam were magnified and "haunted yet authorized by history," charged with Christian values, European modernity, and the perception of an aura of crusade that the British mission in the Sudan had.[56] The memory of Gordon's death and the events that followed in 1885 were kept alive, especially during the first period of the occupation, which saw a number of Sufi, Mahdist, and religiously inspired revolts in the Sudan. Nevertheless, the colonial state "soon discovered that Islam offered not only perils but also opportunities."[57] As Young explains, the essence of the colonial "doctrine of hegemony was a demonological exegesis of the Mahdiyya epoch."[58] Just when the colonial occupation seemed to have finally buried the Mahdist state, the ghost of Mahdism continued to haunt the scene. In the main, however, "religious charlatans, in this view, had exploited popular animosity to Turko-Egyptian rule and had packaged an appeal to rebellion in the religious motif of heterodox Islam. The British design was to supplant the Mahdiyya in exploiting the anti-Egyptian animus they took to be general in Sudan, while using orthodox Egyptian Islam as an instrument to combat and marginalize Sufi Islam from which the Mahdiyya sprang."[59] This dimension of colonizing Islam, which differentiated the Sudanese experience from other experiences, might have borrowed its modified framework from the British colonial experience elsewhere (mainly India).

Different systems of control or ways and means of colonizing Islam and the Sudanese lifeworld were initiated by Slatin, the second-highest-ranking person in the colonial state after Wingate. Armed with his wide knowledge of the country, different Sudanese Islamic representations, and the who's who in the political and religious fields in the country, Slatin initiated two processes of political inclusion. The first was to "encourage orthodox Islam while striving to lessen the impact of Sufism," which "cannot be allowed to be re-established, as they generally formed centres of unorthodox fanaticism."[60] This is not to say that kind of policy sympathized with orthodox Islam, but rather that it sought to establish "a Sudanese Muslim leadership which would find itself aligned to the interests of the established administration."[61] This kind of orientation's essential dispositions toward the orthodox discourse about Sufi Islam did not fit with Slatin's "nature" and his open "hostility towards Mahdists, especially the family of the Mahdi,"[62] but it did fit very well with Slatin's "nurtured" Mahdist ideology, for which one of the representations of such opposing discourses was fundamental.

In reordering the religious hierarchies, the inspector general relied on the board of the 'ulamā', which was instituted by the government in 1901, and on several Muslim leaders such as Sheikh al-Tayyib Aḥmed Ḥāshim the mufti (a Muslim scholar and a legal authority employed by the state to issue *fatwa* (decree) and interpret the shari'a), whom he regarded as trustworthy. The inspector general asked the advice of the board whenever a religious problem occurred, and they became the sole interpreters of orthodox Islam. Moreover, the promulgation of the "Sudan Mohammedan Law Courts Ordinance of 1902 established a central Islamic court of three members, the Grand Kadi (*Qāḍi*), the *mufti*, and another judge."[63] The Sudan Mohammedan Law Courts ordinance "vested in the *Grand Kadi* the power to make rules regulating the decisions, procedure, jurisdiction, composition and functions of *Shari'a* courts."[64] Slatin was responsible for the appointment of *al-quḍāt* (sing., *qāḍi*), "many of whom were of Egyptian origin, and thus was in a position to supervise their activities in the Sudan."[65] The promotion of orthodox Islam as a state religion and later the evolution of this policy was reflected in the government's integration of Islamic studies into the curriculum of Gordon Memorial College. Together with the institutionalization of the orthodox 'ulamā' as the only interpreters of Islam, this policy produced an uneasy ideological conflict. This conflict occurred between what was perceived as modern official Islam, which is orthodox, and that brand of Islam described as traditional and backward, composed of the Sufi orders whom Kitchener described as "heretical Moslem sects." As a consequence of that disposition, the Sufi majority were relegated to minority status in terms of stratification of power and prestige. Such an attitude has remained recurrent within the consequent developments in the Sudanese political arena and continues to play an important role in the political theory and practice of the Sudan's elites, both civilian and military.

Slatin was also the architect of the second process of control through inclusion of "what the colonial state understood to be the local institutions of tribe and kinship into the grassroots foundations of colonial domination."[66] These local institutions were also regarded "as a means by which it could derive a degree of legitimacy from association with 'traditional' social forces."[67] Reorganizing the administration of this sector of the population by appointing what is described as a "tribal" or "native administration," Slatin selected "men of his own acquaintance over those preferred by local British officials." Although, he was described as favoring "the restoration of traditional values of tribal authority,"[68] Slatin was, in fact, the architect of another system of an indirect form of colonization of the lifeworld of the Sudanese that fashioned a "decentralized despotism."[69] He established this structure through a group of handpicked personalities assigned the duties of local chiefs. Their appointment or restoration at the helm developed into what was called indirect rule. This structure fit very well with the stipulations of the military rule of the colonial state and its attempts at legitimizing "relations of authority."[70] This form of indirect colonization constructed a new order of "tribal" settings and ranking. Slatin formally instituted all that by locating this new order and differentiation in the local traditions of the colonized "natives" to indicate continuity with the past. These different forms of invented tradition were modified replications of a British ruling experience established in India based on "the notion that 'authority once achieved must have a secure and usable past.'"[71] That past, as Cohn further explains, was being codified. It required representation to both the British (whether in the colony or at home) and the colonized. Furthermore, it had both British and local components and a theory of the relationship of the two parts.[72] Later, the colonial and postcolonial states and political orders experienced different forms of acceptance and denial of the construction and invention of "tribal" structures as a necessary part of, not in, the political process and nation building.

The fourth attribute of the colonial state relates to the racial construction and differentiation of the colonized human landscape. When the British invaded the Sudan in the closing days of the nineteenth century, they drew upon the "Victorian doctrine of racial degeneration," which "supported views of 'oriental' history as a legend of decay, of the erosion of Islam and decline of its once glorious civilization to ignorance, indulgence, and excess. But if Arabs were deemed backward, fallen from levels they had once attained, they were nonetheless more highly evolved than Africans."[73] The "African" or the "Negro," within that concept, as Sir Harry Hamilton Johnston—one of the leading of the British Empire builders—noted, "more than any other human type, has been marked out by his mental and physical characteristics as the servant of other races."[74] The Negro, according to Johnston, "is possessed of great physical strength, docility, cheerfulness of disposition, a short memory for sorrows and cruelties, and an easily aroused gratitude for kindness and just dealing. He does not suffer from home-sickness to the over-bearing extent that afflicts other peoples torn from their homes, and, provided he is well fed, he is easily made happy."[75] As R. Hunt Davis concludes, "The result of Johnston's work and that of later scholars such as the ethnologist C. G. Seligman was to create a climate of opinion that led most Westerners to think that everything of value in Africa originated outside the continent, usually from supposed Caucasoid sources."[76]

On this doctrine the British colonial masters superimposed the idea of racial difference between northern Sudanese ethnic groups, described as Arabs, and other ethnicities, depicted as Negroes, in other parts of the country. This ideology of difference, which was intensified by the totalitarian condominium military regime, organized the Sudanese societies "so that it [the ideology] produced on the best possible terms, from the viewpoint of the mother country, exports which provided only a very low and stagnating return to labour."[77] It transformed the population landscape into a system of racial ranking, which divided the people into Arab-Semitic people over Hamites or Nubians, and Nubians over Sudanic and Nilotic peoples (Negroes). This defined ranking was both created by and served the political regime that designed it. Sir Harold MacMichael, a longtime British administrator in the Sudan, editor of "Sudan

Notes and Records," and author of several books about the Sudan, chief among them *A History of the Arabs in the Sudan*, wrote in a different book, "the line of division, geographical, ethnical and cultural, between the predominantly Arab north and purely negroid south is well marked and obvious, and still, as we shall see, potent as a political factor."[78]

MacMichael came to this conclusion after he gave a broad generalization of the country and its people. He described a first group of people as having a "highly educated, intelligent and progressive element" that came to be in towns and large villages, a second group as coming from "aboriginal pagan stock" in the Nuba Mountains, a third group as a "primitive negroid of whose origin little is known,"[79] and a fourth group as "a quick-witted, musical brown folk of medium stature," who are the Zande.[80] But what makes MacMichael's conclusion especially important is that he represents the opinion of a protocolonialist. Maḥmood Mamdani describes those protocolonialists as representatives of "the confluence of two institutions, scientific racism and scientific bureaucracy," which were "key to shaping" the colonial power.[81] Out of such a protocolonialist opinion came the "drive for mastery over men," as Ashis Nandy explains, "not merely as a by-product of a faulty political economy but also of a world view which believes in the absolute superiority of the human over the nonhuman and the subhuman, the masculine over the feminine, the adult over the child, the historical over the ahistorical, and the modern or progressive over the traditional or the savage."[82] Here, "it has become more and more apparent that genocides, ecodisasters and ethnocides are but the underside of corrupt sciences and psychopathic technologies wedded to new secular hierarchies, which have reduced major civilizations to the status of a set of empty rituals."[83]

The fifth attribute of the colonial state relates to its masculine nature, and what I call the secular celibacy that it enforced upon its British employees. As Nandy explains, the British Victorian culture experienced a split between two ideals of masculinity. Within this split, "the lower classes were expected to out their manliness by demonstrating their sexual prowess; the upper classes were expected to affirm their masculinity through sexual distance, abstinence and self control."[84] Two of the three patriarchs of this secular celibacy, "men such as Rhodes, Kitchener, or Gordon—who eschewed family life in favour of the attractions of overseas adventure,"[85] had a direct relationship with the Sudanese state at different times. The colonial state, which was built as a male enterprise, enforced this secular celibacy as a state policy. The Sudanese perceived this state of secular celibacy as incomprehensible, "even granting the exotic proclivity of Britons to marry for life." The Sudanese assumed that homosexuality was a British import.[86]

Within an *elective affinity* between these modes of militaristic, racist, and totalitarian pursuits, different despotic norms, ideologies of difference, identity and religious management, and economic exploitation, the colonial state emerged. This elective affinity manifested itself within an "appearance of structure" and carefully cultivated a myth inside these different forms of "bureaucracy and among political figures as the state's own myth of itself, and is constantly enacted through grand state spectacles, stamps, architecture, hierarchies of rank, systems of etiquette, and procedures within the vast expanse of the bureaucracy."[87]

At the helm of an absolutist system stood the governor general, wielding total power as *al-hakim al-'amm* (the governor general) and sirdar of the army to promulgate laws and regulations and to impose the dictates of private enterprise through a system of multiplied offices and structures, which in the end control, directly or indirectly, the entire population and their ability to make a living. To establish its presence as "both an expression and an extension of British power,"[88] through disciplinary pursuit, the colonial state used all means of soft and hard power, including coercion. The framework of the state was organized to maintain a single supreme and centralized authority over the whole country. The country was divided into twelve provinces each under a governor (*moudir;* pl., *mudarā*), who, like al-hakim al-'amm, were British military officers. They exercised total control as both the governor and the military commander of the troops in their provinces. The *mudarā* were followed by district commissioners and assistant district commissioners (*māmir;* sing., *ma'mur*), then the tribal chiefs, who were ranked from senior to junior as follows: *nuzār* (sing., *nazir*), *shukh* (sing., *shaykh*), and *'umad* (sing., *'umdah*), who worked under the supervision of the Egyptian *ma'mur.* Within this governing structure, "the ubiquitous British District Commissioner became the very important 'roving' administrator who continually sought the assistance of Rudolf von Slatin Pasha, the Inspector-General."[89] As Boddy explains, the colonial regime:

> drew on a disparate array of precedents—British, Turkish, Egyptian, Sudanese—from which there emerged a corporeal culture

> specific to Anglo-Egyptian Sudan. Its spectacle politics concealed a subtle but radical exercise of power. Assuming participants to have acted in good faith, observance of conventions concerning dress, salutes, postures and such would have had both performative effects (where commitment to a canonical order is achieved and sustained by enacting it) and mnemonic ones (where bodily habits of hierarchy and subjective dispositions are mutually informed). British officers were not alone in being subject to disciplines; Egyptian and Sudanese subordinates also lived them day by day. Differences of rank displayed on the human body hid salient if unspoken disparities of race and ethnic affiliation beneath the garb of individual achievement, subtly facilitating participants' "consent" to a hegemonic order that their very practices created and maintained.[90]

The new colonial state developed its aberrant constitutions and formations of its regimes of order as a private economic enterprise with "disciplinary institutions that establish authority, encode moralities, and order social relations."[91] Each particular aspect acquiesced to the demands of the state in favor of this whole colonial economic enterprise project. The new state took shape—different in appearance, violent in nature, and efficient in involving "the mental as well as the political and economic subjugation of the colonized, a subjugation that did not end with the independence movements of the late 1950s and early 1960s."[92]

3

The Malignant Tumor of the Colonial State

The Antibodies

In his last poem, Aḥmed wad Sa'd, the greatest of the Mahdiyya bards (*muddaḥ*), painted an extravagant picture of the time, the society, and the state he admired the most, bemoaning its end in a prophetic, apocalyptic vision full of affectionate intensity. After lamenting the demise of the great society of the Mahdiyya, he grieved over its brutal obliteration. In what could be considered a requiem par excellence for the death of a society, wad Sa'd pleaded with the martyrs of Karari to wipe away his tears. He concluded his poem by crying loudly:

ya ahl al-juba jala shofo al-Kuba
Islamna Iraba hab dina insaba,

Oh wearers of *al-juba*,[1]
hearken and see what a disaster
[this is where] our Islam has grown murky and our religion been cursed.[2]

Here, one will disagree with Robert L. Tignor, who asserts, "Often the voices of the invaded are silent. We look in vain for their reactions to the trauma of invasion and occupation."[3] The Egyptian Muslim scholar and chronicler 'Abd al-Raḥman al-Jabarti (1753–1825)[4] and others, such as wad Sa'd, noticed that "the exceptional nature of that [colonial] power lay not so much in military prowess, but in the order established in the aftermath of the conquest."[5] This new order has had specific characteristics and serious consequences. Most important of all was its attempt to prevail by shaking what Peter Berger describes as "the taken-for-granted certainty" and the "worlds of fate" to transform the entire social world of the colonized. Not all the Sudanese supported, or even sympathized with, the idea of Mahdism or its state. Different individuals and groups contested the idea that Muḥammad Aḥmed was the Mahdi; others took up arms against the Mahdist regime at different times. Nevertheless, great numbers of the population represented the engineering of the latent and manifest forms of resistance to the colonial state and its order. Nothing could have saved Sudanese society from the penetration and violence of the occupying system. However, the lives of the Sudanese people and their society would have been annihilated had it not been for the protective countermoves (both latent and manifest) that buffered, to a certain degree, the action of such destructive force, its order, and its mechanism of obliteration.

Two opposing forces struggled to reshape Sudanese society, its population, and their material life. The proliferation of these processes gave rise to a malignant tumor that begot and grew into the colonial state and has stayed alive ever since, guiding the disciplinary and coercive forces of the postcolonial state.

A Social Capital-in-Circulation: Mobilizing the Resources and Symbols of Resistance

Where intense destructive forces subjugated resistance and other forms of hostile engagement and the order of a colonial system was endured, inventive reactions and types of struggle assumed different modes within the wide-ranging scope of continuing resistance. A variety of social and political modes of operation capable of manufacturing additional factors that support and maintain the means of resistance from one side and social integration to the other, buttressed the production of self-identity and contributed to the sound and fury of an uneasy rebirth and suffocation of a civil society in the face of the colonial and postcolonial states and their coercive order.

Central to wad Sa'd's feeling of loss is what could be perceived as the countertransformation, the destruction of a good society he described in one of his poems as *al-jira al-'ammana khiera* (the neighborhood whose virtuous wealth we all relished). The virtue of that society had shaped the imagination of those who appreciated the kind of social change that was perceived as constituting the practice of a good and righteous Muslim society. Wad Sa'd's argument in this respect was speaking to the moral disposition of that society, appreciating its social practice rather than reflecting on the political differences of opinion, however repressive the regime that ruled over the population. His argument found meaning in the societal relations that the Mahdist revolution created for itself, its state, and the determinants of the founding of the Ansār as the core builders of what they perceived as a good society. The goodness or civility of that society became integral to people's lives across the country as they were drawn into the labyrinth of its revolutionary and moral authority. It was a society whose powers that be were determined by the everyday practice of its members, which were, in turn, fashioned by group prayer and the ideological regimentation of specific readings. These readings included *Ratib al-Imam al-Mahdi* (Prayer book) and the *Munshorat* (a collection of al-Mahdi's pamphlets), and writings such as *Nasiḥat al-'awam, Al-ayat al-byinat, Al-anwar al-saniya al-mahiyatu li dalam al-munkreen li al-Mahdiyya,* and *S'ādat al-Mustahdi fi sirat al-Imam al-Mahdi.* These textually based ideological enforcements of the Mahdiyya were reinforced by the work of bards like wad Sa'd, Aḥmed wad al-Twaim, Aḥmed abu Sharia, Aḥmed abu Kasawi, Aḥmed al-Qala'a, Muḥammad wad Surkati, and al-Manboor Muḥmmad, to name a few. Their oral feed of action orientations and performing arts came out of an expressive culture attractively crafted by their poetry and advocacy, on behalf of the regime. Such poets and bards had been important for centuries, even before the Mahdiyya. As Neil McHugh explains, they "were an invaluable resource because their skill as composers and eloquence as reciters inspired faith in the supernatural gifts of their masters" and their subject matter.[6] The Mahdiyya poets not only made their *madīḥ* a "central motif of sacred literature in the Sudan," but they gave that art and their subject matter an additional value by immortalizing the Mahdi who died in 1885, celebrating his successor al-Khalifa 'Abdullahi, and venerating the followers of the Mahdi, the Ansār. They continued to propagate the message of the Ansār's religious observance, self-assurance, audacity, and the uniqueness of the virtuous community they instituted. Such vociferous written cultural prerogatives and political utilities, together with an imminent belief in the Mahdiyya, have had deep social, political, and ideological consequences that greatly shifted previous boundaries and consolidated new powerful patterns of culture.

Thus, in sensing the expansion of the new range of enigmatic and unwarranted alternatives by the encroachment of a disaster (*kuba*) on that good society, wad Sa'd and other latter-day Mahdists, together with other groups of Sudanese in different parts of the country, set in motion an anticolonial impulse and activity disseminated through different forms of communicative systems. For example, wad Sa'd and like-minded protoreligious nationalists used an old music-lyrical activity through mobile groups of *muddaḥ*. These groups acted for and entertained the ordinary person by performing a vibrant poetic and musical tradition that stretched back more than five hundred years in the history of the country and propagated their audience's religious and political identities. Concerned about the good society and the material life of their Ansār community, they evoked anticolonial attitudes in popular terms, illustrating and disseminating them for public utility through a vocal, theatrical, face-to-face popular medium. This created a new human environment, in which growing communities of conversation opened up different methods of voicing an ever-growing, serious concern. That concern was translated into different forms of resistance to, and confrontation with, the new colonial order.

This attitude and its developments added to the multilayered forms of other emerging communities of conversation. Hence, the entire external world became not only uncertain but also extremely menacing and dangerous for all these communities. Their own internal world became more and more complex and they became prone to active and passive reactions. These groups were forced to pull themselves together and act, as they all felt that their material and social worlds were threatened. Some of these communities of conversation were shaped by their mutual discontent, hostility, and antagonism toward alien invaders. Others withdrew from the fields of the colonial presence altogether (especially Omdurman), while a third group pursued uneasy forms of relationship with the structural, colonial, or institutional dimensions of the regime, but not necessarily with its cultural order. These efforts and their resulting empowerment and constraints had an effect beyond their end results to those who opposed or took positions according to conditions and circumstances among the population. The very fact that different forms of insurgence and discontent were alive was an empowering political statement to many sectors of the population. This signifies, in fact, that conflict in itself embodies, in principle, a discernible form of social interaction, while hostile or antagonistic attitudes represent, in essence, "predispositions to engage in action." Such engagement could help generate an energy inspired by the strength of these societies and their social capital in circulation to both transform and reproduce a strong or a weak link between different forms and modes of resistance.

The separate and concurrent processes of the development of the colonial state, together with the impact of the formation and progression of resistance, and the resultant changes of scale in both Sudanese society and the state represent a complex event in history. That is, the development of this phenomenon represents the relentlessness of both the state and the society—each within its own terms—as they exercised their power on each other, on the one hand, and the incompleteness of each according to its own capacity to act, on the other. The resistance that Sudanese society produced had two important characteristics: its continuous nature and its inventiveness in producing different strategies.

It is important to consider the environment in which this resistance found itself. During the resistance, Sudanese society was both subject to destabilization and threatened with total destruction. This destruction and destabilization was the direct result of two things: the growth of the state as a primary mode of organization of domination, and the obliteration of emerging forms of civil society. During the half-century lifetime of the colonial state, three important forms of resistance to the colonial order and its state took place. These experiences were important not only for their scale, but for the enlargement of the development of nation building within the external and internal circumstances of the growth of the state and the civil society. It is important to look first at the underlying forces and the structures of relations that made up the emerging formations of resistance and the conditions it found itself in. Next, one must examine their associations with different groups' sentiments and the traditions from which they emerged, as well as the reactions and correspondence of these groups with each other. For this, each of these three developments, in its very essence, represents an important point of divergence and convergence in the form of struggle out of which profound changes then took place.

The First Form of Resistance

It did not take long for Wingate to discover that it was wishful thinking when he cabled his wife jubilantly in November 1899 to say, "Hurrah! Mahdism is finished." It did not take al-Khalifa 'Abdullahi and those defiant Mahdist communities of conversation long to develop into armed insurgents of various sorts. After the battle of Karari, al-Khalifa 'Abdullahi and a number of amirs headed west, calling on his remaining forces to regroup and his people to rally around him and begin again fighting the invading army. His plan was to summon his commanders and their troops from different parts of the country. At that time, "there was still the army of Aḥmad Faḍīl in al-Qadarif, al-Khatim Musa in el-Obeid and 'Arabi Daf' Allah in al-Rajjaf. He would call on them to join him. They would take Omdurman by storm and enter the city as victors just as he had done with the Mahdi thirteen years before."[7] In January 1899, Lt. Col. Walter Kitchener, brother of the sirdar, was near al-Khalifa 'Abdullahi's camp, but he retreated when he discovered the khalifa's army was more than ten thousand strong. The presence of 'Abdullahi with such a growing army was therefore neither inconsequential nor frivolous. It was a daily reminder to everybody that Mahdism was still alive, an aspect that neither coincided with the ambitions of, nor fit with the new colonial regime and its order. The khalifa was a threat to the colonial state's presence and its self-image. It was evident that whatever remained of the old order, subject though it was to all unfavorable conditions, had the vitality not only to resist but also to challenge the new order, its military state, and its power. Hence, by October 1899 rumors stormed the city "about the Khalifa's movements and about a supply of buried weapons in Omdurman, to be used to prepare the way for a renewed revolt in his support."[8] At the same time, reports "were repeatedly reaching the Intelligence Department of the preparedness of the men of Omdurman and the neighbouring villages. An atmosphere heavy with rumours hung over the city. The rumours finally took shape in definite news. Al-Khalifa was on the move, heading for Omdurman."[9] By November 1899 a force of 3,700 men with artillery and a company of the new British weapon of mass destruction—the Maxim machine gun—under Wingate himself engaged with the khalifa at Umm Dibaykrat. It was another fierce battle where superior organization and unmatchable weaponry won the day, which ended when "one thousand of the Khalifa's men fell, either slain or wounded. 3,150 men and 6,250 women and children were taken prisoner."[10] In his official report, Wingate wrote that when al-Khalifa saw the destruction of this army, "he called on his Emirs to dismount from their horses, and seating himself on his '*furwa*' or sheepskin,—as is the custom of Arab Chiefs who disdain surrender,—he had placed Khalifa

'Ali Wad Ḥelu on his right, and Aḥmed Fedil [Faḍīl] on his left, whilst the remaining Emirs seated themselves around him, with their bodyguards in line some 20 paces to their front and in this position they had unflinchingly met their death."[11] The heroic death of al-Khalifa 'Abdullahi and his men has rendered them everlasting admiration, not only among the Sudanese but even within the ranks of his enemy. Later, Wingate's son Roland wrote, "even a European country will tolerate despotism in its most atrocious guise if the despot to the people represents their country resurgent, their religion and their place in the world. The Khalifa 'Abdullahi represented to his followers all these things; he also had courage, and he was not afraid to face his end in battle."[12]

Compounding oppositional developments were those arising more immediately from the destruction of what remained of the Mahdist state and the death of al-Khalifa 'Abdullahi. Those who were imbued with the spirit of the Mahdist revolution and nurtured by the jihadist teachings and practices of its state pulled together to encounter the colonial state on the field of its military superiority and challenge its new order. The ideological impulse of these rebellious groups found marked affinity with the spirit and capital within and beyond wad Sa'd's sense of loss to produce hostile violent actions toward the new colonial state and its new order. For their rejection of the new regime, those resilient Mahdist communities of conversation initiated and mobilized symbols of a newfound religious identity by which they related to binding ideas in order to define themselves, their modes of operation, and ways they could respond to new challenges. Of the most militant upsurges that took shape at that time were those that evolved around ideologies of post-Mahdism (for example, the credo of *al-nabi 'Isa*, or the second coming of the prophet Jesus Christ). These movements continued with modest intensity for almost the first two decades of colonial rule. Some Mahdists saw in the invasion and its leader, Sirdar Kitchener, the fulfillment of the appearance of the Antichrist (*al-Masīḥ al-Dajjal*) and asserted that both the Mahdi and al-Khalifa 'Abdullahi had prophesied his appearance. "They also appealed to the prophecy of Sheikh Faraḥ wad Taktūk [an ancient Sudanese Sufi] who said at the 'end of time the English will come to you, whose soldiers are called police, they will measure the earth even to the blades of the edges of grass. There will be no deliverance except through the coming of Jesus.'"[13]

In 1908 'Abd al-Qadir wad Ḥaboba and some of his followers spearheaded other attempts to restore the Mahdiyya. Millenarian upsurges were encountered in different parts of the country from just after the brutal suppression of wad Ḥaboba's uprising until 1921. Songs of mourning (*manaḥāt,* sing. *manaha*), gratifying wad Ḥaboba's courageous confrontation of the colonial state and his defiance until the moment of his execution, spread like wildfire. Wad Ḥaboba's sister, Ruqayya, composed more than one of these *manaḥāt*. In a passage that has echoed through generations and has become an anthem for the nation, Ruqayya proudly describes her brother walking toward the gallows:

> *bitread al-litām assad al-khazaz al-zām hazeat al-balad min al-Yaman li al-Shām*
> You welcome combat, ye ferocious lion of the thick forest,
> You shook the country from Yemen to Greater Syria.

Ruqayya's *manaḥāt* added a new dimension to that spirit of resistance and defiance by connecting it to the collective memory and to a rich reservoir of an expressive culture of such creative contributions as hers, wad Sa'd's, and others' to create a literature that praise singers and entertainers continue to transmit through traditional and new media. What started as an anticolonial narrative has become consolidated throughout the lifetime of the colonial period as an important addition to the national and nationalist anticolonial discourse.

Abel Gadir wad Ḥaboba and all the other opposition incidents and movements emerged, locating themselves in "some eschatological traditions" and in commitment to jihad. As Ruqayya said in her *manaḥat,* their jihad cry was: *al-din manṣūr,* Religion is victorious. This new ideology of jihad joined wad Sa'd's nostalgia for that good society in the national consciousness. The two strains of thought influenced one another, one favoring passive but defiant expression of sentiment in poetry and song, the other tending toward violent action by armed groups. These groups associated the termination of the Mahdiyya, and the brutal murder of al-Khalifa 'Abdullahi and his closest lieutenants, "with the appearance of al-Dajjal, the anti-Christ who, in turn, [would] be destroyed at the return of al-Nabi 'Isa, the Prophet Jesus." This was of particularly serious concern to the British colonialists, "who found themselves seen not only as alien rulers, the *Turuk* [as the Sudanese labeled them], who might be overthrown like their nineteenth century predecessors, but even as *al-Dajjal* against whom *Nabi 'Isa* would arise and lead the people into battle once more."[14]

It might be difficult, if not completely erroneous, to look at the Sudanese resistance to the colonial state and its order as a northern or Islamic enterprise or both. The resurgence, with its diverse forms and ideological and nationalist claims, especially within the first two decades, was a clear resistance to the occupation, the colonial state, and its order.

Other violent hostilities dominant over the first two decades of the colonial period had taken place in the southern part of the country, the Nuba Mountains, eastern Sudan, and Darfur. The nature of resistance to the colonial regime was different in each of these places. Sometimes it did not revolve around eschatology or religion, while in other times it did. Generally, it did revolve around the most cherished and fundamental human right of rejecting outside interference. Because of this propensity for independence, the colonialists encountered a different but unwavering resistance in all parts of the country. Each of these insurgencies or resistance movements seemed to have a life of its own. Nevertheless, the synergy of that independent impulse was similar to the religious impulse in calling for a "language of ultimate order."[15] In addition, the colonial administration continued to subdue these forms of resistance "through ever-widening use of force, which tended to deepen alienation and resitance."[16] The oppressive grip of the colonial state encompassed the entire Sudanese population, regardless of their location or religious affiliations, in very different ways.

Accordingly, one sort of violence—the Sudanese resistance—turned into "an emblem of protest" while the other form of violence—that of the colonial state—became "an emblem of control." Moḥamed 'Omer Beshir has recorded the history of resistance to the colonial order in the southern part of the country and the violence with which the state met that resistance:

> Expeditions and patrols were sent from time to time to quell a revolt of a tribe refusing to submit or suffering from inter-tribal feuds and fights. The Nuer were the most difficult of the tribes to pacify. In 1902 a force was sent against the Nuer witchdoctor Mut Dung. Other expeditions against this tribe were sent in 1910, 1911, 1914, 1917, 1920, 1923, 1924 and 1928. It was not until the early 1930s

> that the Nuer finally submitted. Other patrols were sent against the tribes: in 1907 against the Awok Dinka, 1912 against the Bier, in 1911 against the Twig Dinka, in 1912 against the Bier, in 1914 against the Anuak, in 1916 against the Latuka, in 1918, 1919, and 1920, 1921, 1923 against the 'Aliab Dinka, and in 1922 against the Toposa and the Didinga.[17]

Douglas H. Johnson adds another aspect to a system of punishment and control followed by the colonial state in order to "pacify" the southern population. According to Johnson, the colonial administration "took the simplest form of maintaining government prestige and authority through the continuation of coercive policies. Among most of the pastoralist societies of the central clay plains and swamp area of Upper Nile and Bahr al-Ghazal, cattle were extracted as tribute, not primarily for their economic value, but as a practical demonstration of government authority and as an obligatory sign of submission by the pastoralist people."[18]

A momentous corollary of the violent resistance to the colonial rule was the persistent and fierce opposition the British encountered in the Nuba Mountains. In a similar vein, to the south, the Nuba Mountain communities that resisted the Turko-Egyptian intervention also defied the heavy-handedness of the Mahdiyya, who considered the Nuba Mountains to be *dar al-Hijra*, location of Jebel Qadir (Jebel Massa, according to al-Mahdi), which sparked the Mahdist revolution. Here as in the north and the south—different forms of rebellion took place against the colonial state, such as the Talodi insurgency in 1906, where "forty-six people, including the *ma'mur*, were killed."[19] The government reacted violently, and "about 400 of the rebels were killed during the insurrection. In August two rebel leaders, 'Faki Awri and Abd Sham Sham,' were executed after a court martial, thus precipitating a controversy similar to that caused by the hanging of Muhammad al-Amin in 1902."[20] The Nuba resistance continued, only to be followed by punitive patrols. In 1915 Faki 'Ali wad Almi organized a revolt attacking the government's post at Kadugli. Between 1917 and 1918, massive operations were launched against the Nuba highlanders, burning and entirely destroying their villages, hanging rebel leaders, and cutting off their water supplies. The government was making an example of the Nyima Nuba, and in order to make sure other groups got the message, they "brought in notables from other hills to witness the operation."[21]

Another example of resistance, 'Ali Dinar joined together a similar spirit of resistance and the spirit of independence with his own ambitions: "either just before or just after the battle [of Karari] he ['Ali Dinar] gathered a few Fur followers, and headed west to regain the throne of Darfur."[22] 'Ali Dinar was neither a Mahdist, like wad Ḥaboba or 'Arabi Dafa' Allah or even *Faki* Sanin Hassan, nor was he a collaborator with the new colonial regime. In one sense, 'Ali Dinar's "presence in Darfur was an insurmountable obstacle to the Khalifa in the west."[23] The veiling and unveiling of 'Ali Dinar's ambition, attitude, and resistance to the colonial state was not far from the anticolonialist's impulse and its antithetical nature.

First of all, being aware of Wingate's determination "to avoid a military fiasco reminiscent of Hicks Pasha's expedition to Kordofan in 1883,"[24] 'Ali Dinar continued to "show the same skill at interminable evasion, the same fertility in producing excuses, that he had displayed years before when Mahmud Ahmed was waiting for his submission."[25] Wingate did not send troops to fight against 'Ali Dinar directly. Yet, Dinar was not completely ignored.

The first aspect of Wingate's policy led to the second: to avoid another expedition like Hicks Pasha's, Wingate tried first what Alex de Waal would describe as "counter-insurgency on the cheap." Plans were carried out to supply groups hostile to 'Ali Dinar with weapons. The supply of arms came in handy to the "Rizayqat of southern Darfur, who for years had been at odds with the sultān but received little support from the Sudan government. Bassett, an inspector in Western Kordofan, arranged for the supply of three hundred rifles and thirty thousand rounds of ammunition to the tribe to arm a special irregular force. In December the loan of two hundred rifles to 'Ali al-Tom of the Kababish was approved."[26] This informal resemblance between Wingate and 'Umar al-Bashir's counterinsurgency on the cheap might draw our attention to the similar strategies of domination regimes pursue and the decentralized forms their counterinsurgencies take, regardless of dissimilar players, times, and circumstances.

'Ali Dinar was aware of the internal and external anticolonial movements in Africa and in the Muslim world. He paid particular attention to the anti-British sentiments within the Sanusi *jihādi* movement in neighboring Libya, together with the Islamic alliances, which went beyond ethnicity to rally Arabs, Tuareg, Tibbu, and other ethnic groups. All that unveiled to Wingate 'Ali Dinar's most alarming form of defiance to the colonial regime in the country: forming alliances within his neighborhood and with other Muslim entities like the Ottomans. While the Sudanese religiopolitical chain of memory was vibrant with the successful rebellious experiences, the British and their colonial state focused their "ultimate objective"—to capture and occupy the Darfur capital, al-Fashir—"'on the Omdurman precedent, causing the final overthrow of 'Ali Dinar and the collapse of further organized resistance.'"[27]

The war against 'Ali Dinar ushered in the period of "colonial policing" in the Middle East, where aerial bombardment provided a better and more cost effective way to win the day. Nevertheless, it was not the end of resistance to the colonial order, as Darfur after 'Ali Dinar proved to be more dangerous than expected. Indeed, "'Ali Dinar's rule had checked the influence of individual *fakis*,[28] but following his downfall their influence kept recurring, as it had in other parts of Sudan before the First World War."[29] The revolt of faki 'Abdullah al-Siḥayni, which occurred in Nyala in 1921, resulted in the death of British officials and was a new proof that the impulses of resistance and Mahdism were still alive. Al-Siḥayni successfully rallied behind him the Masalit, the Merarit, and the Borgu, in addition to some West African immigrants. In his report to the civil secretary in Khartoum, the British governor of Darfur quoted southern Darfur district commissioner McNeil's observation that "'all the neighbouring tribes were sitting on the fence awaiting the result of this attack and had it been successful they would have joined the enemy whose numbers are estimated at five thousands.'"[30] 'Awad al-Sid al-Karsani adds that the Arab groups of the Habānia and Bani Helba "were in continuous revolt during the time of the Mahdist state" and, in McNeil's words, "'not going to join in—though of course they probably would if the *Faki* had a success at Nyala.'"[31]

This diversity in the ideological millenarian visions and other different motivations of collective identities for all and each form of resistance to the colonial state, together with the counterviolence of that state, which James Currie described as "the blood stained policy,"[32] became permanently instituted as different—but progressive—forms and modes of the exercise of power. Within such an environment, however, the Sudanese mode of resistance to the colonial state had transformed into a new form of solidarity.

The Second Form of Resistance

By the mid 1920s, the Sudanese clearly felt that the era of the first Mahdist and non-Mahdist modes of resistance to the colonial state and its order were coming to a close. However, a reinvention of "the al-nabi 'Isa doctrine took amongst Mahdists, Fulani [Muslim West Africans] and other Sudanese [from western Sudan] was the belief that 'Abdel Raḥman al-Mahdi, the son of Mohammed Ahmed, would have the spirit of 'Isa manifest within him at the appointed hour."[33] The Ansār believed *al-ishara*, or the pronouncement to begin jihad, to be that appointed hour. By that time Sayyid 'Abd al-Raḥman al-Mahdi had consolidated his power as the absolute leader among the Mahdist families, earning him the title of imam of the Ansār. 'Abd al-Raḥman's vision depended on a policy of peaceful resistance. Through an alternative to confrontation, as he explained in his memoirs,[34] he engaged himself and his people in a common effort to build an economic enterprise on the bases of collaboration with the new colonial regime. In doing so, he bent the Ansāri spirit of jihad and resistance to fit the aims of neo-Mahdism within a well-defined economic institutional mechanism.

At the same time, it was the colonial state's new policy "to 'absorb' and win over to permanent allegiance this large portion of the community, the neo-Mahdists, as he [C. A. Willis] called them, by granting them 'slightly greater freedom.' By doing this, the authorities would so closely identify the interests of those people with that of the government that their leaders could be relied on to keep it informed of any adverse movements."[35] On the other hand, the colonial regime's new policy toward neo-Mahdism and its leader had placed that state as the power center that dominated other Sudanese groups. Hence, "the removal of the restrictions on al-Sayyid would immediately alarm his rivals in other ṭuruq, particularly the leaders of the Khatmiyya, Tajanniyya and Isma'iliyya, and drive the Ansār in certain places 'to make themselves and their beliefs undesirably conspicuous.'"[36] Willis, who replaced Slatin as the country's chief intelligence officer, sensed that old Mahdism was no longer a threat, and he himself even proclaimed, "'the most fanatical dervish can meet the Government on common ground.'"[37] The main sign of that, according to Willis, was what "Sayyid 'Abd al-Raḥman had 'shown by his loyalty and good will.'"[38] Accordingly, the colonial state offered him a conditional freedom of movement and a license to develop and pursue his agricultural enterprise. The "gradual drift," as R. Davies described it, or the turnabout effect of such a development, was extremely significant.

For the colonizers it was one form of "managing dissent." As Nandy explains, in different but similar settings, "a colonial system perpetuates itself by inducing the colonized, through socioeconomic and psychological rewards and punishments, to accept new social norms and cognitive categories."[39] The governor general of the Sudan, Sir Geoffrey Archer, summarized the orientation of that policy by ordering his government "to treat him ['Abd al-Raḥman], certainly with firmness, but also with the greatest personal consideration and respect as the best means of preserving the loyalty of his followers."[40] He later added, when Sayyid 'Abd al-Raḥman was recommended for a KBE in 1925, that "it looks as though the position may restore itself to this, that he is an accredited and highly esteemed hostage in our hands, and I only hope, in the manner of the East, he will appreciate that we can judge the tree only by its fruits."[41] For Sayyid 'Abd al-Raḥman, as he explains in his memoirs, *Jihad for the Cause of Independence*, it would be a mistake to confront the colonial state and continue to fight it in the old way.[42] Such a confrontation, according to Sayyid 'Abd al-Raḥman, would be catastrophic for the Sudanese people. As a leader who rarely showed a tendency to use physical force or violence, Sayyid 'Abd al-Raḥman was "pragmatic enough to realize that the British were arrogantly supreme, and that his father's extreme tactics would not unseat them."[43] Hence, his logical alternative to the jihadist mode of insurgency, revolution, or any direct form of confrontation, was to gradually organize the Ansār, protect them from the government's oppression, and help them live in peace "until God eases their plight and . . . [they] emerge stronger to regain the rule of the country."[44]

Sayyid 'Abd al-Raḥman successfully attracted and organized the Ansār almost throughout the entire country and employed large numbers of them in different levels of his new agricultural enterprise, which spread across Aba Island, as well as the areas of the Blue and White Nile. This involvement forever changed the functions of the Ansār as a group, neo-Mahdism as a movement, and the obligations of its leadership to the goal their forefathers gave their lives to fulfill. In his quest to reconcile these essentially contradictory or potentially conflicting aspects found within the accumulation of wealth and the ideals of austere life and Mahdism's *jihādi* reference point, Sayyid 'Abd al-Raḥman's vision was clear: political and religious strength require financial power. Practical means of changing the jihad against the colonial state took the form of a systematic commitment to *ishara* by Sayyid 'Abd al-Raḥman himself. Until that time came, the Mahdist morality of hard work, diligence, and self-discipline was to be followed; delayed gratification was promised, saved, and sometimes reinvested. The successful movement of the Ansār from western Sudan en masse to Aba Island and the White Nile areas closer to Aba enhanced the capitalist success of Sayyid 'Abd al-Raḥman and helped form the nucleus of the new capitalist agrarian class of neo-Mahdists around the Sayyid. In correlation to the new function of the Ansār, neo-Mahdism, and Sayyid 'Abd al-Raḥman's leadership, the colonial state shifted its attitude toward him. According to the consideration of the Sudan's governor general, Sir John Maffey, "as al-Sayyid is behaving reasonably in the religious and political field, we ought, as a measure of political expediency, to bind him to us by economic fetters" (quoted in Ibrahim, *Sayyid 'Abd al-Raḥman*, 74). But no matter what the objective of 'Abd al-Raḥman's collaboration with the regime, nor the type of fetters he was bound with, the emergence of neo-Mahdism and its leader was in itself neither a political nor a religious movement in the truest sense. Rather, it was an economic move that turned work into a sacred calling and set in motion a religious spirit in that direction. The reproduction of an asymmetric field of power in which the effects of competition with the colonial state itself as a capitalist enterprise and with the other collaborators, who had already forged an uneasy relationship with that state, opened new vistas for political rivalry. Some of the players reconciled and collaborated with the colonial state's self that offered instantaneous gratification, while contesting the other colonial cultural self of that state.

The Third Form of Resistance

In particular, most of those who constituted that uneasy relationship with the colonial state were an essential part of religious Sufi, 'ulamā' (scholars), or other regional or ethnic groups with old and irreconcilable differences and frequent ideological objections to Sudanese Mahdism and its different forms of representation. Most of these groups, with their divergent outlooks and interests, neither denied the eschatological tenets of the Mahdiyya nor resented the independence or integrity of their country. Despite the challenge and the refutation some of these groups expressed openly or took into account with regard to the authenticity of Muḥammad Aḥmed in person as the Mahdi, they did not deny or argue his personal qualities of piety, nor did they disagree with the reasons for his rebellion. Three forms of asymmetrical synergy emerged between these different Sudanese communities and the progression and growth of Mahdism and its state.

The first form of synergy was created between the Sudanese revolution and its leader, Muḥammad Aḥmed al-Mahdi, without creating serious cleavages among the ranks of the Sudanese population. The second form of synergy grew between some of these Sudanese groups and the Mahdist state during the tenure of al-Khalifa 'Abdullahi, while the third form arose from the conflict between the Mahdist state's ideology and practice and Sufi beliefs. The residue of this complex situation was the main and fundamental issue that made the withering away of a Sudanese institutional impulse of resistance to an alien order as a function of the realization of the colonial state an unattainable task. Within this context, it was clear that ideological differences among Sudanese groups had never developed into ideological or social fences between these groups or into a civil war. It is well known, for example, that the Sufi ṭarīqa al-Tijaniyya continued to repeat what their sheikh, Muḥammed wad Doulib, had said in his prescient poem, claiming

> *la khier fi al-Sudan ba'ad al-ān*
> One cannot expect something better from the Sudan from now on.

Time and again al-Tijaniyya, together with other groups, have channeled their dislike of the Mahdiyya by citing and reciting that poem, especially the verse that says

> *akhir al-zaman kulhu asf wa al-Ingleez amrahum akhuf*
> The end of time is all sorrow and the English (British) ordeal would be scarcely discernible in comparison.

Nevertheless, none of al-Tijaniyya as a group or on an individual level acted against the Mahdist state. Not only al-Tijaniyya, but also the followers of the Sufi ṭarīqa al-Qadiriyya followed al-Mahdiyya without abandoning their own beliefs. They quoted the noncommittal statement of Sheikh al-'Ubeid wad Rayya, about al-Mahdi: "*kan Mahdi jeed layena wa kan ma Mahdi shin layena*" (if he is the Mahdi, that would be good for us; otherwise, it would not be our business). Apart from these groups, the Khatmiyya, whose leadership suffered voluntary exile in Egypt, openly disagreed with the Mahdi and refused to join the Mahdist ranks and its violent pursuit "on two grounds: the leader of the Order did not believe in the religious mission of the Mahdi as the 'Expected One' and the Khatmiyya saw in the political domination of the Mahdists a threat to its position and privileges."[45] Throughout the Mahdist era, different forms of disagreement with the doctrine, the state, and its leadership were symptomatic of the crisis that manifested itself in varying degrees and forms of dissent against the state and its autocratic rule. Some of these groups showed their dissent through progressing propensities to engage in violence. Others found themselves confronted with dissonance as the Mahdist state began to lay its foundation on an oppressive form of governance characterized by enshrining the ideology of the Mahdiyya as a state religion and by denying other Sufi ṭuruq expressions the freedom to operate either openly or without restraint. One never knows whether the anti-Ansār poems of the most prominent Sudanese poet, al-Hardalu, with their racial epithets, were a reflection of an ethnic (*shukri*) or a doctrinal (*khatmi*) unsympathetic sentiment, as in the following verse:

al-waga'at 'alay taqa' 'alaī al-Ansār
What has befallen me, I hope will befall al-Ansār.

Nevertheless, the colonial regime was sympathetic neither to the Sufi communities of believers nor their ṭuruq. On the contrary, both Kitchener and Wingate perceived them as sources of trouble, regarding them as "little more trustworthy than the Mahdists."[46] The fear of any potential or imagined movements, or a resurgence that might arise from Sufi Islam and constitute a new threat to the new colonial state, took many different incarnations. From its first day, the colonial state and its propaganda machine acted aggressively and indiscriminately against all forms of Sufi representations or ṭuruq, their institutions of learning, and all forms of religious private practice, which Kitchener described as "the deepest threat to the Sudan." Hence, the government favored prompt, hard-hitting suppression of any rebellion without giving its leaders a chance to escape, "lest their followers 'credit them with supernatural powers.'"[47] Another strategy in this regard was the unrelenting efforts to replace Sufi "seats of authority and learning [which] were spread out through the villages and towns, and whose teachers were individual sheikhs of sufi orders, . . . by one central authority, one official seat of learning, in the capital, under the watchful gaze (and indirect administration) of British authorities."[48] In addition, the state as a colonizer of religion and the lifeworld of the population, describing itself as the sole agent of Islam, imposed and institutionalized an "Orthodox Muhamedanism" as the state religion and the only religion recognized by the government. As early as 1901, the colonial state appointed the Board of the 'Ulamā' as the sole arbiter of all things Islamic. Wingate saw its role, or the colonization of Islam, "as a way 'quietly but firmly' to deal with the *tariqas*, by which he meant *fuqara* generally, who, he said, had 'been rather on the increase.'"[49]

But Sudanese resistance to the colonial state was provided with another model of reference and soft resistance when Sayyid 'Ali al-Mirghani, after persistent and patient work, succeeded not only in countering the colonial policy toward Sufi Islam, but also in reinstating al-Khatmiyya ṭarīqa as a legitimate socioreligious practice without much constraint. In itself, this move was significant. The colonial state branded al-Khatmiyya as the government ṭarīqa, but the Khatmiyya and their leadership saw themselves as creating a dent in the colonial body of state religion. By this, they counterbalanced the policy of a state religion with a private one. Sayyid 'Ali's move opened a new space that enabled other actors within the other ṭuruq to reinstate themselves in an asymmetric form to the newfound state religion. Thus, they reestablished themselves within their historically and religiously pluralistic and differentiated forms and practices within the Sudanese religious private sphere. The change in the Sudanese religious field was swift and complete, as other ṭuruq proliferated in the open. The upshot of this change was that the Hindiyya, Tijaniyya, Isma'iliyya, Qadiriyya, Samaniyya, and other ṭuruq reestablished themselves as religious private practices within a revitalization of sorts "to collectively restore or reconstruct patterns of life that [had] been rapidly disrupted or threatened" before.[50] Importantly, the new emergence of the Khatmiyya under the leadership of Sayyid 'Ali revitalized and attached this ṭarīqa to newfound communities that began to rebuild themselves in urban Sudanese society in general and within certain rural areas in the northern and eastern parts of the country.

The religious and social impact of this development was far reaching. The Khatmiyya became strongly established as a religious organization that fit Mayer Zald's description of a social movement by providing an "infrastructure of social relations that are mobilized for other purposes."[51] Specifically, they provided "a repertoire of skills and a protected social structure, so that when a larger political ideology and movement impinge[d] upon the group, the religious organizations and personnel [could] easily be mobilized."[52] In addition, their biweekly religious participation, as well as their inner socialization, created "networks of relations and similarities of perception that help[ed] unify later behavior."[53] Finally, that religious organization affected "the readiness to participate in political social movements" in a more indirect way.[54] The Khatmiyya, in its new mode of action and resource mobilization, fostered and maintained contacts with diverse social groups from different parts of the country, including merchants. This group suffered under the hand of the "Mahdist state[, which] not only put Khatmiyya traders out of business, it also came down heavily on trade itself."[55] In addition, among the internal immigrants from different parts of rural northern Sudan, who constituted the vast majority of an emerging working class in the "railways and docks in communications, exports, and imports. . . . With the exception of the Danaqla, almost all of these immigrants were Arabic speakers who belonged to the Khatmiyya Sufi order."[56] To most recuperating urban centers in the country, expanding farmers' communities in the north, and nomadic groups in eastern Sudan, the Khatmiyya reintroduced and reinforced, in an organized manner, a strong sense of brotherhood, solidarity, and an orderly socialization system where cooperation was observed and which produced different tangible rewards. These processes, which turned the Khatmiyya into what its activists described later as *safienat Noah* (Noah's ark), have produced social cohesion and a collective identity that have turned the ṭarīqa into a new socioreligious movement and to a great extent a new and a growing countrywide network of merchant groups. The introduction of the railways as both a communication and a transportation system revitalized the urban center, enhanced the growth of trade, and propagated the circulation of capital.

The new emerging entrepreneurial groups who found refuge in the security of the ṭarīqa raised the professional and social status of entrepreneurship. It soon became apparent and believed by its followers that the ṭarīqa's *baraka* (blessing) became the source of an emerging accumulation of capital institutionalized and organized around Sayyid 'Ali with significant transformative potentials within the religious, social, and political fields of power. Consequently, "In a short while there was comfort when it was reported [in the meeting of the northern governors of the Sudan] that 'Ali al-Mirghani's prestige was rising 'owing to greater activity and the efforts of the Omdurman merchants'; though he increasingly kept his distance from the British, and as early as 1933 began to reactivate the *tariqa*'s links with Egypt."[57] In other words, those other forms of discontent that did not agree with the Mahdist impulse gave rise to different modes of mobilization. These modes of mobilization captured a complex dynamic of social interactions that felt at home with an uneasy form of resistance to the colonial order, which affected the accumulation of capital. This accumulation of capital enhanced the readiness to participate in political social movements from more indirect to direct forms of resistance.

This complex Sudanese situation, which began to express itself at the turn of the twentieth century, was the foundation of a long-standing existential experience of a country that "was not a new state, and some resistance was essentially a replication of earlier resistance to experiences of state-building, which had been exploitative and remembered as such."[58] In addition, a new consciousness of collective religious and national belonging cross-fertilized these new anticolonial resistance movements and their communities of conversation with social-capital-in-circulation as a resource mobilization. The new colonial state's institutions, its hierarchies of soft (hegemonic) and hard (military) power, its structures of violence, and their reproductions were deeply influenced by the ghost—the real, potential, and imagined threat—of a rebellious Sudanese anticolonial stimulus, which finally reached its apex in the Mahdist revolution, in 1885. The Mahdist revolution "was no peripheral revolt, but at the core of the colonial state and, far from being suppressed, it had established a new state of its own."[59]

However, in entering the new Sudanese social world, the colonizing process at its center point—the state—emerged as a centralized, violent, governing entity with a total monopoly on all physical and symbolic violence and the means and processes by which the conduct of the population could be governed and disciplined. Through this governing system, the state became "a major manufacturer of inequality," racial engineering, and social stratification on a grandiose scale. In consequence, a center reproduced around the capital, a peoplehood—visible and invisible marginalization entities that included regions, women, and rural poor—was fashioned. Meanwhile, as an economic enterprise and as a hegemonic and a coercive system of domination, the state developed the capacity to organize that which it deemed profitable within the labor and production processes. It also had the upper hand in the reproduction of the constitutions of a dominant ideology, the fashioning of the peoplehood, and the shaping of the geographical structure of the country as a whole. Here the state emerges as a fetish or new deity with its worshippers, priests, and prophets and its community of the state. These arrangements, within their permanence and the camaraderie of the sociopolitical relationships that emerged and persisted within the growth of the state, have continued to reproduce.

First, the colonial city Khartoum was the prime example and an expression of colonial dominance in the country. It was the citadel and the center of operation of the British institution of direct rule, which constructed "an integrated state apparatus and [which] resembled the form of state domination that developed in Western Europe over the previous five centuries." This system, contrary to its auxiliary form of governance, indirect rule, "required the dismantling of preexisting political institutions and the construction of centralized, territory-wide, and bureaucratic legal-administrative institutions that were controlled by colonial officials."[60] But what set Khartoum apart from other colonial capitals to the British collective memory was that it represented a Golgotha of sorts, and its ruined palace represented Gordon's crucifix.[61] Khartoum was a day-and-night hymn that rang down the long trek of the invading army:

> Then roll on, Boys roll on to Khartoum,
> March ye and fight by night or by day,
> Hasten the hour of the Dervishes' doom,
> Gordon avenge in old England's way!

The distinction between Khartoum and Omdurman, which lies on the western side of the River Nile, is more than the growth or emergence of cities under direct or indirect rule. Omdurman was built as an anticolonial entity. It fought the invading colonial army vigorously. As a city in a colonized society, it remained as the symbolic production and continued reconstruction of modes and means of resistance to the colonial order. Omdurman was conditioned by its history, ideology, and place of formation. (For the wider contribution of Khartoum, Omdurman, and Cairo to civil society, see chapters 4–6.)

Another very important development was the creation of a multitier system of differentiation that created not only the geographical structures and routes that connect and disconnect the center and marginalized visible sectors of the country but also its invisible margin, which includes women and rural poor. Among the different endowments of these uneasy relationships, violence, counterviolence, and ways of negotiating passage across different boundaries were exercised. At the same time, the embedded capacity of the social capital in circulation has continued to influence and nurture the foundation of the distinctive formations of each emerging civil representation, the Ansār and their Umma Party and the Khatmiyya and its Unionist Party, in addition to other political entities and associations.

The rebirth of the Ansār as an enduring religious group restored that social-capital-in-circulation and the Umma Party as a political entity operationalizing an ideology inspired by that capital. Born as a player within the nationalist community, the Umma Party has succeeded in bringing together the Mahdi family and the Ansār with other sectors of urban elite at the helm of the leadership of the party. These distinctions between the Ansār and the Umma Party are of practical importance. The resilience of the Ansār as a group, and their material power as a player in the Sudanese political and social scene, has imbued the party with a significance, a solid base, and an order founded on the social and religious solidarities of brotherhood and cooperation.

The political corollaries of these two formations have collectively proven very complicated and have remained implacably subject to persistent negative views from other communities born out of the conversations of the colonial and postcolonial states who continue to label the Ansār and the Umma Party as the harbingers of sectarianism (*ṭaifiyya*), looking backward (*raj'īyya*), and conservatism (*taglīdiyya*). With the introduction of mass public education, and to a certain extent church-based education, a new sense of citizenship and characteristics of other different political formations emerged. This development brought together three different communities of the state.

The first includes regular and civil service personnel, the army, and members of trade union organizations (white- , blue- , and khaki-collar and white-*'arrāqi* groups). Public education brought out political organizations that include the Islamists, Communists and other leftists, and pan-Arabists, while church education produced most of the southern political elite. Each of these political groups and organizations committed itself to certain exclusivist ideologies that followed or propositioned doctrinaire order for the state and society and entertained self-assurances as self-contained models of political representations. By virtue of their upbringing, these different political schools and their representations among the community of the state openly reject or discreetly undermine the rules and the results of the democratic game as long as it puts the Umma Party (or their other "sectarian" rival, the Unionist Party) in an advantageous position. This elitist self-regard has created a culture of external power based around the military coup and the regime that emerges out of it. That culture has always antagonized all other political representations, and even the democratic process itself, as long as the coup—a tool for political change—led those groups to power. Within this group's internal discourse and pursuit of power, the coup became the favored mode of operation. It is not inconceivable, then, that all these self-imaged minority progressive, modern, Islamist, conservative, and regional political entities from all colors would use the state through military coups to annihilate both the Ansār and the Umma Party and the Khatmiyya and Unionist Party, as they did several times.

In many respects, these exclusivist groups in their different colors—"neotheologians," reductionists from the left—not only directed their depredations and military coups to induce violence toward the Ansār and the Umma Party, but also toward the Khatmiyya as a ṭarīqa and the political parties it established or supported. The Khatmiyya, who opposed the Mahdiyya from the beginning and suffered immensely from it, entered the twentieth century with the same dislike of the Mahdiyya, but not necessarily any affection for the new colonial order or its state.

However, the anticolonial sentiments of these different communities and the reactions by which the colonial regime tried to disrupt the material worlds and the institutional arrangements of these communities created conditions under which the colonial state became a violent adversary not only to anticolonial struggle but also to all forms of civic engagement. In this way the continuity and the growth of the colonial state was a homogeneous "construction of machinery of permanent domination"[62] through "self financing hegemony and security [that] demanded effective resource generation from the primary factor of production."[63] As these processes continued to produce their fields of power, violence became a habitual state utility. And as the colonial state continued to progress, this hegemony translated itself into two particular developments: The first has to do with what Antonio Gramsci describes in the third volume of his *Prison Notebooks* as an association of several groups. The first of these groups is composed of "traditional" intellectuals, including scholars and writers; the second, "organic" intellectuals; and the final, "functionaries," such as civil servants, military workers, businessmen, and political leaders. These all combined to transform outright "domination into a variety of effects that masked both conquest and rule."[64] The second relates to the emergence of the state itself as a force that could shape people's lives and confer power, wealth, and prestige. In both cases the state as a primary regulator played the role of restructuring the entire society while its community of the state simultaneously played the role of its "intimate enemy." Consecutively, through these processes the community of the state emerges. This community of state represents the generations of educated elites that colonial institutions of learning have produced to serve the state. Those elites later inherited that state and became its surrogate mother.

4

A Tale of Three Cities

Khartoum

The colonial communities of conversation in the Sudan, their regime, and its new disciplinary order emerged not only to put down all forms of resistance in the Sudan but also to establish a new state as "a corporate institution,"[1] firmly connected to the British mini-imperial system. Builders of that system and of the colonial state in the Sudan came of age when "the flowering of the middle-class British evangelical spirit, began to ascribe cultural meanings to the British domination, and colonialism proper can be said to have begun."[2] In all these instances, the colonial state had continued to develop as a contradiction and an antagonist of all forms and representations of an emerging Sudanese civil society. At the same time, "the cultural technologies of rule . . . and the brutal modes of conquest that first established power"[3] in the country had acted violently against all the emerging modes of mobilization of moral and normative resistance to the colonial system. Violence became a tool of control, symptomatic of a malignant tumor, which arose on the first day of the invasion, continued to take different shapes, and increased in intensity only to remain a prominent part of the heritage of the colonial state. From that point on, the eminence and attributes of a powerful, power-bestowing, and power-denying centralized state apparatus continued to grow throughout the lifetime of the colonial state, eventually transferring that ascribed status to the postcolonial state. At the same time, the integrity of the colonial regime had been frustrated from both inside and out; this frustration transformed it into a violent "contact point" with unmatched "technologies of domination."[4] That is, the colonial experience engaged and shaped the postcolonial state as well as the lives of the colonizers.

Over the past century, the colonial state—and its heir, the postcolonial state—have killed, banned, and violently devastated several individuals, peoples, and civil institutions. Through these developments, an uneasy relationship between the colonial and postcolonial states and the very foundation of a civil society were continually shrouded in conflict. This history of both discursive and physical violence constituted the postcolonial predicament. Ultimately, no single event has had such a profound influence on the sociopolitical life of the Sudan as the colonial experience. Both the structured and the amorphous forms, the magnitude, the "ghostly residues"[5] of the colonial experience, and the growth of the state's malignant tumor that plagued institutions and technologies of domination and their collective effects on Sudanese society continued to influence not only the most particular, but also the less particular forms of violence by adding more barriers to resurrecting a civil society. In its physical form, the colonial regime withered half a century ago. Nevertheless, the inherited state, the ghostly residue, and its innate malignancy of violence that divisively reshaped anticolonial communities of conversation have continued to develop and to fight back in an attempt to expand, or at least maintain, the postcolonial state, its space, and its fields of power.

The synergy and resource mobilization that endowed all Sudanese movements with their violent and nonviolent modes of resistance to the colonial state and its orders took more than two decades to effectively appropriate a force that was engaged with both rural and urban developments of capitalism and elective affinities that enthused and revitalized competing sociopolitical movements. At the same time, as much as it had been resisted, the colonial state and its constituent community continued to develop, employ, and force structures through the course of their activities, in order to build up the state's system of domination as an enterprise. This enterprise grew within what Anthony Giddens describes as the powers of the "allocative resource" and the "authoritative resource." Giddens explains, "By the first of these I refer to dominion over material facilities, including material goods and the natural forces that may be harnessed in their production. The second concerns the means of dominion over the activities of human beings themselves."[6] Over time, the colonial regime was able to create the state we know today as a regulator of most aspects of life, an order-endowing and order-enforcing entity, a disciplinary power, and, as perceived by most, an eternal body. This chapter addresses the development of the colonial state and the construction of the colonial capital city, Khartoum, as well as its extensions as progressive forms of colonization and modes of control. Khartoum was the colonial city, the citadel, and the dual center of operation for British direct and indirect rule. Through these modes of control, the simultaneous operation of differential arrangements of identity management, which produced peoplehoods, and differentiation, which produced different spheres of power, the most dramatic developments and growth of different Sudanese community of the state groups working together and with other emerging social groups with and against that state took place. They all worked as "intimate enemies" both to build and to impede the very existence of that state.

Identity Management as a Mode of Control

Given the situation in the Sudan, during the establishment and consolidation of colonial rule, it follows that there were two related yet distinct tendencies. The first hid underneath the totalitarian canopy of the colonial state and reflected itself within specific violent and nonviolent hegemonic collective actions of the state and its progressive forms of colonization. The second found its strategies within the logic and modes of operation and counterviolent acts and expressions, which were directed against the colonial state, together with what has been described as collaboration with its new order. Accumulative endowments that were used and reinvented to confront the new militaristic and totalitarian colonial order inspired these multilayered strategies and tendencies to take steps to further incorporate concrete collective actions and forms of politico-economic and socioreligious organizations. The battle lines of this complex situation had simultaneously set in motion several different progressive forms.

First, "these struggles, their starts and stops, methods, and motivations, owed their beginning and their tenor to the encounter between Anglican Christianity and Sudanese Islam that Gordon's clash with the Mahdi set in train."[7] Second, not only did the Anglican-Islamic aspect of the conflict exist, but it also had "much to tell us about the nature of imperialism, even in our supposedly postcolonial times. Empires exert dominion not only from above, but, by engaging and seeking to mold subjects' sensibilities, they also rule by colonizing consciousness, to the extent they are able, from within."[8] Finally, the essence of the colonial regime was persistent in its attempt to order the private, public, and official lives of the country's population. The colonial regime's functions and orders went hand in hand with the reconstruction of a Sudanese culture of resistance. On both sides, some people perceived Mahdism as the political and religious core of this culture of resistance, which was supposed to curate the inner souls of the people who were, in contrast, opposed to all forms of colonialism.

Hence, from the first day of the occupation, both the Sudanese and the colonizers set their preoccupations in different types of arrangements, through which the latter fought vigorously to establish an order on one side, while the former struggled as best they could to disorder the occupation and its order, as a reality, on the other. With a serious degree of difference of power relations between them, these two entities fought cultural wars and armed confrontations. Over the spectrum of facts on the ground and the iconic power of a proliferating colonial state, Khartoum was rebuilt and reconstructed as the shadow theater—the model and the representation of the "symbol of Imperial Britain." However, in a more exceptional mode, the name Khartoum was as suggestive and reminiscent in its day as Timbuktu once was for the European imagination. Khartoum invoked all the effects that led to the Anglo-Egyptian invasion of the country between 1896 and 1898, which, Daly confirms, "was often described as simply the re-taking of the town."[9] Daly continues, "Whether primarily for its symbolism, its hallowed status as the place of Gordon's 'martyrdom,' or the legitimacy the site derived from the previous, Turco-Egyptian regime, there seems never to have been any doubt that Khartoum would be rebuilt and that it would again be the seat of power."[10] Khartoum symbolized to the British "crusaders' mind," and to their collective memory, a Golgotha of sorts, and its ruined palace represented Gordon's crucifix.

A few weeks after the battle of Omdurman the colonizers started to build a new capital for the colonial regime. They constructed the capital to be a fortress of the new military system, the headquarters of an enterprise, both the seat of and the apparatus through which that state was to be governed. The new Khartoum was "a planned town, famously laid out in a grid pattern by Kitchener himself, and was embellished not only by squares and roundabouts, intersections, vistas, and a 'corniche,' but, more importantly, with monumental buildings far in excess of anything that the dusty little town needed or that the embryonic regime could afford."[11] Khartoum's avenues and streets, designed in the shape of the Union Jack, "were more than emblems of Christian saints; they were tangible extensions of imperial personae named after Kitchener, Cromer, Victoria, [and] Gordon."[12] For the colonizer, "Khartoum was a persuasive, evocative city, both a crusader fortress and an outpost of reason in a barbarous land."[13]

The Sudan's colonial capital was divided into different wards. The palace, which Daly described as never ceasing to amaze its first-time visitors, "almost embodied legitimacy; it was in a way a tomb, or at any rate a memorial to Gordon, who had died there." He continued, "But the key to its political significance (in addition to its all-important hallowed site) was its size. It remained for years the largest building in Khartoum, and, from the river, dominated the town, exuding solidarity, triumph and permanence." Not only "was this merely an office block: the Palace was the center of the regime, and the Governor-General lived there, like Louis XIV at Versailles."[14] Further, the Anglican cathedral "was not only large and impressive, but was built within the precinct of the Palace, achieving a perfect assertion of Divine right."[15]

In the strip between the Blue Nile and Khedive Avenue (currently Gama'a, or University Avenue), colonizers built the palace, the government's administrative and communication departments, the British residential ward, the cathedral, Gordon Memorial College, and the British Sudan club, in addition to the barracks. In these places the British Empire's functionaries—or the citizens of the colonial state—resided, worked, strategized, socialized, and maintained the colonizers' roles. The city's commercial sector, al-Suq al-Afranji (the European market), which consisted of company headquarters, banks, professional offices, bars, hotels, and rings of wholesale and retail shops, was south of the colonial city. Gamal Ḥamdan noticed "the locational contrast within the business center between the legal and medical professions. The former cluster[ed] chiefly in the very heart, the nucleus; the latter [were] in the main more peripheral."[16] Al-Suq al-Afranji—which stood in contrast to al-Suq al-'Arabi and physically separated al-Suq al-'Arabi from the official sector of the city—was a "fashionable, modern shopping area clearly dominated by foreign businessmen, mainly Europeans, but also Levantines and Egyptians."[17] Within the colonial discursive tactics of urban designs and the built forms of zoning, al-Suq al-'Arabi was designated a separate zone that told its story through its rank, which "the colonial discourse literature has made the useful step of highlighting the intersection of language with geography, through the place-names and the naming power of colonizers or explorers."[18] Al-Suq al-'Arabi was "more like an 'Oriental'—that is, Arab or Middle East—bazaar than a typical 'African' market of, say, the Omdurman type. The strict localization of each type of product, and each group of related trades, is a characteristic feature. This is in striking contrast with the European market and is in common with the Middle East towns. The bazaar caters to traditional native domestic consumption."[19] Another important factor about this division and containment: "The noticeable relationship in location between the Arab market and the religious center is a reminder of the religious character of the native society. The market depends considerably on the weekly visits of the faithful to the mosque, from localities well outside the Three Towns."[20]

Like the Forbidden City of imperial China, for a considerable period of time, the colonizers would not allow common Sudanese people to enter colonial Khartoum or its places of entertainment. While the official sector and the European market of colonial Khartoum's zones hid and sheltered the colonial residents from what they perceived as the inconveniences of life in the Sudan, these zones also isolated the colonial community from Sudanese society. Both terms of such relationships described the colonial system's tools, which were created for the formation of separate zones inhabited by different races, each designated a well-defined space, as frameworks for a system of the exercise of power differential and control. Accordingly, in the new city of Khartoum, "all the cultural groups, including the British, other foreigners and the natives with their subgroups, were spatially segregated."[21] The eastern sector of the city—which was higher (about 378 meters above sea level), better drained, more healthful, and in possesion of more pleasant landscaping than other sectors of the city—was the zone occupied by the middle-class Europeans, especially the Italians and Levantines. That sector included "little Greece," a highly concentrated well-to-do Greek community; their medical clinics, clubs, retail shops, bars, schools, and churches served the community specifically rather than the whole town. Mainly Europeans of the higher standard occupied Khartoum One, the highly stylized and most colorful quarter of the city. The western sector was the Egyptian Copts' "capital in the capital," home to their schools, cathedrals, and residences.[22] The design of Kitchener's capital "aimed for easy defense of the town and easy movement of people from place to place, through wide and well-connected streets using orthogonal and diagonal street geometry. All main and secondary roads radiated from the focal point of the colonial city, the Governor General's Palace."[23] Even the trees had to be imported from India and were lined and well planned within the streets and avenues of the colonial capital. An ironclad borderline, which consisted of a rail loop, two steel bridges that connected the city to Khartoum North and Omdurman, and a series of army barracks encircled Khartoum—the seat of the colonial enterprise.

Outside the zone of the fortified, "gated" community were the residential areas of the "natives," which were also ranked according to the status of their inhabitants. The Sudanese at the top of the economic hierarchy were closest to the colonial city, with the lowest-ranking dwellings (*diūm*), singular *deim*, in areas farthest from the city center.

Khartoum—the colonial city and its gated community—stands as the grand model of planning and most important contribution to the "colonial built environments and urban forms by public authority" in the Sudan.[24] Builders followed similar patterns and architectural designs to construct new sectors in other urban centers to house the state's British community and to accommodate their administrative, military, religious, and social needs. Towns such as Wad Medani, El-Obeid, 'Aṭbara, Juba, Kassala, Malakal, and Waw functioned as district headquarters. It was there the colonizers built most of the new architecture. The colonizers' planning and urban design policies in each city were intended for *al-ḥai al-Britani*: the British sector.

Each of these British sectors and their Khartoum master plan followed a certain style and a vision, which Thomas Metcalf described as "a manifestation of an interconnected structure of power and knowledge that informed colonialism everywhere."[25] At the same time, the colonial architecture and its landscape reflected serious concerns. Chief among them was the fear of further revolts along the lines of the Mahdist revolution, in 1875. Mainly, the aim of this architectural segregation was to create a new zone and framework that would physically and socially separate the Europeans from the Sudanese population and use the space in a markedly distinctive form that reflected and reinforced the colonial order. The colonizers built each of the colonial minicities in the urban provincial centers of the Sudan as extensions of Khartoum, the flagship of the colonial state. They designed and built the governor's house to visibly signify the power and prestige of the imperial regime. The planning and the structure of these colonial minicities and their residential and administrative pattern generally had the same design, house form, and building material to preserve the feeling that the colonial community lived, worked, worshipped, and socialized within one clearly defined space. As in Khartoum, an army surrounded and was connected to the railway line or river port in each minicity. Other forms of communication, such as the postal and telegraph systems, were integrated within the arrangements and designed to protect the colonial minicities. Most of the colonial minicities were separated in one part by a green belt, a *khor* (a creek or tributary), or even a large empty space that could play a defensive role if the need occurred. The new strategically designed market stood as a buffer zone between the colonial minicity and the local population's commercial and living zones. Colonial villages in smaller towns followed similar designs and were connected to their urban centers through a telegraph communication system, as well as forms of traditional communication, such as runners.

This function of the state and its grand grid of colonial minicities and villages did not reside only in the general organizing capacity of the regime but also in structuring zones that clearly reflected, and, in effect, reinforced social and racial differences. The colonizers, in so doing, successfully made the differences between the colonizers and the colonized a natural fact of everyday life. The settlement, assignment, and mapping of space also reflected a system of meaning—a process devised to maintain power relations and a form of domination—representing and recognizing both of them officially and legally. Within the racial, ethnic, and regional aggregates of that state of affairs, a system of meaning and a process of segregation that crystallized the British community of the state as the signifier of the superior race emerged. Within that system, some European settlers were placed second, while others followed according to a ranking system that the state itself devised. The implications of these imaginative geographies, race, and history, in their power relations, as Edward Said explains, "help the mind to intensify its own sense of itself by dramatizing the distance and difference between what is close to it and what is far away."[26] At the same time, that grid of colonial architecture and its imaginative geography was planned to affirm a symbolic significance and an additional material effect. It remains a reminder of the violent zeal of the state, how it could be deployed whenever needed toward any rebellious "natives," and as a warning of how collective violence coming from those distant "subjects" would be a costly endeavor.

For a regime concerned with security and its total control over the population and the country, the results of such a complex situation of resistance and multiple encounters of forms of insubordination were imbued in the process of the creation of the state as the representation of a violent, self-sufficient, centralized power foundation. Likewise, modes of domination and coercion in effect shaped the formation of that state as the focal point of accumulation and distribution of resources. These developments of the colonial state as a centralized power and a resource-accumulation enterprise found their expression through different forms of violence, symbolic and hegemonic zeal, and policies of confinement that ever since have relegated the "subjects" of the state to a lower status. The constitutive elements and periods that relate to these forms and structures of the colonial experience continued to characterize the postcolonial state and, at the same time, to have profound bearings on the plurality of the internal and external dynamics of conflict. These constructions remain subordinate to the following conditions.

The British colonizers reconstructed the city of Khartoum as the seat of colonial power in order "to create agencies of rule and to invent extractive devices imposing on the subordinated societies the cost of the unsolicited governance proposed for them."[27] In January 1899, Governor General Kitchener laid the foundation for the first of these agencies, Gordon Memorial College. Kitchener's haste to call for the establishment of the college impressed the poet and "the prophet of British Imperialism in its expansionist phase," Rudyard Kipling.[28] In his famous poem "Kitchener's School" (1898), Kipling wrote:

> They terribly carpet the earth with dead,
> And before their canon cool,
> They walk unarmed by twos and threes
> To call the living to school.

For James Currie, the college was established as an evocation of "his first appeal to his fellow-countrymen on behalf of a definite educational object. . . . and thus clearly intimated that education and its kindred problems were, for the reconstructed Sudan, a matter of primary concern,"[29] as the first principal of the college and the director of education in the Sudan explained. Kipling wrote about the violent nature of the "civilizing mission" of the sirdar and his school:

> Not at the mouth of his clean-lipped guns shall ye learn his name again,
> But letter by letter, from Kaf to Kaf, at the mouths of his chosen men.
> He has gone back to his own city, not seeking presents or bribes,
> But openly asking the English for money to buy you Hakims and scribes.

For Kitchener, the sirdar and the first governor general of the Sudan, the essence of colonization presumed such a task: "The responsible task is laid upon us, and those who have conquered are called upon to civilize. In fact, the work interrupted since the death of Gordon must now be resumed."[30] James Currie clearly outlined the sirdar's expressed ideology of colonizing education. Currie defined the role of the college and the system of education in a three-point program that included: "I. The creation of a competent artisan class. II. The diffusion among the masses of the people of education sufficient to enable them to understand the machinery of Government, particularly with reference to the equitable and impartial administration of justice. III. The creation of a small administrative class, capable of filling many Government posts, some of an administrative, others of a technical, nature."[31]

Hence, the reconstruction of the new Sudan as a country could be achieved through the creation of an abundant underclass of cheap labor, a small class of artisans, and a small English-speaking male community of the state as a continuum within a new class structure. This new system helped create the conditions in which the Sudanese identity management was fashioned and maintained to fulfill the main requirements of the colonial state as an enterprise: a supply of cheap labor and the demand of an open market for products coming from the core state, Great Britain. In theory, any Sudanese person could have become a part of that class through the new system of public education; however, very few Sudanese people in urban areas of the country could have achieved such a goal.

In other instances, not only those substantial state considerations but also other deliberations about the functions of such education were raised immediately after the battle of Omdurman, in 1898, when "Kitchener received an offer of laboratory equipment for the future Gordon Memorial College and stores for the school's dispensary from Henry Wellcome, an American entrepreneur living in London who, in partnership with Silas Burroughs, had made a fortune marketing tablet medicines in Britain."[32] From this perspective Wellcome perceived the educational system at large and the college in particular. Wellcome "dabbled in archeology, befriended explorers of Africa, and championed British imperialism." He quickly recognized the educational system as a viable inoculation of "the empire's commercial prospects."[33] How these commercial prospects materialized and how they were to be maintained and reproduced would be the function of the colonial state. However, the first step that needed to be taken in Gordon's name, according to Wellcome, was "the rescue, education and uplift of the natives from their state of savagery and disease."[34] It might not be sufficient to read the meaning of Wellcome's philanthropy apart from his vision of the Sudan, which Boddy describes as "salvific." The colonialist alone might accept Wellcome's logic, which he expressed in clear terms: "All Central Africa is going to be made perfectly habitable for the white man. Its agricultural, industrial, and commercial resources will become available." Within that vision, "The Niles and their tributaries will teem with the commerce of a numerous and happy people."[35] In the process, however, alternative insights from other segments of the Sudanese population had to be integrated in the concern for how the basic institutions of learning should be designed to construct "social frameworks that enable and limit ways of thinking and acting."[36] These insights were expressed in what Kitchener called "amusing" English verses:

> And pray you never will endeavor
> To make the Sudanese too clever.[37]

There is no reason to doubt that this impulse not to make the Sudanese "too clever" was intended as a colonial policy and a permanent state arrangement earlier described as salvific. Mo'awia Muḥammad Nur (1909–41), who graduated from the American University in Beirut, wrote that he was denied a teaching job at Gordon Memorial College because he was "not the type, too clever" according to the director of education who interviewed him for the job.[38] Nur describes the peculiar nature of the system of education that the college followed at that time. He writes that in the curriculum of the college "there is no place for natural sciences or modern history or arts, but most of its [courses] are exercises in typewriting or practical engineering or accounts to prepare the student for filling junior positions in government."[39] Nur quoted a Syrian professor, who used to work for the college and claimed that the colonizers wanted to keep the Sudanese youth ignorant of contemporary nationalist movements. In doing so, they were following the educational policy of Lord Lugard,[40] which attempted to produce a self-respecting gentleman who knew nothing about what was taking place in the world and cared not in the least about it.[41] In all cases, this reproduction of new status and rank, which perpetuated a different form of social stratification, could explain the speed by which the arrangements of identity management and social reproduction of colonial racialization both started and progressed. Within the first days of the occupation, the memorial service in front of the ruins of Gordon Palace was described: "The Royal Engineers were ordered to commence the arduous task of rebuilding the city [Khartoum] within one year. The prisoners taken at Kereri were put to work clearing the rubble and filling in the potholes."[42] Khartoum was built as a colonial city and was meant to be so from its origin and first day of its reconstruction. "Using sketchy plans prepared by Kitchener himself, the expedition's surveyors and engineers cut into the old urban fabric and opened new roads and public squares whilst disregarding the old plans."[43] Kitchener's haste to build the governor's palace—as a means "to inscribe the signature of power" and absolute rule—and the Gordon Memorial College—as an institution—not only exhibits what Wellcome illustrated, but also that Kitchener sought to define the routes of entry to the new, growing milieu and fields of power and authority that were "crucial in entrenching the supremacy of the colonialists."[44] An element that Ngũgĩ wa Thiong'o articulated eloquently, was his argument that what he called "the colonial cultural bomb's" aim "is to annihilate a people's belief in their names, in their languages, in their environment, in their heritage of struggle, in their unity, in their capacities and ultimately in themselves."[45] He continued, "It makes them see their past as one wasteland of non-achievement and it makes them want to distance themselves from that wasteland. It makes them want to identify with that which is furthest removed from themselves; for instance, with other peoples' languages rather than their own."[46]

Royal engineer Maj. Gen. George Gorringe designed Gordon Memorial College to be similar to the palace.[47] Kitchener officially opened the college in 1902. The college was another expression of the colonial ideology of difference and geography, knowledge and power. Two similarities between the college and the palace were the college's prime location as the second most distinctive building in the colonial city of Khartoum and its representation of hegemony as power exercised. Like Gorringe's other grand schemes, the college occupied a captivating space with a double-winged, arched building constructed with concrete and red bricks. The structure, image, and function of the college worked together to complement the power of the new colonial state and to bestow prestige on the actions of its students and teachers. The college was detached from where the locals lived, however, and Sidney Peel—British soldier, financier, and conservative politician—told how "its commanding position at the east end of the town makes it a conspicuous landmark for many miles round."[48] Peel described the college as "a handsome structure of native red brick, built in the Moorish style, but retaining the collegiate character. It occupies two sides of a square, the front facing on the river. In the centre is the principle entrance, and over it a tower. . . . Along the inside runs a cool and airy cloister, with winding stairs leading to the upper story; the class-rooms are spaciously designed."[49]

Over the years the college came to be surrounded with an array of green lawns, flowerbeds, soccer playgrounds, dormitories, and houses for faculty and staff. For many years, "the college also hosted two affiliated educational programs—the Instructional Workshops (operative from 1904 to 1932) for training artisans and technicians, and the Khartoum Military Academy (operative from 1905 to 1924), which trained Northern Sudanese officers for the Egyptian Army in the Sudan," as well as "several government research organizations, including, for example, the Wellcome Tropical Research Laboratories and the Antiquities Service."[50] Unknowingly, perhaps, the students contributed to the symbolic domination exercised on them as they began to develop an affinity for the hierarchies of difference achieved through the academic space and the function through the social and disciplinary aspects of their new experience and new self-image, which, in comparison, was perceived as superior to their ascribed heritage. Here, all the traits by which the new educational system was recognized were firmly connected to a new taste-endowing system of education. Furthermore, to consider the universe of all social and academic properties in addition to the added value of isolating them within what Amin al-Tūm describes as "spacious, pretty rooms entirely furnished, that had been prepared for us . . . , the dining hall for seating hundreds of students at one time . . . , the clean, elegant bathroom for everyone . . . , the fields of greenery and verdant trees, and the flowers, and the piped water ([through] faucets)." All these amenities, together within such confinement, produced a homogeneity that increased over time by virtue of continued socialization. Moreover, although the British college administration continued to categorize the "native" students into the following categories: "Arabs," "Blacks" (or "Sudanese"), "Berberies," and "Muwallads,"[51] the most attractive aspect of the system maintained an important myth of the equality of chances, as one of the main factors behind progress within the rank and recognition among the state employees was seniority within the group.

From this experience, an elite and new structure of social and cultural stance emerged and became the essential element of a different economic and social capital and a base for sociopolitical differentiation. Thus, within its acquired specialized knowledge, education was connected to a practice tied to progressive economic rewards. The state and a higher social recognition within the community endowed that practice and its privileges with a gradational status. The progress and development of the college and its symbolic and actual connection to the British educational system was positioned within Sudanese society in order to select a state-manufactured elite with a shared self-image, a monopoly status on the group level, and the mutual conviction that each member of the group shared such a status. This particular educational institution and its graduates continued to dictate the rules of the space of possible virtues or vices attributed to state endowment of power and prestige together with the social rewards, and lack thereof. No other form of public education played such a major role in the structure of merit, social space, and distribution of cultural capital, power, and prestige.

The college continued to grow into a university and became increasingly active in producing and adding to the professional, cultural, and religious groups of the state's community. The human capacity that developed within that community, and the ideological models, the worldview, and the self-image they established as a modern community, was carefully crafted with the intention of establishing its members as a class, created to adhere to the rules that served the state. Those rules were harmonious with the colonial ideals to "meet the approval and support of the British public and of the English-speaking race," and civilize the

Sudanese.[52] The population of the country was enticed to see the future of their children transformed into positions of power and prestige through public education and to trust that they would be better informed through the new media. The same new system of communication and knowledge dissemination and instruction, however, was firmly fitted in constituting a system of domination as an extension of the state power and hegemony. The new educational system has set the boundaries and fault lines between the elite and different groups of the population. The colonial state was not only able to define certain routes to upward mobility, status, power, and prestige, through which colonial radicalization historically structured social realities, but it was also able "to propound canons of taste, [which] are among the most significant instrumentalities of rulership."[53] Within these developments, the growing Sudanese cultural, economic, and political communities of conversation or community of the state developed their own courses of action and ways of thinking about themselves, their colonizers, and the world. Considered together, the colonialists were able to exercise their material and hegemonic power to construct a form of institutional state structure and to determine its directions and deeper effects on Sudanese life.

As Bernard S. Cohn wrote of the British in India, those who "came under the imperial gaze were frequently made to appear in dress and demeanor as players in the British-constructed theater of power, their roles signaled by prescribed dress, their parts authored by varied forms of knowledge codified by rulers who sought to determine how loyal Indian subjects were to act in scenes that the rulers had constructed."[54] With the constitutions of these developments in the Sudan, a new class relationship emerged in which fields of power gradually started to organize within the fields of political, economic, and social orders. By privileging the new system of public education over the indigenous system of education, and firmly tying the former to the demands of power and status, the colonial state remodeled a few of the *masā'id* (sing., *masseed*) or *khalāwi* in the urban areas into vernacular elementary schools, thereby leaving the rest to dwindle in meaning and eminence, and eventually to die a natural death. The accumulative effects resulting from the new British educational system were far reaching, as through this process the Sudan and the Sudanese started to see a number of incompatible but serious implications and ever-growing effects of radicalization and identity management.

Sudanese society began to experience a new form of organization of power out of the rise of the small class of publicly educated citizens (the community of the state) that continued to grow through the expansion of public education. This community of the state continued to find its legitimization within its invention of a progressive self-image and cultural identity as being an important part, if not the only part, of modernity in the country. These inward-looking groups and their exclusivist self-image developed a worldview and political ideology of self-affirmation that was reflected in the practice and the discourse of the elite of political parties in their multiple centers and in the civilian groups who collaborated with the military regimes. The reproduction of this class within its self-image, as they continued to enter the political sphere, introduced a new form of stratification that devalued the majority Other as backward.

There were additional implications that directly resulted from the seemingly improved and modernized sphere of public education and the degradation of the indigenous system of both education and work across the board. As a result, the interest in and attention to public education as a tool for upward mobility influenced the livelihood and image of indigenous education. Accordingly, this steady lowering of the standards of all types of indigenous schooling and professions meant that the growing numbers of individuals still involved in both remained poor. One result of this structural poverty was a lack of interest in the old system of education, work, and their resulting products. As more people plunged into poverty, the majority of the population plummeted into all-encompassing illiteracy and poverty. More people were transported away from their homes to be turned into workers in the colonial government's emerging capitalist project in the creation of the infrastructure, such as railways and river transportation. In addition, dams and other construction projects, as well as the Gezira irrigation scheme and other colonial extractive economic activities, allowed wealth and poverty to take on a different shape. Within this new development, public education and government jobs were made the criteria of modernity. A new form of stratification and aggregates of poor people emerged as a new structural social phenomenon as a result. At the same time, the colonial state formed its homogeneous system, salient characteristic, and propagated image as the main job provider for both the educated and the uneducated, a situation that caused most groups to become dependent on its opportunities and "goodwill." Within this development, all sectors of the population, rich and poor, educated and uneducated, became increasingly dependent on what the government provided in the field of employment, transportation, education, medical care, and other services. Machines powered by steam, coal, and electricity, which were a monopoly of the state, and the growth of their material production, in addition to new more efficient communication and transportation systems, had a profound effect on the power, security, and capacity of material production, together with the marginalization of the structural production of and regions and sectors of the population. The connection between poverty production and the government's mode of operation points to the distance between the colonial system and its institutions on one side, and various groups of the population on the other.

Another effect of this new system on Sudanese life was that most of those left behind within the realm of traditional work or production—including rain-fed agriculture, rural economy, and menial jobs—remained poor and turned into an underclass. Thus, when Sudanese society was viewed from the bottom, it might be even clearer to see the progress of structural poverty, marginalization, and the human sacrifices offered at the altar of the colonial state. Most profoundly affected were the rural poor throughout the country, who were rapidly driven to the bottom of the new social strata. In a short time, the colonial state was not only the original core of the capitalist development, which dominated and transformed the social structure, but was by far the most important agent in the importation of the most pressing needs—from the train to the pencil—and the sole exportation body for all raw material, from cotton to gum arabic, sesame, and groundnuts.

By design, space, marginalization, identity management, and new forms of stratification had specific roots in the development of the colonial state. This colonial experience, its consequences, and its inherited institutions continued to ramify, through Sudanese society, colonizing the fate of its population and contributing both directly and indirectly to the high cost of devising and creatively maintaining an independently evolving social relation that had the potential to lead to the growth of institutional structures of governance and civil society.

Colonizing Islam

Symmetrical modes of reproduction within the colonization of Islam accompanied the modes of reproduction that acted within the colonization of education. The struggle to win everything in the war against Sudanese Mahdist political, social, and cultural Islam started as early as 1891. Francis Reginald Wingate, the Sudan's director of military intelligence, initiated this war. Wingate's book *Mahdism and the Egyptian Sudan*, which he completed as governor general of the Sudan, started the strategy, which developed and progressed through the campaign, or what Mamdani has described as "a full-blown pornography of violence."[55]

A series of books, reviews, and commentaries followed in 1892 with the translation and publication of Father Ohrwalder's *Ten Years' Captivity in the Mahdi's Camp*. It was Wingate who facilitated the escape of Father Ohrwalder and Sisters Elisabetta Venturini and Catterina Chincarini, the three members of the Austrian Roman Catholic Mission who had been prisoners in the Sudan since 1882. By publishing Ohrwalder's book, Wingate renewed the memories of the death of Gordon and the fate of European prisoners in the Sudan. In 1894, Wingate facilitated the escape of Rudolf Slatin from Omdurman, and early in 1896 he translated into English and published Slatin's book *Fire and Sword in the Sudan*. With all these concerted efforts, Wingate was successful in unearthing, and effectively keeping alive in the collective and individual memory of the British public, the several memoirs and works published since Gordon's death. Those new publications, in addition to the old ones, represented literature "whose stunning success owed much to the fact that their descriptions of dervish cruelty confirmed European images of Islam."[56] This, in one sense, was not only necessary in order to revive British interest in the reconquest of the Sudan but was also used to provide a perception of what Islam was, and what it was not, to the empire's riveted audience. In this way, the colonizers employed the strategy of colonizing Islam to solve the issue of the involvement of the state in manipulating and controlling religion in an attempt to empower hierarchies of hegemony over the Muslim social world.

One of the major aspects of colonizing religion in general, and Islam in particular, during the colonial period was that the state created in and of itself a new religious entity via its monopoly and control over the Sudanese open religious space with its different representations. The state could deploy its authority strategically to regulate, impose certain roles on, and deny access to particular religious markets. The enforced social, political, and religious fragmentation turned different religious representations into appendages of the state. The colonial state, from its first day, embarked on a four-tiered strategy that monopolized and organized the course of action through which the regime could pursue its policy to impose control over the entire population.

The first aspect of this strategy arose out of a policy of inclusion, while the second was derived from arrangements of exclusion. The guidelines of this policy were carefully drafted in Kitchener's famous memorandum to the new military rulers (*moudara;* sing., *moudir*) of the different districts of the Sudan. Kitchener made a clear distinction between "good" Islam, which would be accommodated, and "bad," which should not be tolerated.

Sir Auckland Colvin wrote that these guidelines "lay down the principles which should be followed by a foreign, and for the most part, a Christian power, in dealing with men of alien race or religion, and far removed in the scale of civilization."[57] Tracking what Sir Colvin described as space in the scale of civilization could lead to a conclusion that might be translated into processes of differentiation, thereby turning religious representations into geographical affairs to be dealt with differently than what could be considered as part of religious rights or the separation of church and state. In the broader sense, the open zone in the north, where "Mohammedan religion" prevailed, material colonial power would be augmented to colonize Islam from without, while in the closed zone, where "heathens" dominated, the state, through religious power, would be given a free hand to colonize from within.

Governor General Wingate and his right-hand man, Inspector General Rudolf Slatin Pasha, employed these considerations as the predominant determinants of the state policy that they initiated. Slatin was not only the second-ranking person in the colonial state but also the de facto Grand Mufti par excellence. Armed with his wide knowledge of the country, different Sudanese Islamic representations, and a who's who knowledge of the political and religious fields, Slatin, who had accumulated vital insights, was the most instrumental person in the colonial regime. He helped design and oversee the implementation of the course of action of colonizing Islam from without. Slatin perceived the first step in that direction as a venture to "encourage orthodox Islam while striving to lessen the impact of Sufism,"[58] which, according to Kitchener, "cannot be allowed to be re-established, as they generally formed centres of unorthodox fanaticism."[59] That is not to say that policymakers sympathized with orthodox Islam, but rather that colonizers used such policies to establish "a Sudanese Muslim leadership which would find itself aligned to the interests of the established administration."[60]

The form of state interventionism and control of Muslim life was conducted as a function of the state through reordering the high-ranking 'ulamā' as state employees. The inspector general handpicked and relied on the Board of the 'Ulamā', which the government instituted in 1901, and on several Muslim leaders, including Sheikh al-Tayyib Aḥmed Hāshim, the mufti whom Slatin regarded as trustworthy. Wingate and his regime defined the Board of the Civil Secretary as to "concur in any action taken by Government to suppress those unorthodox religious preachings or conventicles, known as 'Tarikas,' which profess a reformation of religion, which generally lead to grave political trouble."[61] The board would allow the government to act "as, ostensibly, the approved agents of orthodox Mohammedanism, rather than the Government acting on its own imitative."[62] The inspector general asked the advice of the board whenever a religious problem occurred; thus, they became the sole interpreters of orthodox Islam. Moreover, the promulgation of the Sudan Mohammedan Law Courts Ordinance of 1902 "established a central Islamic court of three members, the Grand Kadi (Qāḍī), the mufti, and another judge."[63] Simultaneously, "section 8 of the Sudan Mohammedan Law Courts Ordinance vested in the *Grand Kadi* the power to make rules regulating the decisions, procedure, jurisdiction, composition and functions of *Shari'a* courts."[64]

Slatin was "responsible for the appointment of *qāḍīs*, many of whom were of Egyptian origin, and thus Slatin was in a position to supervise their activities in the Sudan."[65] The promotion of orthodox Islam as a state religion and the later evolution of that policy, as reflected in the government's integration of Islamic studies into the curriculum at Gordon Memorial College, and the institutionalization of the orthodox 'ulamā' as the only interpreters of Islam, produced an uneasy ideological conflict between what was perceived as modern and official Islam, which is orthodox, and that brand of Islam that is described as traditional and backward, composed of what Kitchener described and Cromer confirmed as "heretical Moslim sects," namely Sufis. As a consequence of that disposition, the Sufi majority was relegated to minority status in terms of stratification of power and prestige. Accordingly, such an attitude has remained recurrent within the consequent developments in the Sudanese political arena and continues to play an important role in the political theory and practice of Sudan's elites, both civilian and military.

In addition, another tool of what Boddy describes as a "quiet crusade" was the government's own press, which started the publication of the *Sudan Gazette* in 1899. In 1901 the government opened the Sudan Government Press in Khartoum, where the *Gazette* was published. The government press expanded through time, and government-owned papers have continued in different names and forms to outlive the colonial state until the present. In October 1903, *al-Sudan*, the first privately owned pro-government paper, was established in Khartoum. The paper was founded and owned by Faris Nimr, Yaqoub Sarrouf, and Shaheed Makarious, who also owned *Dar al-Muqattam* and *al-Mugtatf* in Cairo and were ardent supporters of the British policy in Egypt.[66] As Heather Sharkey explains, "The British gave official support to *al-Sudan* because they appreciated it as a vehicle for government news."[67]

A number of general conclusions in the history, growth, and influence of Khartoum as the center of spaces of power can now be ventured from the assortments of this multifaceted saga. Khartoum represents, and continues to read as, an open book for the meanings and ways of how the forces at work in the colonial and postcolonial state instituted the beginning and end of many internal relations within the complexities and the oppositions of the construction of the Sudan as a whole. These complexities and oppositions, seen in sociopolitical terms, as will become clear in the coming chapters, represent the tensions between a state trying to find ways to control and exploit and the different streams of defiant moves of a society trying to resist them. The way these different styles the state developed to retain control persist and strengthen themselves forced a system of differentiation and a progression of obstinate evolution and growth of what could be described as multitiered and complex developments. These developments and their representations include the creation of a titanic vision of the state, the emergence of its community, the meager severance between the center and the periphery, and the designs and schemes that affected the internal and external dynamics that either contaminated or added to the growing pains that afflicted the ascent and fruition of a civil society. The next chapter explains how that struggle was wrapped in many forms of consciousness and pathways of an emerging Sudanese society and in the being and becoming of another city—Omdurman—and the space and the impression of demands for civility—freedom and the value of their human dignity—that their society attempted to attain.

5

A Tale of Three Cities

Omdurman

Opposite the new colonial capital at Khartoum, on the west bank of the Nile, "defying it across the Nile lay Omdurman—the Mahdi's bastion, 'the Orient,' Islam."[1] For the invading army and its every wish, "the name is like the groan of a great gong rolling mournfully across the desert; a sound redolent of all the mystery of Arabia; of shadowy latticework in still, secretive courtyards; of ancient temples; of great markets where camel caravans brought in the scents and silks of China and Circassian slave girls exhibited their charms before the lustful sheikhs."[2] In retrospect, the invading army was disappointed to find a less romantic place than they had imagined. Philip Ziegler concurs: "It is hard to believe that any city can have less charm, less dignity, less distinction than this squalid accretion of mud hovels and straw-walled huts."[3] However, these two views that reflect the orientalists' anecdotes confirmed their own conflicting forms of reproduction of knowledge about the place and its social universe. Omdurman's lack of charm was not the only aspect of the city that disappointed those whose plans were to invade and colonize it. The city disappointed those who met there, and their colonial presence further reproduced different forms of profound resistance by the people of Omdurman to the colonial incursion and hostilities before and after the invasion.

The triumph of the Mahdist revolution raised serious challenges for the entire colonial scheme. Nowhere were such challenges more serious than in imperial Britain and royal Egypt. While liberation movements were visibly developing in both the African and Asian Muslim worlds against colonial rule, the Mahdist revolution in the Sudan had already reached its successful end. As anticolonial activists were apt to admire and sympathize with the Sudanese Mahdist movement, Omdurman became the mecca where "pilgrims arrived from Samarkand, Bokhara, India, and Mecca, to examine Mahdieh with their own eyes."[4] To this must be added what Holt described as the numerous delegations from Morocco, al-Ḥijāz, Nejd, and Yemen who either visited Omdurman or communicated with al-Khalifa 'Abdullahi to be his agents within their particular regions.[5] Al-Khalifa 'Abdullahi was "full of ideas of conquest and pretensions; he used often to announce publicly that the end of the Turks' rule in Egypt was approaching. He was most anxious to obtain possession of that country, and thought the time had now come."[6] Where royal Egypt was at its most immediately vulnerable was, as Aḥmed wad Sa'd said in his poem praising al-Khalifa 'Abdullahi, *mink khaf Tawfiq 'ala qusro;* that is, the Egyptian khedive Tawfiq was terrified to lose his palace or seat of power. More alarming to the official Egyptian and British colonial forces was that "several of the sheikhs and ulemas in Cairo and in other parts of Egypt had written to him [al-Khalifa] inviting him to take possession of the country where, they assured him, he would be most cordially received."[7]

But the danger Omdurman presented to both Egypt and Britain was that it could aid the emergence of a competing empire with potential ambitions to spread and advocate a civil, Islamic, ideological war against the competing Ottoman and British empires. Hence, all within the grand scheme of the expansion of the British Empire, the invasion of Omdurman inaugurated a project of a colonial state and absorbed a Mahdiyya-free Sudan into the British colonial system. Thus, the end of that non-European nation-state or that frustrating and threatening jihadist African empire "on the way to Cairo, Damascus or some yet more glorious destiny," as described by the Mahdi's vision, was the apparent triumph of an empire on which the sun never set.

But what the British had never pronounced was that both the triumph and the defeat had set in motion the conditions, the central stakes, and the different modes of struggle for the liberation of the country from that scheme of domination. Omdurman itself, with its population and other Sudanese in the country, which was described as the national capital, was incorporated into the new Sudanese experience. Past momentous events of the city were imbedded in the history of the Sudan motivating the deeper trends of the anticolonial movement.

Omdurman before the British Invasion

In essence, Omdurman was a liberation movement that wrote its transcript in a "squalid accretion of mud hovels and straw-walled huts."[8] The invention of the city was directly related to the Mahdist revolution, its allegories, sociopolitical and religious memories, and one of the propensities of its potential groups to innovate and wield human and material resources to build a nation. Together, the triumph of the Mahdist revolution, the total collapse of Gordon's colonial state, and the contemporaneous move toward a national-religious based regime helped rejuvenate the Mahdist state as a form of a nation-state. Hence, as Roland Barthes puts it even more succinctly, within a general context, "The city is a discourse and this discourse is truly a language."[9]

Omdurman was "a physical statement of the political and religious/mystical ideologies of the Mahdiyya movement."[10] Omdurman, which the Ansār described as *buq'at al-Mahdi* (the place of the Mahdi) and *al-buq'a al-mubaraka* or *al-buq'a al-mushrafa* (the blessed place), was created overnight to acquire the prestige of a special moment in the history of a radical communicant shift of a movement into a new regime and into a different state. It was an event on a par with the revolution itself and was the last in the series of evolving encampments that were developed during the long Mahdist march that included Qadir, el-Obeid, al-Janzara, al-Rahad, and Abu Si'id.[11] The city's associated sacredness was thrust upon it by the religious, national, social, and political allure of its founder. Omdurman, *dar al-Hijra* (the place to where believers immigrate) and home of the Ansār, witnessed the commencement and the difficult fortification of the regime, its system of governance, and its statecraft.

The Mahdist poet Moḥammad wad al-Twaim said in his poem "Omdurman":

> *sahab al-raḥma ya qabl 'alaa Omdurman nazal wabil*
> the clouds of mercy, Oh arriver,
> have heavily rained on Omdurman.

Ever since, other Sudanese followed wad Sa'd's designation when he said in one of his poems, "Buq'at Omdurman aman al-khayif" (Omdurman place, the site of safety for the frightened), to call it "Omdurman balad al-aman" (the city of safety). No other city in the country has become such a repository of different sentiments, as it has been articulated in all forms of Sudanese expressive culture praising the place as a center for felicity and national pride.

Muḥammad Aḥmed al-Mahdi—who chose the place as his army's headquarters during the 1884 siege of Khartoum—settled on it as the destination and central event of one of the longest jihadist marches in history, a march that started with a small group of his Ansār, who gathered around him in 1881 on Abba Island. The grand human panorama was composed of more than "'100,000' Arabs," according to Wingate,[12] or 150,000 people, as Ohrwalder estimated, or, in the words of a recent scholar, "upwards of 400,000" men, women, and children from every sector of the population,[13] in every section of the country, who were bound together ever more closely by the cause of revolution.

This unique experience transformed and hardened the people of Omdurman to become not only the common bearers of the revolution but also the builders of the new state and the inhabitants of its new capital. This long march had turned that small group into one of the largest and strongest armies in the continent. In the reorganization of the army "almost all the male population of the Sudan was involved. All men were warriors, though some only volunteers in the reserve army."[14] The three-part army, with 'Abdullahi al-Ta'aishi as its commander in chief, included: "the permanent regional garrisons," "the volunteers," and "the military expeditions."[15] Omdurman became the headquarters of a military system and the expression of its trends that organized and divided the country into *'imalāt* (administrative units), each with an appointed commander in chief, or *'amil*, responsible for its civil administration and its military duties.

The Omdurman garrison was organized into three parts. The city itself, which spread for about five miles, or, according to Wingate, "nearly six miles along the bank of the Nile and, at its largest, extended almost three miles inland from the river."[16] The city's population, according to the estimate of Father Ohrwalder, who was there from the early days of the settlement of the new capital, was more than one hundred and fifty thousand people. The metropolis of Omdurman was "a conglomeration of every race and nationality in the Sudan . . . [in addition to] Egyptians, Abyssinians, Turks, Mecca Arabs, Syrians, Indians, Europeans, Jews, and all these various nationalities [who] have their own Quarters, and marry into their own tribes and sections."[17] Functionally, the Mahdists planned and built the spaces of Omdurman, as in other cities, in a way so that they could perform their social, religious, and other material practices. At the same time, it was incomparable to other cities because all these needs were part of a grandiose ideological scheme. This ideological scheme was put together in the landscape of a city that was constructed overnight to house a large and highly diversified army that represented the entire population of the country, along with their families, possessions, and transport animals. It compromised one unique, extended, and aggregated zone that rapidly transformed into an urban capital of a different sort.

The city's official sector combines the administrative, the spiritual, and the state disciplinary institutions that expanded as a multifaceted, open compound. This sector casts itself in accordance with the spatial system, architectural considerations, and framework style of the official city and the character of the new place. Bayt al-Khalifa 'Abdullahi (al-Kahlifa 'Abdullahi's house), which the inhabitants of Omdurman described as *al-bāb*, or *al-qaṣr* (palace), was the official residence of the head of state and the center of the administrative and executive Mahdist compound.[18] This two-story building commanded the highest part of the terrain and overlooked the entire city, as far as Karari, to the north, and Fort Omdurman, to the south. However, the tallest building in the city was Qubbat al-Mahdi (the Mahdi's tomb).

Isma'il 'Abd al-Qadir al-Kordofani, Father Ohrwalder, and Slatin, who witnessed the development of construction of the building of Qubbat al-Mahdi until its completion, described it in their books as a square white building, thirty feet high and thirty-six feet long, each wall surmounted by a hexagonal block rising another fifteen feet, and crowned by a dome forty feet high. The Egyptian engineer Isma'il Effendi—a Mahdist prisoner after the fall of Khartoum—designed the building. Later, the khalifa assigned Chief Engineer Omer to assist Isma'il Effendi in building the palace. Isma'il Effendi was the designer of al-sayyid al-Ḥasan al-Merghni tomb at Kassala before the Mahdiyya. The stones for the construction of Qubbat al-Mahdi, whose walls were upwards of six feet thick, had to be brought all the way from Khartoum. Father Ohrwalder expanded on the ambience and other features of the place: "Every night, and all through the night, quantities of candles are kept burning; and it is impossible not to be impressed with the solemnity of the tomb. The walls are so thick that the tropical sun cannot penetrate, and there is always a cool refreshing breeze inside. The rich perfumes with which the tomb is continually sprinkled fill the air with the most agreeable odours."[19] Yet the idea of the tomb extends beyond the tall and majestic building. Its impact is threefold.

In its initial impact, the tomb has been the expression of the immortalization of that impressive person and the ideology he advocated, an ideology that continued to be the focus for diverse groups of Sudanese people in pursuit of a complexity of goals, some of them universal and others local. These goals continue to inspire those groups, within the historical legacy of the group itself, the character of the leader, and generations of Sudanese people who have come after. Since that day, for more than a century now, some Sudanese celebrate the man and recognize his teachings as the path that kept them unwavering in their ideology when they were confronted by difficult political circumstances and that protected them in desperate situations.

Second, as Deemer argues, al-Khalifa 'Abdullahi "was seeking through the construction of [the] Qubbat al-Mahdi complex to legitimize his position as the rightful successor to the Mahdi by perpetuating the personality cult of his predecessor and perpetuating his own identity with it."[20] He adds, "it can be argued that the construction of the mausoleum was an attempt to maintain the validity of the movement in the absence of its charismatic leader."[21]

A third, and continuing, impact of the tomb is an everyday reminder of the Mahdi's sudden and untimely death, before he fulfilled the Mahdist promise that "the Apostle of God" had given him in the prophetic vision. He left behind a situation in which it became difficult to reconcile the ideological claim and the actual fact among the skeptics and those who already doubted the claim. According to al-Mahdi, the prophet promised him he would possess the whole world and he would pray in the mosques of Mecca, Yathrib, Cairo, Jerusalem, al-'Irāq, and al-Kūfah.

The constraints that came with such a development have weakened that claim and eroded the ideology over time to open the door to all forms of political competition, personal and group conflicts, and different forms of dissent. Some vital dimensions of the transformation that marked the history of Mahdism since the death of the Mahdi involved what was described as the revolt of the Ashraf, according to most historians, or the Danaqla revolt, according to others, including Babikr Bedri.[22] Bedri, who knew some of those Danaqla since his childhood, claimed that they lived "in great prosperity in the days of their power, while the

Mahdi was yet alive, and after his death, too. They lived in great houses with servants and retainers, and the finest horses; they were the influential patrons of their friends, who placed their hopes in them."[23] Here, one would assume that the characterization of the conflict in terms of *awlad al-balad* (riparians, or settlers) versus *awlad al-gharib* (inhabitants of western Sudan) or *awalad al-'Arab* (nomads) pales in comparison to the class, power, and prestige aspects of the conflict.

The ethnic equation, in its different forms, cannot be applied or generalized to a privileged few of high status who happened to make up a sector of the Danaqla ethnic group. Moreover, the Mahdist state's history of conflicts and its culture and other internal wars demonstrated different forms of collision within or between groups that one day supported the revolution or contributed to the building of that state. The Mahdist movement in its state formation in the sudden and shocking absence of its spiritual guide, whom "'Reis el-Gesh' (commander in chief of the army)" succeeded, turned into a space of governance with a complex structure, brought some groups together in different kinds of alliances, and formed and enforced a militaristic, authoritarian, and hierarchal regime.[24]

The internal and external factors involved in the development of the new regime forced it to cope with and respond to difficult challenges, prompting its leader to tighten the grip of authority and persuade the regime to intensify the centralized power of the state apparatus. Because freedom of Sufi practice and association, unrestricted local and regional trade, and the unconstrained movement of individuals and groups were an existential necessity for most Sudanese, the regime's sumptuary regulations, and its jihad needs, forced certain resentful and dissenting individuals and groups to resort to collective violence against the Mahdist state. In these different fields, the initial and the continuing impacts—solidarity on the one hand and conflict on the other—continued to occur, sometimes in tandem, and each by itself insofar as religion has been used as a mobilizing resource or functioned as a mode of imposing or opposing forms of construction of sociopolitical realities in Sudanese life ever since.

Closer to the Mahdi's tomb was Jāmi' al-Kaun (the Mosque of the Universe), or the fourth mosque.[25] The mosque, as described by Wingate, "is merely an enormous rectangular yard, about 1000 yards long and 800 yards broad, and quite uncovered; a number of labakh trees (*Acacia albizzia*) are enclosed at the western end, which marks the position assigned to women, and which is partly roofed in by matting."[26] The Mahdist chronicler Ism'ail al-Kordofani described the mosque as having eight entrances, which stand for the doorways to Paradise. He added that the construction of the mosque took only seventy-three days and was one of the miracles of divine support that al-Khalifa 'Abdullahi enjoyed.[27] According to Ohrwalder's account, the mosque could hold up to seventy thousand parishioners, in long rows of one thousand people each, whose collective moves during prayer sounded like distant thunder.

This idea of having one central mosque for the entire male population of the capital to attend regularly for the five daily prayers goes along with the idea of one centralized ideology of the Mahdiyya, which banned other Sufi representations and associations and attempted to control and reshape the society and the state. Within the new state mosque, each individual was to keep to his own spot, within the same row, permanently. The abiding physical motive of regulating prayer that way was to keep track of the attendance of each individual. A police guard who never let anyone out of his sight made sure that individuals attended the mosque five times a day, otherwise absentees might suffer the strictest punishment. Male attire was also strictly regulated; the Mahdist rules required the Ansār to wear the *jiba*. In addition, there were strict rules for marriage ceremonies and for *mahar*, the display of grief for those who have died. There was a ban on tobacco and alcohol consumption, and a form of sumptuary regulations emerged. Disciplinary action was taken toward suspects or noncompliant persons; "educational" measures could progress from *mulazamt al-farwah* (sticking close to the khalifa's prayer sheepskin in the mosque for an indeterminate period) to spending an indefinite term in *al-saier*, the state prison. Named after Idris al-Saier, the chief jailer whom the Mahdi appointed as its commissioner, the prison was called *bayt al-Saier* (al-Saier's house). Charles Neufeld explains that al-Saier "eventually replaced the proper word for prison, all prisons being called 'Saier,' and the head-goaler 'Saier.'"[28]

Whether in jail or sticking to the *farwah*, the educational process was primarily confined to reading *al-rātib* (a prayer book the Mahdi prescribed for his followers). In accordance with the educational plan, illiterate people were taught how to read and write. All these disciplinary measures were enacted in order to give suspects and noncompliant individuals a chance to redeem themselves by changing their behavior. Seen in this light, the mosque appears to play a crucial role in the disciplinary system of the regime in two complementary ways.

To the south of the mosque three units stood together as part of a single compound called *bayt al-amāna*. The first of these units was for the production storage for the war material that included ammunition, rifles, guns, and powder. The second unit was where hundreds of flags were planted in the ground. Ohrwalder described these flags as a forest of staves with the khalifa's black flag rising above all of them. The third unit was a two-story building in which war drums (*nugara*) were stored. No residential houses were to be built near the *bayt al-amāna*.

Within the official city, near the dock on the Nile and surrounded by a brick wall, stretched extensive buildings that housed many government departments. This multifaceted compound was the *bayt al-māl* (state treasury). Ohrwalder devoted a good part of a lengthy chapter of *Ten Years' Captivity* to describing this compound. He illustrated that Ibrahim 'Adlan (*amīn*, or commissioner, of *bayt al-māl*) "built an extensive yard of sun-dried bricks, which he divided off into sections for the various departments of administration. He made a large corn-store, in which a mountain of dhurra was collected—indeed, so high was it, that it could be seen from a considerable distance."[29] In addition, the compound was organized to include "a soap manufactory, several treasury stores including the granary, sections for keeping booty, animals and slaves, the lithograph press, the national mint, and many offices for bookkeeping and accounts, for purchases and sales. There was also a museum (*Antīkkhāna or Bayt al-antikā*), and a dispensary."[30]

The *bayt al-māl* was the controller of the trading activity. The commissioner had the power to confiscate goods, to enforce different types of high taxes, and to act as the state monopoly over many main local products, buying them from their producers only to resell them for high prices to those who were permitted to export them. Around the core city were barracks (*al-mulazimin*), which hosted the khalifa's bodyguard. This small army was "made up of eighteen *rub's*. Most men were armed with Remington rifles. Each *rub'* was commanded by an *amir*. The *rub's* were divided into between eight and twelve standards, each standard containing one hundred men."[31] The barracks had its own *bayt al-māl*, or treasury. The khalifa's bodyguards received "a monthly payment in cash for themselves and in kind (grain) for their families from this treasury, which drew its revenues from the Jazira (Gezira) area and the east bank of the Nile."[32]

The second army that resided within close proximity was the regular force or the hard-core units of the Mahdist army: the Jihadiyya. The Mahdists recruited these troops from previous private units of bazinger originally from the southern parts of the country and the Nuba Mountains, and reorganized them with their generals headed by Ḥamdan Abu 'Anja. The Jihadiyya had their own *bayt al-māl*, responsible for their salaries and maintenance, that "derived its revenues from the west bank of the Nile in the province of Omdurman."[33] In other parts of the city resided the irregular national guard units, who transformed the small village of Omdurman into the largest garrison in the continent and the capital for the new Mahdist state.

There was a special match between the growing capital and the largest emerging Omdurman bazaar as well as a degree of difference. The same way the Mahdist state organized *bayt al-māl* as the center of the public enterprise, it too organized the Omdurman market as the center of private enterprise. It was divided into different markets and "separate areas for each important category of commodities or services, i.e., an area for old women who were engaged in the selling of oil, grease, beans, vegetables, *dhura* (Sorghum), milk; an area for blacksmiths, etc. Each zone included a number of huts or sheds for protecting the merchants and their merchandise from the sun. The users of these sheds were required to pay a monthly rental fee to the Bayt al-māl."[34] For its part, the state gave much attention to the market by assigning al-Khalifa 'Ali wad Ḥilu, Khalīfat al-Fārouq, the second-ranking person in the state, in charge of the place. According to Ohrwalder, "One of the most important places in Omdurman is the market, to which a broad road leads from the mosque."[35]

The country's largest bazaar was the main meeting place for the jallaba "from Kordofan, and the Gezireh, from Berber, Dongola and Sawakin, all earnestly occupied in learning each other's news."[36] Although the human landscape of the market encoded what matched the newly diversified Mahdiyya's society, nevertheless it excluded representatives of those in power and included some relatives and close class associates of the groups of the Mahdi's wealthy relatives whom the khalifa had forced out of power. Ohrwalder observed that the market "is a place full of life, abounding in buyers and sellers, as well as idlers, who come to tattle and pick any news they can. The proof that Mahdieh is not considered to be a durable régime is evident from the feverish anxiety of everyone to hear the latest news, and the market is the rendezvous for all news-seekers."[37] He adds, "It is impossible to give an idea of the wild rumours which are continually flying hither and thither. It is equally impossible to separate the false news from the true. On this account the market is looked upon by the Khalifa with the utmost distrust, and he would really abolish it if he thought it was possible to do so."[38]

Hence, the excessive measures of taxation, duties, arbitrary confiscations, and monopoly privileges that the state placed on the *bayt al-māl* constituted a serious hindrance for the stable growth of the market and capitalist development. That unique experience united the new community of the new state more than their common location or mode of living. This new community finally inhabited the place and continued to grow as "the biggest collective effort" of the human war machine in the country that could be utilized or deployed in part or as a whole at any time.

The southern residential zone of al-Rayya al-Zarga (Black Flag) of al-Khalifa 'Abdullahi extended from the mosque and stretched west to the bank of the White Nile. This part of the city was the main residential area of the western Sudanese of Darfur and southern Kordofan. West of the mosque was the residential zone for groups affiliated with al-Rayya al-Khadra (the Green Flag) of al-Khalifa 'Ali wad al-Ḥilu.

The Mahdists established the new city, society, and state to satisfy the demands of a system of war rather than of agricultural, trade, or industrial production that could maintain any form of functional accumulation. In many ways these demands were extensions of the jihadist ideology and the revolutionary experience on which the Mahdist movement had embarked. But the massing of citizens deployed as armies fighting these continuous wars became a major impediment to the Mahdist collective effort to reach those universal goals or sustain the demands of the Mahdiyya. One of the further consequences of massing citizens in Omdurman was the neglect of farming, which subjected the country to famine and severely damaged the power of the state and its ideology. Hence, the empire's promise was unfulfilled, the state was weakened, and the colonial threat came creeping from all directions. But when the sound of the empire fizzled out, nationalist fury and a spirit of independence remained alive.

Omdurman after the Invasion

Martin Daly has rightly stated, "No events in the history of the Sudan since the death of General Gordon in 1885 have attracted more attention in the outside world than the battle of Omdurman (or Karari) on 2 September 1898, and the Fashoda Crisis that began later in the same month. The former marked the destruction of the Mahdist State, the last important African polity to be subdued by the Europeans."[39] Moreover, the battle of Omdurman, which "was an execution,"[40] its aftermath of violence, and the performance of the invading army, which committed atrocious acts against the Sudanese, led to an indictment of human brutality as it was of those who executed it. Neither the victor nor the vanquished, however, was saved from the deep scars and the implacable hostilities and violence that followed; the historical and political circumstances blemished them all.

Since the day Omdurman fell into the hands of the conquerors, its houses of mud and sun-dried brick and narrow lanes were reduced to a reimaging of everything inferior and alien in the colonial discourse. Philip Ziegler describes the ideas that cast that image and its enduring legacy: "Some at least of the British troops were still dreaming of exotic splendour and glanced from side to side in the constant hope that great palaces or mysterious temples would burst upon their eyes. They saw nothing but the nondescript squalor of what must then have been Africa's largest slum."[41] Victorious, Kitchener vowed to empty Omdurman of its useless mouths.[42] Underlying these assumptions were all the forms of the foundation of the colonial thinking about Mahdism, the Orient, and Islam.

Yet for the Sudanese, the impact of the Omdurman moment was a continuum of reinvented forms of resistance to the occupation. What Omdurman's moment brought to the anticolonial movement or the potential resistance to the new regime was essentially an audacity of defiance and a new invented collective arrangement that took different shapes and modes for the society to reconstruct itself and produce meaning to its new exertions. Neither the three years that Kitchener took to finish the invasion nor the period that followed the battle of Omdurman settled affairs for the colonialists in the Sudan. Hence, Omdurman provided the material support for resistance and social infrastructure that continued to insure the revitalization of all memories—both positive and negative—of the past from where it sprang. Out of Omdurman thousands of Sudanese, who did not accept the defeat, followed al-Khalifa 'Abdullahi west to regroup for a new round with the invaders. Two momentous changes took place as a result.

First, the Mahdist state, which stayed in power for thirteen years, again turned into a fighting force. Second, although the state's forces suffered significant limitations, the teachings and spirit of the Mahdiyya, for some, had far from exhausted its assurances and promise. It inspired new forms of resistance even after the defeat of al-Khalifa 'Abdullahi's forces at Omdurman. So, as in Omdurman, Umm Dibaykarat, the second temporary Omdurman (the temporary capital of a defiant Mahdiyya), turned into a new encampment where there "would be no compromise with the invader: Wingate was never to forget that [though] militant Mahdism had been beaten down, it had not given up; that the Sudanese had surrendered not to the inexorable force of European arms, but to the unarguable will of God; and that more than Maxim guns would be needed to win the battle for the respect of the Sudanese."[43]

For those who stayed behind and did not join al-Khalifa 'Abdullahi, the city remained a reminder of a past that flourished in history, but it continued to feed the present with a shared meaning of a contiguous glory. The quarters of the city stand as a reminder of everything that symbolizes the power and authority of the Mahdist state, its warriors, and its system of rule. It was quite an experience, the changeover from making history and participating in all aspects of the human lived experience to dwelling in the symbolic reminders of that human experience within its diversified ramifications. The most inspirational heirs to that experience were the Mahdiyya, Omdurman the city, its inhabitants, and those who lived by the values of that city.

The Mahdi's tomb, or what Khalil Faraḥ described as "the mausoleum which perfumed the place by its gentle breeze" or *bayt al-Khalifa*, *al-Mulazimin*, *al-'Arda* (the parade ground), *bayt al-Māl*, *Ḥai al-Umrā* (the princes' quarter), *Ḥai al-sayyid al-Makki* (Sayyid al-Makki ibn Islamil al-Wali, from Kordofan), *wad Nubawi* (Amir Moḥammad wad Nubawi, from Kordofan), *Abu Roaf* (Amir Al-Mardi wad Abu Roaf, from al-Buṭana region), *Abu Kaduak* (Amir Ḥasan wad abu Kaduak, from Darfur), and *al-Msālma* (the Coptic sector); all were reinstated as heirloom residences of that history as well as of human beings who had settled or continued to settle there. Each of these histories turned into neighborhoods and those princes, dignitaries, and leaders of the Mahdist era, from whom these neighborhoods took their names, served as a reminder to the ordinary person and the colonizer alike. It was a signifier and a reminder of the reality and the symbolic meanings of the Sudanese private, public, and official life, which stood as an element of defiance to the image and truth of an imperial outfit in its recent past and current ruling orders.

While Khartoum continued to grow as the headquarters of the administrative network of the colonial capitalist system and its military guard, Omdurman also continued to grow, as the home of the largest bazaar in Africa, the home of a growing urban capitalist enterprise, and the flagship of an emerging and resilient anticolonial Sudanese spirit. In some respect, it was a tale of two cities that faced each other as polar opposites, as representations of the most critical dissimilar forms of symbolic realities and meanings within the new colonial system of power and cultural and social relations in the Sudan. The confrontation between the two had constrained the colonized through contempt and aggression as the colonizer continued to define himself and his mission as the spokesperson and the sole provider of an enterprise of modernity and modernization to a "savage" race. The other side, the Sudanese colonized people, continued to redefine themselves within an undeniable cultural, religious, and moral supremacy. Within such collusion between politics, religion, and culture, incompatible self-images of cultural, religious, and moral supremacy of new communities of conversation continued to grow. On the Sudanese side particular "terrains of resistance" found their representation in different styles of expressive culture that complemented other forms of resistance and developed into what was described later as *al-ḥaraka al-waṭaniyya* (the nationalist movement). The complexity of this movement entails the whole host of political, cultural, and economic developments that were by no means directed only toward the resurrection of the Mahdiyya, but also toward an emerging civil society.

From the beginning of the Sudanese counterattack on the colonial invasion, Mahdist poets such as wad Sa'd and wad Ḥaboba's sister Ruqayya laid the foundation of an expressive culture, influenced by, but not congenial to, such terrains of resistance. Similarly, the resisting military admixtures continued to resurge in different parts of the country within their different rubrics and endured up to the 1920s. In certain ways, many aspects of Omdurman after the invasion were evolutionary, while others were revolutionary and new.

The Evolutionary Trend: Mainstreaming a Conservative Orthodoxy

The historical transition for some commercial groups into the post-Mahdist era represented something significant about the ways in which some activities were organized or certain opportunities presented themselves. Given their positive and negative status during al-Khalifa 'Abdullahi's reign and their discontent with the Mahdist state's regulation of trade, citizens in the market sector felt liberated from the restriction of the Mahdiyya. Yet, as explained before, there were considerable numbers of people who had followed the Khatmiyya ṭarīqa before the arrival of the Mahdiyya and who never believed in the Mahdiyya at any time. With or without the pressure from the anticolonial environment, the Omdurman merchants politely rejected Kitchener's offer to act as agents for British companies. Some of Omdurman's merchants, however, were eager to reinstate an independent source of socioeconomic power around the Khatmiyya ṭarīqa and Sayyid 'Ali al-Mirghani, the group's spiritual leader.

Sayyid 'Ali's efforts to reinstate the Khatmiyya ṭarīqa in its new mode of action and resource mobilization fostered and maintained contacts with diverse social groups from different parts of the country and placed the Omdurman market and merchants at the center of the trade activity in the country. Hence, new forms of accumulation grew among those who remained in Omdurman after the invasion, and those who continued to build on the relationships that existed between the functioning of the religious ṭarīqa (Khatmiyya in particular), the family, and the jallaba networks. The new communication and transportation systems that brought different parts of the country together in the form of economic action enhanced opportunities in local, regional, and international trade by using local (Egyptian) and international (British) currencies. Within the new development of the largest bazaar in Africa, the new form of capitalism stratified their social life and shaped the way they saw their world. Through the value-adding economic capital and the value-imposing cultural capital, new forms of knowledge, taste, practice, and an overall societal order started to emerge.

It was the invisible hand of the ṭarīqa, the unified currencies, new systems of communications, and an open market that regulated the emerging community of Omdurman and defined its self-image and self-esteem. Such a disposition was deeply imbedded in the values and demands of general education and sometimes in specialized forms of knowledge. Hence, both the social and the knowledge-bearing universes of all possible forms of education that continued to operate in Omdurman before that time, together with the new ones, which the colonial state introduced, were in high demand, as they had functional necessity. This explains the persistence of the trading community, which normally sustained the traditional *masseed* education through donations, to keep that form of education operational. At the same time, the colonial authorities saw a need to colonize the entire educational system.

The prime example of those conflicting attitudes was al-Ma'had al-'Ilmi (an Islamic school established in 1901), at the Omdurman mosque, where some of the 'ulamā' would teach Islamic studies as part of the new regime's plan to colonize Islam. As 'Abdullahi 'Ali Ibrahim explains, the colonial regime agreed to "establish al-Ma'had at the Omdurman mosque in which clerics would teach instead at their private residences."[44] In 1912 the colonial state appointed Sheikh Abu al-Gāsim Hāshim as the head of Ma'had, which was to be upgraded under the supervision of the "Legal Secretary of the Governor General. Bowing to modernity, the clerics introduced arithmetic, Arabic composition, and dictation into the purely theological curriculum of traditional education."[45] As in other colonies, however, the introduction of the British system of education took place "in institutions, meaning buildings with physically divided spaces marking off one class of students from another, as well as teachers from students," in addition to other policies and processes of regulation, which marked the students' progress, using rewards and certifications to attest "to the student's command of a specifiable body of knowledge. Even with the undoubted good will and best intentions on the part of [the British leaders] . . . a British metalogic of regularity, uniformity, and above all fiscal responsibility could not help but participate in the erosion and transformation of what the British wanted to preserve; that is . . . Muslim learning."[46] The modernization of al-Ma'had had institutionalized the inferiority and marginalization of that type of learning.

The new generation of Omdurmanis who gained modest masseed education, or either al-Ma'had al-'Ilmi in its different developments or moderate public education, and who operated through such social image, started to add to an inherited cultural capital within new and diverse forms of expressions. Different forms of learning, the ṭarīqa, and the market values became separate and sometimes collective conditions and entries to new socioeconomic and political universes. The construction and stratification of this emerging society of Omdurman, and gradually other jallaba communities at large, was socially, politically, and culturally conservative by way of conformity to the ṭarīqa and its leader. This conservative impulse is reflected in a newly constructed identity, jallaba identity, with its very distinctive guarded sphere. More than the colonial minicities and villages that followed the pattern of Khartoum, major jallaba cities and neighborhoods refurbished themselves and expanded nationwide. The division of the family house into closed and open zones to guard and exclude women has become an insignia of the conditions created by the new form of conservatism. Yet, at the same time, controlling the jallaba women and keeping them dependent, while taking pride in competitively high marriage costs, was one of the most effective ways of rooting wealth and people within the confines of social space and economic class.

Social distance is produced to fit the function of class more than race, ethnicity, or religion. Gender differentiation and gender identity that conform to such conservatism created a musical genre later called *ḥagibat al-fann*. The *ḥagibat al-fann* emerged as a form of entertainment parallel to the *madīḥ* [religious praise] genre in praise of an imagined image of the mere physical beauty of a woman who was kept away, beyond reach of any form of social interaction. The writers of the lyrics of *ḥagibat al-fann*—Ibrahim al-'Abādi, Saliḥ 'Abdel seed Abu Salaḥ, Moḥamad 'Ali 'Abdullah, Moḥammad wad al-Radḍi, Aḥmed 'Abdel Raḥim al-'Umari, and 'Umer al-Bana, to name a few—represented a paradigm shift notable for idealizing outward female beauty. These poets radically changed the lyrical form, style, and language of the Sudanese song. They presented neither a specific female nor living females in general, but forms of the female identity and the difference that would characterize that particular Sudanese woman. The identity indexes the physical beauty and attractiveness of that silent female. The difference of that person lies beyond time and place, while her virtual presence can be ascertained only in dreams or through her toward a fascinated male, who consequently suffers sleepless nights.

The two musical legends who gave this genre its influence on Sudanese life were the performers 'Abdal Karim Karoma and Moḥammad Aḥmed Suror. It was the phonograph (originally the Gramophone), followed by the radio, that introduced this kind of entertainment to wealthy urban Sudanese families and spread the conservative message. The popularity of these new communication devices turned that form of art into one of the major currents of that time. It was the radio revolution that gave that art nationwide attention and "when [its] language first entered history its masters were already priests and sorcerers"[47] who extended that conservative taste all around.

Yet, the enormity and consequences of the subtle dissension and the restrained resistance to colonial rule within Omdurman's emerging conservative communities evolved around the neo-Khatmiyya and its urban accommodations, as well as the neo-Mahdiyya and its rural adaptations, which should not be glossed over. What happened, in actuality, was that Omdurman became the counterhegemonic pole of a new Sudanese social and political culture evolving around both conservative and progressive civil trends.

The Revolutionary Trend: Unconventional Conventions

Yet, at the heart of the city of Omdurman, new forms of resistance started to brew by the time that militant insurgency started to wane in the rural parts of the country. By 1920 a new generation of Omdurmanis, whose parents had outlived the Mahdiyya and who were among the earliest graduates of Gordon Memorial College, began to enter fields of prestige, though not of power, as government employees, new members in the community of the state. However, they might have instinctively felt an early group consciousness, as acting as a group would transform them from a descriptive class into a transformative one. The developments that emerged out of those conditions and the consequences of the relationships of the community of the state within the colonial field of action were crisis riddled, inconsistent, and contradictory.

The crisis for that generation was embedded in a loyalty toward their nation and nationals that can never be eliminated under colonialism. The growing community of the state in the complexity of their relationships with the state that had created them was similar to what Marx described as the "hideous heathen god who refused to drink nectar except from the skulls of murdered men." That is, as Nandy explains, "history would produce out of oppression, violence and cultural dislocation not merely new technological and social forces but also a new social consciousness in Asia and Africa."[48] Drinking that nectar took different forms within different phases of development that brought together numerous recourses for the realization of that goal. There were wide-ranging changes in the emerging façade that reproduced different voices and characterized these developments; nevertheless, the underlying logic of the anticolonial movement was the same. Three of these developments represent the different forms of continuity and change that Omdurman experienced.

First, by 1920, and for the first time since the early days of the Mahdist revolution, a new nonreligious trend introduced itself as a challenger to the monopoly the religious leadership enjoyed in the field of resistance to colonial regimes. This new trend played a part in stimulating other emerging groups, such as the new labor formations, and at the same time created different uneasy relationships and culture wars with Sufi religious representations, particularly, Sayyid 'Ali al-Merghani, 'Abd al-Raḥman al-Mahdi, and Yousif al-Hindi. This trend came together under the name of Jam'iat al-Itiḥad (the Union Society).

In all probability, Jam'iat al-Itiḥad, which was organized as early as 1920, was one of the first clandestine societies in the colonial Sudan. Its founding members were 'Ubeid Ḥaj al-Amin, a nephew of Sheikh Abulgāsim Hāshim; Muḥi el-Din Jamal Abu Seif, son of a chief clerk; Tawfiq Saliḥ Jibril, a government employee; Ibrahim Badri, son of the famous Mahdist and educator Babikr Badri; and Sulayman Kisha, like Ibrahim Badri, the son of a wealthy Omdurman merchant. All five members of the organization were known as poets, writers, and independent-minded intellectuals. Four of them were Gordon College graduates and government employees. The fifth, Sulayman Kisha, was a young merchant. Later, chief among the graduates of Gordon College who joined the group were Khalf Allah Khalid, al-Amin 'Ali Madni, Makawi Yagoub, 'Abdullah Khalil, Moḥammad Saliḥ al-Shinqīti, Babikr Qabani, and Khalil Faraḥ. Another group included 'Ali 'Abd al-Laṭīf, Moḥammad Saliḥ Jibril, and Saliḥ Abdel Gadir, along with Moḥammad al-Umarabi, one of the few al-Ma'had al-'Ilmi graduates who joined the organization.[49] It was not clear if the term *al-itiḥad* (union) in the group's name refers to a union among Sudanese groups or a union with Egypt.

Al-Itiḥad was less cohesive in structure than other Sudanese organizations. Each member was assigned to recruit five new individuals known only to him. As the picture of the organization emerges from the writings of Ja'far Moḥammad 'Ali Bakhiet,[50] Yoshiko Kurita,[51] Elena Vezzadini,[52] and Moḥammad 'Omer Beshir, it was clear that al-Itiḥad's members were well known to their *affendiyya* (government employees), peers at the Omdurman Graduates' Club, and to some colleagues in the workplace. In its early days al-Itiḥad focused on literary and cultural endeavors and on mailing pamphlets and letters from the religious leaders criticizing the British administration and those who were accused of collaborating with it—in particular, al-Sayyid 'Ali al-Merghani, 'Abd al-Raḥman al-Mahdi, and al-Sharief Yousif al-Hindi, who according to Obeid Ḥag al-Amin, "worshiped King George and his apostle Sir Lee Stack the Sudan Governor General." In addition,·members of al-Itiḥad continued to publish articles under pseudonyms in Egyptian newspapers attacking the British colonial regime.[53]

On the other hand, an important part of the intellectual discourse among these groups was centered on a Sudanese identity pushing back in defiance. Al-Itiḥad member and poet of the 1924 revolution Khalil Faraḥ articulated these terrains of resistance in song. A new generation of poets and writers—including Moḥammad 'Abdullahi al-Bana, Ḥamza al-Malik Tumbal, Saliḥ 'Abdel Gadir, Moḥammad Aḥmed Mahjoub, Saliḥ Boutros, Yousif Mustafa al-Tinai, Ḥasan Taha, al-Amin Madni, and Aḥmed Moḥammad Saliḥ—informed and motivated the Sudanese anticolonial movement. Most of those Sudanese poets embodied the symbols of such an identity by drawing attention to the corrupted and corrupting identity or the "status symbols" of the colonialist, which Faraḥ described as *tufiali dakheel* (a parasitical intruder), in contrast to the "prestige symbol" of the Sudanese, which he portrayed as *al-sharaf al-badhikh* (the well-established honor).

The general progression of these terrains of resistance had evolved on the Sudanese side of the divide, articulating the basic standards by which the Sudanese made their judgments and pursued their strategies. This despite the fact that the correspondence between the colonial system and these forms of resistance were on the formation of each of the two entities: colonial (the state) and local (civil society), neither of which was evenly balanced or simple. Another aspect of this train of resistance, which was embodied in Khalil Faraḥ's most famous poem, "'Azza fi hawak," was the call for the Sudanese woman to wake up and join the struggle. In large measure, Faraḥ and some of his compatriots shared it as an advocacy for a different role in which Sudanese women could lead the struggle. In his song, the Sudanese "La Marseillaise," 'Ubeid 'Abd al-Nur beautifully wrote:

> *ya umm ḍafyir qodi al-rasan wa ahtifi fl yḥya al-waṭan*
> O Ye with the braids, [go ahead and] lead the caravan and loudly chant:
> long live the country.

The real novelty of al-Itiḥad emerged out of its leadership's ability to represent the vision and dynamism of 'Ali 'Abd al-Laṭīf and 'Ubeid Ḥag al-Amin. Their ability took it a step further to the heart of the new fields of accommodation to include other communities such as the labor organizations, the military, young urban retailers, and tribal chiefs forming pragmatic alliances. 'Ali and 'Ubeid's collaboration came in the form of reform for the organization to come into the open and accommodate other social and professional organizations; it envisioned an association within the Egyptian nationalist movement. The new organization that replaced al-Itiḥad, called Jam'iyat al-Liwā' al-Abyaḍ (the White Flag League) was founded in 1923. 'Ali 'Abd al-Laṭīf became its leader and 'Ubeid its secretary general. The league's insignia was a map of the Nile Valley with the Egyptian flag in its left corner.

Within these new alliances of the Sudanese groups, new leaderships were created, organizations were adapted, and strategies were devised to face colonial challenges. Although the league's activists, according to 1924 British intelligence reports, did not exceed 150 members, its sympathizers and supporters were widespread across the country. According to Vezzadini, "the secrecy and the necessity of trusting each other were obviously linked to the political, anti-establishment nature of the League work. For that reason, the number of League members had to remain limited. The League was not a mass movement, and did not aim at becoming one."[54] The league members were fairly well connected through the numerous government employees who worked in different offices for the postal and telegraph departments, and who used those communication systems to disseminate news to other members of the league. The league's strength "was among the army officers where 'Ali 'Abdal Latif was respected and among the clerical staff who admired 'Ubied Ḥag al Amin."[55] According to Moḥamed 'Omer Beshir, of the 104 names listed by the intelligence department as members of the league "there were 40 junior government officials, 27 army officers or ex-army officers, 10 workers, 8 merchants, 6 clerks, 4 students, 4 *kadis*, 3 teachers and 2 sub-mamurs."[56] At a more profound level, however, three important developments emerged that shaped Sudanese politics ever since. First, the new modes of communication and transportation—such as the telegraph, the telephone, the postal services, print media, and the train—heightened the hegemonic force of the colonial state, which owned and deployed them to increase its power to exploit and control. Second, at quite another level, the introduction of these new agents of change gave their workers increasing efficiency of dissemination of information, provided more opportunities for political exchange, and extended the boundaries of those who had been using these communication and transportation machines. These new forms of social interaction turned the league's members, inside and outside the field of operating these machines, into "almost 'agent saboteurs,' to spread anticolonial unrest among the people to whom they were connected or affiliated. Affiliation could be ethnic, professional, educational, or related to a location and even a neighbourhood."[57] Third, as for the growth of the army or the new khaki-collar workers, the heart of the matter lay elsewhere. Communication efficiency was determined by its autonomous nature and secrecy at the same time. For that reason the armed resurgence caught the colonial state by surprise, as "in several locations the British officers seemed to be unaware of the existence of a League branch and unprepared to respond efficiently to its political actions."[58] All these new developments in the field of growing and structuring a new power group had upset the conservatives and drawn attention to marginalized Sudanese women, whom the emerging Sudanese middle class and the colonial state had assigned an inferior status. The new leaders, such as 'Ali Aḥmed Saliḥ and al-Tuhami Moḥammad 'Osman, and labor union organizers suggested that al-'Azza Moḥammad 'Abdullah, 'Ali 'Abd al-Laṭīf's wife, should organize the widows of the war veterans' society using different organizational techniques and different forms of resistance, including organized demonstrations and strikes.

The revolutionary trend, for its part, reached its high point when the league's military wing confronted Khartoum, the citadel of the colonial state, and some of its minicities. Not only did the civilians of the community of the state emerge as the "intimate enemy" of the state, but the army, too, came forward as a dagger pointed toward the heart of the state. During the 1924 revolution, not only did the league achieve the goal of uniting different sectors of the Sudanese for a common cause but it did so with remarkable speed. At the same time, the colonial state was able to crush the movement by delivering a devastating blow; 'Ali 'Abd al-Laṭīf and 'Ubeid Ḥag al-Amin were able to command a new space for a neonationalist movement to compete effectively with the neo-Mahdiyya and the neo-Khatmiyya for the same goal. In this new space, a new self-validation and a common group identity of an emerging and expanding middle class that included what the British described as "negroid but detribalized" government workers, merchants, and labor groups coalesced into a "Sudanese" nationality, or *al-umma al-Sudaniyya*, as 'Ali 'Abd al-Laṭīf described it. These emerging groups were adversarial not only to the colonial order but also to what they labeled "sectarian and tribal" entities and their leadership.

But the consequences of the 1924 revolution are more complex than a shift from a clandestine to a military confrontation. That happened, for the first time, after the end of the rural resurgences, which followed the invasion and shaped the first two decades of the colonial state's life. This new development laid the foundation for an ongoing argument about the role of the national army in politics. It is interesting to trace the growth of that special gloss and the positive shiny finish that has painted the connection between the role of the national army and the social and political change built in the Sudanese political psyche ever since. It was, at the same time, an experience that unfurled into quite different trends of bitterness, disenchantment, and mayhem within Sudanese political sensibilities. The bitterness reflected itself particularly in the feelings of those groups of Sudanese people who supported and genuinely believed in the idea of the unity of the Nile Valley. Saliḥ 'Abdel Gadir later expressed "his feelings and those of his colleagues in a famous poem with strong anti-Egyptian overtones."[59] Those bitter Sudanese groups "accused the Egyptians of betraying the [1924] revolt and thus bringing about the defeat and subsequent sufferings."[60]

At the same time, *taifiyaphobi*—or thought, fear, and action against the Ansār and the Khatmiyya, which are labeled as *tawāif* (sects), rooted in politics and religion—started to show a slow but steady growth among different organized sectors of the emerging middle class. These included exclusivist groups of various stripes: "neonationalists," "neotheologians," Islamists, reductionists from the left, and modernists. Concurrently, the entire issue of a Sudanese nation and its struggle against the colonial system was turned upside down when a homodeferential impulse reflected itself in the ugliest of forms in the *Ḥaḍārat al-Sudan*, a newspaper owned by the three Sayyids 'Ali al-Mirghani, 'Abd al-Raḥman al-Mahdi, and Yousif al-Hindi—and subsidized by the colonial state. *Ḥaḍārat al-Sudan* then proceeded to publish an article as part of its campaign against the 1924 revolution and its leadership. The article claimed, "The country is insulted when its smallest and humblest men, without status in society, pretend to come forward and express the country's opinion."[61] The writer added, "the row that the trashy [part of the population] stirred up has annoyed the merchants and the business sector."[62] Another article stated, "Low is the nation if it can be led by 'Ali 'Abdel Latif." The writer asked, "Who is 'Ali 'Abdel Latif who became famous all of a sudden? To which tribe does he belong?"[63]

But the most serious culture wars, polarizing tendencies, and cleavages to be found at the heart of Sudanese sociopolitical life developed around one of the most fundamental issues, as "ideologically the experience of 1924 deepened the subsequent generation of the intelligentsia, making them more introspective and prone to self-examination and, as with most frustrated ideological movements, full of factionalism as well."[64] A wide range of actors participated in making the Sudan question "a question for Sudanese nationalists as well as for British and Egyptian diplomats, and ideology as well as pragmatism contributed to the outcome."[65] But the outcome was marred by disagreements, differences, and conflicts that were deeper than ever before.

Fundamentally different views, for example, surrounded the union with Egypt, which "was to become not merely a convenience against the British but a sense of attachment to a world that made as much sense ideologically for some as that of 'Sudan for the Sudanese,' a slogan the British were beginning to encourage."[66] The neo-Mahdists, who started to forge their definition of the Sudan around a position that was hostile to Egypt, opposed the politics and the vision of the meaning of unity for the Nile Valley, promoting "Sudan for the Sudanese." *Ḥaḍārat al-Sudan* and its editor, Hussien Sharif, a close relative to Sayyid 'Abd al-Raḥman al-Mahdi, set the tone for this slogan to embody a natural expression of the Mahdist spirit that signified the independent identity and aspirations of the Sudanese people. In four long articles, Sharif laid the foundation for this discourse even before the 1924 uprising.

Whether or not that discourse was "fostered by the Sudan government to counter Egyptian propaganda," as was widely believed, a strong trend and hierarchies of discourses were established around it to build the ideological foundations for a mobilization resource, which reached toward the goals of neo-Mahdism and later the Umma Party, indicating where they had already been and to where they had yet to go. Accordingly, "in their actions the intelligentsia were influenced not only by the sense of opposition to the British that the years after 1924 revealed, but also by the recognition of the importance of the emergence of Mahdism and the growing counterforce of the Khatmiyya."[67]

In light of these developments, Omdurman emerged as the site of the Sudan's "nationalist moment," where a new generation of Sudanese gathered to build a diverse structure of civic organizations, newspapers, magazines, and discussion groups. Chief among the literary groups were the Hāshmab and the Abu Roaf Society. The "intellectual aspiration [of these groups] was drawn from both European and Arab sources: they read and discussed the books and pamphlets of left-inclined European authors (making ample use of Fabian Society and Left Book Club publications), as well as Egyptian journals and the works of Arab scholars."[68]

The first group, the Hāshmab, consisted of young Gordon College graduates from the al-Hāshmab family, whose members were active in the Sudanese social and political scene since the Mahdiyya. It included some of their friends from the nearby al-Mourada neighborhood. Of primary importance in this group were Moḥammad Aḥmed Mahgoub, 'Abdal Ḥalim Moḥammad, Yousif Mustafa al-Tinai, and Moḥammad and 'Abdullah 'Ashri el-Siddiq. Some of the members of this society, especially the 'Ashri brothers, were inspired by the spirit of the 1924 revolution. "Their experiences shaped their political outlook and led them to become staunch advocates of a Sudanese identity that differed from their colleagues' interpretations. In particular, they cherished a vision of Sudanese nationalism that transcended differences of both ethnicity status, 'Arab'-ness and 'Black'-ness."[69]

Among the members of the second group, the Abu Roaf Literary Society, were Mekkawi Suliyman Akrat, Ḥasan and Ḥussein Osman al-Kid, 'Abdullah Merghani, and Khidir Ḥamad.

Other groups of young graduates established similar cultural organizations in other urban centers like Wad Medani, el-Obeid, and 'Aṭbara. At the same time, some members of the old generation of graduates grouped in the Graduates' Club at Omdurman around Sayyid Aḥmed al-Fil and al-Dridiri Moḥammad 'Osman. The other group rallied behind Moḥammad Aḥmed Shwaqi and Moḥammad Aḥmed al-Shingeiti. Both Sayyid 'Ali al-Mirghani and 'Abd al-Raḥman al-Mahdi were active in supporting these groups.

Khartoum, the headquarters of the colonial state, was successful in establishing its grand grid of colonial minicities and villages that embodied the general organizing capacity of the regime that ordered the zones. That organization reflected and, in effect, reinforced social and racial differences to make the differences between the colonizer and the colonized a recognized natural fact. The same was not true in Omdurman. Unlike Khartoum, Omdurman was successful in expanding a parallel sociopolitical grid of cultural civic units. Omdurman's parallel structure mapped space and reflected the emergence of a system of alternative meaning and a process that was devised to challenge power relations and the colonial forms of domination. These Sudanese colonized groups worked together and separately, as J. C. Penny, the British controller of public security, remarked, to "put Sudanese nationalism on the map."[70]

But if these distinctions that conferred upon Omdurman the status of national capital in the eyes of the Sudanese and made Omdurman the flagship of nationalism, then, in the eyes of the colonizer, they became the fountainhead from which the state project and system of control were devised to constrain these forms of neonationalism.

By the early 1940s, the first political parties started to form in Omdurman. Al-Ashiqqa was formed in 1943, to be followed by the Umma Party in 1945. Principal support for the former came from Sayyid 'Ali al-Mirghani and the Khatmiyya, while the latter found its support in Sayyid 'Abd al-Raḥman al-Mahdi and the Ansār. Isma'il al-Azhari (1900–1969) emerged as the first national leader and, in 1954, the first prime minister of independent Sudan.

6

A Tale of Three Cities

Cairo

The rise and fall of Omdurman involves the complexity of Cairo's destiny in the last two centuries. Between 1821 and 1956, Cairo took center stage in Sudanese life. Within its multilayered political, cultural, and ideological character and content, which influenced the state of affairs in the Sudan, these events' developments substantially transformed Cairo itself.

By invading the Sudan in 1821, Muḥammad 'Ali and his heirs turned Cairo into the seat of an extended "empire that was half the size of Europe,"[1] controlling almost all the major waterways of the region, including the entire Nile Valley, from Alexandria to the Great Lakes, and the Red Sea, from the Gulf of Suez to Bab al-Mandab. Before the invasion, since time immemorial and until the last days of the Sinnār, Musba'at, and Darfur sultanates, the Sudanese were accustomed to traveling to Cairo for trade or study at al-Azhar al-Sharief (present-day al-Azhar University). Sudanese and Egyptian traders established a long and formidable relationship that linked the Mediterranean Sea to the heart of Africa. Both ends of the trip offered great opportunities, which encouraged them to build caravan routes and trade stations that became homes for the men and women whom the changing worlds of the two ends affected. The 'ulamā' and Sufi sheikhs regularly came from Cairo to stay in the Sudan. It was their knowledge and the experience, "conjoined with their mystical divinatory talents and literate-magical abilities, that made them valued associates, particularly of ruling elites."[2]

Before and during Muḥammad 'Ali's reign, the Sudanese al-Azhar students were assigned to dormitories named after the regions from which they came. The two oldest such buildings were named Rowaq al-Sinnāria and Rowaq Darfur. In addition, the merchants from different parts of the Sudan and Egypt created their caravan routes and stations across the desert (Darb al-Arba'in, or Forty Days' Road) and closer to the Nile. These and other factors suggest that these areas and spheres of human activities within that part of the world conformed to human needs. In other words, both Egyptian and Sudanese people socialized and acted in patterns that "were a familiar part of the demographic landscape."[3]

Muḥammad 'Ali's invasion was a point of departure. It involved more than a mere event in history. It was the very essence of that event, its functions, and its constitutions that turned Cairo into an instrument of the nature and ambitions of the prevailing power of Muḥammad 'Ali's state. The target of that power contested policies and practices and was the centrifugal machine for simulating and portraying the Sudanese "as no more than an empire of domestics."[4] This vicious circle produced a prevalence of violence and promoted conditions of social, civic, and hegemonic discourses. These developments and their consequences continued to rely on patterns of conflict and homoreferential racist impulses, which stimulated and maintained a system of differentiation. In this respect the Cairene element in Sudanese affairs might demand considerable analysis.

Muḥammad 'Ali, the Invasion, Slavery, and Its Consequences

Muḥammad 'Ali's invasion of the Sudan came with its own ideology of difference. In all their political and social ranks and locations and from the beginning, the Sudanese rejected any form of invasion or annexation of their country to the Ottoman Empire. In the fifteenth century, 'Amara Dungas, the first Funj sultān, wrote to the Ottoman sultān Selim the Grim (1512–20). Dungas rejected the notion that the Turkish ruler could annex his country to Egypt and adamantly objected to the idea of adding his sultanate to the Ottoman Empire. 'Amara wrote, "I do not know what has incited you to fight me and take my land. If it is to aid the religion of Islam, then I and the people of my kingdom are Arab Muslims, following the religion of the Apostle of God. If it is for some material aim, then know that most of the people of my kingdom are desert Arabs, who have migrated to this country to seek a livelihood, and have nothing from which you may collect an annual tribute."[5] Four centuries later, the Kordofan ruler Muqdoom Musalam rejected Muḥammad 'Ali's invasion on the same Islamic grounds.

The Sudanese resisted the invasion, and, even after their defeat, they did not submit to the conquerors. Both Mekk Dirwish and Mekk Ḥamad, two leaders of different resistance groups in the Shaiqiyya region, confronted the invading army. The Sudanese expressive culture and collective memory retained various poetic defiant statements, the consequences of which never dwindled. Chief among these poetic expressions of defiance was the one attributed to Mihera bin 'Abboud's famous verse: *ya al-basha al-ghasheem gool li jidadc kr* (Oh arrogant pasha, drive your chicken away). In 1822, Mekk Nimir, king of the Ja'aliyyin, killed Isma'il Pasha, Muḥammad 'Ali's son and commander of the invading army. Following the murder, a series of revolts broke out in the Ja'aliyyin area, Gezira, and other parts of the country. These revolts were due to discontent with the heavy taxation and the general heavy-handedness and brutality of the government system. A widely known Sudanese saying goes: *'ashara rijal fi turba wa la rial fi tulba* (ten people in the grave and not one riyal in taxation). Yet it took the regime about twenty years to defeat the insurgencies.

The invasion marked a serious point of departure, splitting the world into violent aggressors and helpless victims. The victims were physically and emotionally abused because they were no match for their heavily armed and well-trained counterparts. All Sudanese people were abused, but some were marked for additional mistreatment. Egyptians were victims of an oppressive regime as well, under Muḥammad 'Ali, when Egypt was subject to a strange type of colonization. Egypt was considered to be under Ottoman authority, but, in a sense, it leased Egypt to Muḥammad 'Ali and his family to reign over it. The wāli's administration "consisted of a nucleus of men, the wāli's family and retainers who formed an inner circle, and a large outer circle of Egyptians who were coopted to work for the government and enjoyed a share of the profits, a share they stood to lose were the government to be overthrown."[6] In view of this, Cairo's role can only be understood as part of the historic advancement of, and the Egyptian reaction to, this peculiar form of colonial enterprise. Through a process of coercive governance, the regime implemented its twisted objective to control and dominate all of the Sudanese and Egyptian people. Egypt was depicted as a façade of fellāheen, who were forcibly drafted en masse, while the Sudan was considered a property acquired by right of conquest. Hence, the Sudanese, who were depicted as Negroes, were "fair game" for servitude. Within that continuum of oppression and domination, the Sudanese were the most oppressed, dominated, and abused. In this context, the different impulses and discourses emerged and progressed. Many times different groups within the fault lines presented certain conflicts and battled within or between distinct traditions in the two countries.

In the Sudan, the residue of that abuse and oppression piled up in the collective memory and popular consciousness that shaped an individual and group worldview. All versions of violence continued to have their distant historical resonance. Yet the nature and intensity of each form of violence could offer a starting point for the consideration of the historical result of difference and distance that emerged out of that experience. The symbolic and physical consequences, and the forms of violence that originated and were sustained out of such an impulse, have since reflected and planted their roots in various types of violence over time, which have included conquest and its consequences. Eve M. Troutt Powell has argued, "The outlook of the colonized colonizer began to take shape in the last decade of Muḥammad 'Ali's reign and emerged full-blown by the 1870s."[7] While this is true, it was far more complex. The territorial differentiation that emerged out of that experience, with each region subjected to its own distinctive form of violence, oppression, and control, planted and maintained something that has reached beyond generalities and generations. Within that situation, Cairo battled between its two divided selves. A range of consequences and deeper effects was attributed to each of those selves in the entire region.

Muḥammad 'Ali and his family worked very hard to constrain the Otherness, or nationalist resistance, that Other Cairo developed and from which dissimilar themes expanded, diversified, and augmented into a counterculture that captured the aspirations of the Egyptian fellāheen and other populations in the region. Variations of this counterculture contrasted not only with isolationist Egypt and the unity of the Nile Valley orientations, but also with pan-Islamist, pan-Arabist, and other discourses on secularism. On the other hand, another perceived racial type of difference and Otherness created another form of prejudice toward groups of Muslim and non-Muslim Sudanese people in their neighborhoods. As a consequence, some groups of Muslim Sudanese created their own internal constitution of space, or "extraneousness,"[8] as

Claude Meillassoux would describe it, to create an ideology of distance and difference, separating themselves from those who were destined to be slaves. This ideology of distance and difference recreated two basic forms.

First, it designated those groups as the different, opposing Other. According to Sikainga, northern Sudanese Muslims gave those different groups "derogatory ethnic labels to refer to non-Muslim groups in the south. These generic names included Fertit below Dar Fur, Janakhara below Wadai, and Shankalla below Sinnar. Hence, the slave-raiding frontier was defined in ideological, ethnic, and geographical terms."[9] Second, this construction of inferiority worked on multiple levels—"somatic traits (ugliness, heaviness) and character traits (stupidity, laziness, shiftiness)"[10]—to develop a general theory, which would maintain and reproduce the system of slavery.

The major forms of violence and abuse that filtered through the Sudanese collective memory of Muḥammad 'Ali's invasion were connected to the slave trade and its consequences. Thousands of Sudanese were dragged, kicking and screaming, to the house of bondage in Cairo. There, those who arrived alive and fit to serve in the army were "converted to Islam by religious shaykhs appointed by the Khedive. They were then given education and training."[11] It did not take that long for Muḥammad 'Ali to build a big war machine from the Sudanese slaves. Immediately after the invasion his agents sent more than thirty thousand slaves to Egypt, and, by 1823, "there were six regiments of four thousand men each. Sudanese units were placed under a *diwan al-jihadiyya*, established in 1821."[12] These troops constituted a force six times larger than the one the wāli sent to invade the Sudan.

The Sudanese *jihadiyya* regiment grew and, by 1823, it accounted for a significant portion of the Egyptian army and played a major role in most of Egypt's regional and international military undertakings in Greece, Syria, Somalia, and Ethiopia. Furthermore, the troops were lent to the French emperor, Napoleon III, to participate in the French intervention in Mexico between 1861 and 1867. 'Ali Effendi Gifoon, the commander of that slave force, was of Shulluk origin. He served as a *yousbashi* (captain) and honorary adjutant-major of the twelfth Sudanese battalion, and he enjoyed the respect of every person who knew him. Gifoon was named Lwaldeed, and he dictated the story of his life and his experience as an enslaved person to Capt. Percy Machell of the Egyptian army. In 1889,

Egypt sold about six hundred soldiers from the *jihadiyya* to Germany to put down the uprising of East African coastal Arab resistance to the Germans' colonialism that Bushiri bin Salim had started four years earlier, in 1885. Capt. Hermann von Wissmann stormed Salim's stronghold at Bagamoyo on the coast in 1889, and von Wissmann captured and hanged bin Salim. By 1890 the conflict had spread throughout the colony, which led to the Maji-Maji rebellion, during which, Africans believed, German bullets would turn into water (*maji*).

Cairo, which made its slave army an international commodity, up for purchase, opened the door for hunting and selling human beings as a means to increase business by creating a convenient and robust infrastructure that could handle and supply both a hungry state and private markets. Moreover, there was a growing demand in Cairo itself for domestic slaves, as prosperity increased in Egypt due to the expansion in cotton cultivation. "This demand reached a peak during the cotton boom caused by the American Civil War during which Egyptian cotton was at a premium in the mills of Manchester."[13] It was in this context of state and local demands for slaves that a vast wave of slave hunting and trade crested in different parts of the Sudan.

Muḥammad 'Ali employed Europeans to draw maps and to journey and collect information about the vast southern territories of his empire. In addition, "in 1839, the Sudd barrier [a vast swamp in the southern Sudan, formed by the White Nile] had been penetrated by steamships. The first beneficiary of this enterprise was a flourishing ivory trade on the White Nile, which was dominated by Europeans at first."[14] Yet, as profit in ivory trade declined, the subsequent turn was toward the business of slave trading. For the local inhabitants of that part of the Sudan, the slave form of trade, with the devastations it brought to human life and the environment, became a new menace to fight. The traders, however, used different strategies to keep their trade going. For example, "the traders soon felt compelled to arm themselves to the teeth, and established themselves in zaribas (fortified, armed camps). Once again, the Europeans were in the lead."[15]

Khartoumers, Raiders, and Jallaba Traders

These new developments encouraged Cairene merchants and those from different European, Arab, and other nationalities to establish their headquarters at Khartoum, the capital of the Turko-Egyptian Sudan, and to send their *wakala'* (agents; sing., *wakil*) to join others in these territories and create new settlements, or zaribas.

The first and primary Khartoumer "companies" were seven; "four of which were owned by the French Barthelemy, Poncet Brothers, Vassiere, and Malzac; two owned by the British: Patherick and the Maltese Debono; and the Italian Angelo-Bolognesi-Antognoli."[16] Among the famous Arab owners of such companies were Aḥmed al-'Aqād, his partner, Musa al-'Aqād, Mahjoub al-Busiali 'Abdul Ḥamid, 'Ali abu 'Amuri, Khalil Shami, Shanuda, and Qattas. Those traders were markedly different from the homegrown traders, or jallaba, who migrated to the region from the northern part of the country by the nineteenth century in order to trade with some groups in the area, chief among them the Zande, the Kerish, and the Banda. The jallaba, as previously mentioned, were well known for their long experience in the creation of trading networks that connected the southern region of Sudan to Kordofan and Darfur, as well as West Africa to the Nile Valley.

One of the major differences between the jallaba and the new breed of Khartoumer traders was that the jallaba were not raiders. They were well known for their donkey caravans and depended on the goodwill of locals to sell them commodities in exchange for cash or other bartered materials, including supplies of ivory and slaves. As Robert Collins explains, Arabic became the lingua franca as non-Muslims adopted some aspects of Muslim culture.[17] The trader-raiders, or merchant-warriors, known as Khartoumers, or wakalā', were the ones who invented and fortified themselves behind the zariba. A large number of the local population, who produced food and provided services, surrounded the zariba, a huge thorn-enclosed structure. Thus, the people "embodied the military and commercial nexus which defined the character and extent of the institution of slavery in the Nilotic Sudan" during the nineteenth century.[18] This institution dehumanized and transformed ordinary people from around the world into perpetrators of a morally deficient business of hunting, gathering, and selling human beings.

Each zariba resembled a small town, with a heterogeneous population organized along military lines, as "sailors, pilots, soldiers, and hunters were recruited in Khartoum, each with a renewable one-year contract. Once in the armed camps of the south, the men were organized into military units, adopting the nomenclature of the Egyptian *nizām al-Jadīd* (new system) for the purpose."[19] The merchant-warriors were the ones who built the private slave armies, or bazinger, as they were known in Chadic Arabic. The bazinger were young "recruits," who usually converted to Islam and newly adapted to the Muslim lifestyle. The Khartoumers settled them around their zaribas and, when they were old enough, supplied them with wives who they selected from the young non-Muslim women taken in *ghazzies* (raids). Some eventually became raiders themselves.[20] With the help of new firearms, the merchant-warriors and wakalā', their private armies and other traders, intensified slave-raiding and ivory operations on an unprecedented scale in a wide area that included the southern and southwestern Sudan.

In 1863, Theodor von Heuglin, the German explorer, naturalist, and onetime Austro-Hungarian consul in Khartoum, traveled as a member of A. P. F. Tinne's expedition to Gondokoro, on the White Nile, and explored parts of the Baḥr al-Ghazāl area. He visited an Egyptian trader named Mahjoub al-Busali at his zariba near the Jur River. According to his account, Mahjoub's zariba "consisted of a large square, perhaps 150 paces (unit of length equal to 30 inches) long and almost as broad, surrounded by a high palisade of tree trunks. Within the enclosure stood straw huts housing soldiers under Mahjoub's command as well as the trader's deputy, a black slave named Ali." Slave women, wearing fiber aprons typical of the dress of local people, appeared when von Heuglin took coffee and locally brewed beer in Mahjoub's hut. On the walls and the beams of his hut, the trader hung weapons of every type.

By 1868 the German botanist and traveler in East Africa Georg Schweinfurth visited the region and spent time at a number of zaribas belonging to the Khartoumer trading companies. He visited Ghattas (a Christian Copt) zariba twice and spent considerable time there. He gave a detailed description of the structure, population, and distribution of the zaribas in the region. He claimed that they could be found every twenty miles. Salim Wilson offered a more detailed description of life in the zariba. Salim, or Hatashil Masha Katbish, was a Sudanese man of Dinka origin who was captured and enslaved while he was still a boy. He served as a donkey boy for slave masters in different zaribas, but at a later stage he became the servant of two British missionaries from the Uganda mission, Dr. R. W. Felkin and Rev. C. T. Charles Wilson, who brought him to England, where he became a preacher.

In England, Salim published a book about his experience entitled *I Was a Slave*. In his book, Salim described life in the zariba where he found a number of Dinka, Shulluk, and others who had similarly been captured, but who were armed with guns and knives and worked and fought for some Khartoumers for a small wage. Schweinfurth, however, gave more details about the slave army, their role, and their everyday lives in the zariba: "the natives who may be enlisted are called in the common jargon of the Soudan Arabic, either 'Narakeek,''Farookh,' or 'Bazingir.'"[21] They were provided with guns, from a kind of Nizam, whose duty was to accompany the "natives" in all expeditions, whether for war or trading purposes. Schweinfurth added that the Narakeek "would appear to be the only men who are trusted with heavier guns, of which a considerable number, originally intended, no doubt, for elephant-hunting, are now found in the companies of Khartoomers, and form what might be called their artillery."[22] In addition, they "play a prominent part in time of war. It is the duty of the Farookh to scour the negro villages in search of corn, to assemble the bearers, and to keep under coercion any that are refractory in the wilderness."[23]

By the time of the raids, such acts were much further along and relations were much more deeply established. The expansion of mercantile companies into Baḥr al-Ghazāl eventually led to the merging of two types of commercial settlements in the far west of Dār Firtīt. There, "the established *deims* or *jallaba* colonialists, with their estates worked by agricultural slaves, welcomed the armed camps of Khartoum companies."[24] That transformation "involves a complex interaction between economy, society, and the state in a form that reproduces these relationships" in which slaves turned into the primary mode of production.[25] In time, the slave trade "involved transformations in the mechanisms of slave supply as Africa became linked to an international system of slavery and then severed from its external market."[26] This alternative form of agricultural labor, which turned slaves into a mode of production, gave local groups the means to expand markets and necessitated the expansion of private slave armies. The capacity to link these three aspects of trade, agriculture, and private armed forces turned the zariba into a ministate, or an autonomous decentralized community, described as a deim. The development into the deim, or the amalgamation of deim and zariba, were, according to Douglas Johnson, "in Dar Fartit and Baḥr al-Ghazāl [and] produced a plantation system of slave and semi-free labourers working not just for individual patrons or landowners, but for commercial companies."[27] Different *diūm*, (sing., *deim*) grew within the region. The "largest and most magnificent *deim* was deim ez-Zubair, the capital of ez-Zubair al-Rahma."[28]

Those developments, however, did not change the character of slavery, though they did create new functions for the slaves. Economic interests were connected to markets other than the vulnerable Cairo slave market, which turned the balance more in favor of traders (jallaba), rather than raiders (the merchant-warriors). It is true that "the numerous *jallāba* who went south and west and dealt in small-scale slave trading, rarely made more than a modest profit, because the risks, losses and customs dues were so great. Independent success in the south required private armies to subdue hostile populations and fight off competition from rival 'companies' and *zarība* owners."[29] The jallaba, who found themselves "reduced to middle men, fully integrated into the *zarība* system,"[30] one day were eager to set themselves and their activities free from the restriction of the zariba. The raiders, who were dominated by the nature of their insecure activity, which had always been resented, resisted, and vigorously fought by targeted and surrounding communities, were influenced by two important developments.

These developments included the local resistance and the military expeditions for suppressing slave trade. At the same time, those who benefited from the transfer from raids to different, peaceful enterprises found the new market and agriculture transformation more rewarding and less risky. Another important transformation was the bazinger. As a military force, they also opened their ranks to include voluntary recruits and were thus transformed to function for the security of an emerging state and other productive activity. This mounting new space and the opportunities that came to fruition through the loosening of the zariba and the expanding of agriculture resulted in a growing market and trade activities that went beyond the old restrictive limits, consolidating trends of peaceful coexistence and nonviolent human exchange.

Hence, it was the vested interest of the zariba owners, the jallaba, and the neighboring communities to continue in the expansion of the zariba and to carry on the search for different forms of exchange and coexistence, thereby opening up and securing local and continental roads to Cairo and serving mutual interests by maintaining all these endeavors. The growing economic, security, and mutual benefits of those involved in this new system transformed relations within the region as much as they turned the area into a state-in-the-making and made al-Zubair Raḥma Manṣūr its ruler par excellence.

Al-Zubair: From Zariba to Deim to State

According to Lawrence Mire, al-Zubair's "meteoric rise to predominance among these Khartoumers was due not to his individual daring and intelligence alone, for there were many daring and clever men in Baḥr al-Ghazāl then. His success was largely due to his fortuitous geographical location in the region and the important services he was able to render the Khartoumers as a whole from this position."[31] Mire enumerated these services as "securing an overland trade route as the Nile was being closed by the slave trade through the actions of Samuel Baker and others; opening territories in southern and western Baḥr al-Ghazāl as the Muslim advance was checked elsewhere; [and] defending the rights of slave traders against corrupt representatives of the central government."[32] But the manner of general attainment of al-Zubair's predominance, rise to power, and the manner by which he established his new state was more complex.

Al-Zubair was neither a Khartoumer nor a typical slave trader. He perceived himself, as he told an interviewer, as "a trader, and also that I bought many slaves, but that I never was a slave-trader. I might have been, but was not."[33] He admitted that it was his practice to buy slaves, but not to sell them. He claimed that after his army was organized, he recruited it "almost entirely by slaves bought for that purpose." He added, "when the caravans passed through Mandugba on their return to Egypt I examined the slaves they bought, and took the best and the healthiest to make soldiers. I trained them in the use of arms, dressed them well, fed them, and kept them always into my service."[34] Moreover, the development of the agriculturalists and merchants, and a new system by which people could buy and sell their products, helped make this process incidental to the emergence of these new relationships. When and how these conditions were fulfilled and how such a system was put into place might be a long and complicated enterprise, extending over the period in that region.

On its own terms, the expansion of the Zande states, which were resisting the merchant-warriors' encroachment, was an important development. It was al-Zubair's alliance with the powerful chief Tikima, whose daughter he married, that opened the door for a new relationship within the region. Al-Zubair's organizational skills and his ability to forge coalitions and peaceful relations with local chiefs was an extension of the new trend that had been perfected by the development of local markets, farms, and the opening and securing of local and Saharan caravan roads between his capital and Cairo. What was unique about al-Zubair was his ability to bring together a collective effort of an organized army, which he assembled and headed, that "reach[ed] eventually 12,000 . . . his own soldiers served as a nucleus, and the kings' sons, with their picked followers, who considered it a privilege to be allowed to use European arms, were good material to begin with."[35] With this huge army he "laboured to instill first principles of agriculture and internal trade." Accordingly, his soldiers, "who represented the only Government Officials, were used for many purposes." He made every chief responsible for the farm in his district "and lent soldiers as a favour to help in the work, causing nearly all taxes to be paid in corn." He also opened and organized markets "right through the country, and notions of peace were organized side by side with notions of trade."[36] Viewing the market as a contagious mentality, such a system was "of overwhelming consequence to the whole organization of society: it mean[t] no less than the running of society as an adjunct to the market."[37] Hence, al-Zubair considered himself a trader who organized, built, and headed an army, secured and expanded local and trans-Saharan trade, and created "a nation of farmers," which local chiefs supervised. As Flora Shaw has explained, "caravans arrived three to four times a week, coming from Syria and Egypt, from Tripoli, Tunis, and Morocco. Zebehr traded also with Prussian, French, and Italian merchants. . . . He reckons this as the period of his most complete prosperity."[38]

In places other than Baḥr al-Ghazāl, especially Kordofan, a different system grew out of the lopsided government deficits and added to an expanding system of "a nation of farmers" and slaves as a mode of production, which took a different turn by allowing the slave trade to flourish "even without an export market."[39] Under the financial difficulties, the Turko-Egyptian government experienced a different rate of exploitation, which turned out to be the source of accumulation of wealth for the jallaba. When the Khartoum regime was short of funds to pay its employees—who were in need of staples such as sugar, coffee, tobacco, soap, cloth, and grain—the employees carried government notes to "traders, who took them for exchange for goods. But the traders accepted the notes only at a 40–50 percent discount, giving the government workers goods worth only a fraction of the bills' face values."[40] By exploring the need of the other groups within the population, especially the herders, who possessed little or no cash to pay for heavy government taxes, "the Baqqara promised to turn over a certain number of slaves in exchange for the merchants' assumption of their cash tribute obligations. If the traders paid the herders' assessment of 5000 Egyptian pounds, for example, the Baqqara would supply 1000 slaves to the traders."[41] Out of this triple-tiered form of exploitation, the jallaba in Kordofan were able not only to own and run big farming estates that produced a food surplus in the region, but also to build entire villages inhabited by slaves, who were cultivating millet and other staple grains.

The farming activity added to the longtime trade activities of the Kordofan jallaba. Ignatius Pallme gave a description of that province of Egypt and of some of the bordering countries, with a review of the present state of the commerce, and of the habits and customs of the inhabitants, as well as an account of the slave hunts taking place under the government of Muḥammad 'Ali. Pallme gave a lively description to the development of the market in different Kordofan cities. He described also a multitiered structure of specialization from the large-scale to its gradational scale of other operators including the *samasira* (brokers), *dallalin* (auctioneers), *tashasha* and *sababa* (retailers), and their operations, which increasingly reached into the most distant places, including Cairo. Pallme reported that "caravans brought the produce from Abyssinia, the interior of Africa, and from Egypt, into the two towns of Lobeid and Bara, whence the greater part was again transported into other countries."[42]

Another important factor in al-Zubair's rise to power was the agreement he made with the Rizayqat that opened and secured the road between Baḥr al-Ghazāl and Kordofan. This arrangement was made to provide al-Zubair "with an outlet to the north that avoided the Nile region where Turko-Egyptian authorities had banned slave trade, but it also brought an influx of North African merchants to Baḥr al-Ghazāl."[43] The jallaba traders soon learned of the superior trading experiences and networks through the new trans-Saharan route. Working within this mode of production under different relations, with a common goal of accumulation, the jallaba of the greater Nile Valley—who remained to a certain degree connected to each other—reinstated themselves as a class that possessed wealth together with "the means of coercion, both commanding slave armies and forming alliances with local raiders."[44] The new trans-Saharan route created favorable conditions for the jallaba of Kordofan to expand and diversify their trading activities and to be more connected to others within the Nile Valley, East and West Africa, the Mediterranean, and the Red Sea. Pallme, in his description of the main commercial center of el-Obeid and Bara in particular, and other urban cities of the region in general, reported, "Abundance might be said to reign everywhere, and there was no want of any necessities, whilst all were wealthy, even the women of the less opulent inhabitants wore golden rings in their noses and ears, and many even golden bracelets and silver anklets round their feet."[45]

The market, trade, and agricultural activities transformed some villages of Kordofan into important trade centers and the entire region into a zone of wealth and prosperity. Within these new conditions, Kordofan earned the name *Kordofan al-ghara um kharian bra* (bright-faced Kordofan whose goodness overflows). This phase saw a new form of class and population differentiation as the jallaba dominated the mercantile and agricultural economy, its means of production thereby establishing themselves in an uneasy relationship with ruling entities. Personalities such as Aḥmed Dafā Allah and Alyas Umm Birayr in Kordofan as well as Idris Abtar in Baḥr al-Ghazāl not only gained power, wealth, and prestige but also allied or conflicted with formal and informal ruling regimes. Some assumed very high government positions during the Turkiyya, while others sought social distinction through other means and different associations. Al-Zubair emerged as the protomerchant and the ace of the jallaba.

But the crux of al-Zubair's rise to power was the threat he presented to the Turkish regime that alarmed Cairo. His success in carving out a territory that included not only Baḥr al-Ghazāl but also Darfur drew the attention of other Sudanese, who looked to him as a promising leader. Moreover, he was renown for his ability to defeat the government's attempts to control Baḥr al-Ghazāl and for his crushing defeat of the Moroccan adventurer Muḥammad al-Bilali, for whom Ja'far Pasha, governor general of the Sudan, provided troops in 1872. The pasha's support earned al-Bilali the authority to stand up as the most powerful force outside the realm of the Turko-Egyptian Empire. According to al-Zubair's account, the king of Borku sent emissaries who proposed a treaty and the opening of his roads. The king of Tagali had approached him and offered his loyalty saying, "We have heard a good report of you, and if you will have us we will submit ourselves to you."[46]

Other stories claim that 'Abdullahi al-Ta'aishi, "the seeker," approached al-Zubair "secretly, and announced to him that he had had a dream, in which it had been shown to him that he [al-Zubair] was the expected Mahdi, and that he ['Abdullahi] was to be one of his faithful followers." Slatin continues with al-Zubair's supposed response: "'I told him . . . that I was not the Mahdi; but that when I became aware of the wickedness of the Arabs, and how they blocked the roads, I came to open them and establish trade.'"[47]

Cairo of the khedive and imperial Britain, however, took matters differently. They both were bluntly alarmed, as their representative in Khartoum, Charles Gordon, clearly expressed. The khedive had appointed Gordon to a variety of positions, including governor general of the Sudan during the 1870s. For Gordon, al-Zubair's semi-independent state was an alarming signal and a threat to both Egyptian and European imperial moments. Al-Zubair, the Black Pasha, was described within expanding imperial Europe as "set up as equal and rival of the Khedive himself."[48]

Al-Zubair was set apart as the nemesis of Charles Gordon, and was referred to as "the richest and worst," a "Slaver King," and one "who [had] chained lions as part of his escort." In addition, Isma'il Ayoub, the governor general of the Sudan, soon discovered that al-Zubair had not conquered Darfur to add it the Sudanese government or the khedive's empire but rather to rule it himself as part of his expanding empire. Hence, Cairo reached a critical stage with regard to al-Zubair's expanding ambitions, which were perceived as potentially dangerous and, thus, these ambitions could hardly be tolerated. In Cairo, the khedive told al-Zubair that he had made himself too powerful, and the ruling authorities in Egypt feared that if they gave al-Zubair the authority he desired, he "would set up an empire in Darfur which would rival and perhaps even subjugate. Egypt is not strong enough to tolerate neighbours so strong."[49] Hence, al-Zubair had to resign himself to life in Cairo. There, he was promised two things, "to be practically free, [but] . . . to go back no more to the Soudan."[50] But al-Zubair's confinement extended far beyond his Cairo internment to his exile in Gibraltar.

Al-Zubair's sixteen-year-old son, Sulayman, proved to be more than capable of defending his father's empire. Not only did Sulayman defeat Idris Abtar, who acted on Gordon's behalf, and hold Romolo Gessi, whom Gordon had sent, he also kept "all these troops with a European leader at bay." However, after a number of well-armed merchant-warriors, chief among them Abu 'Amūri, defected to the government's side, and two years of fighting later, Gessi was finally able to defeat Sulayman. Gessi promised Sulayman and his lieutenants security of life and property. Trusting him, Sulayman surrendered on July 15, 1879; however, Gessi ordered Sulayman and his uncles to be gathered under a tree, where he "spoke with them very kindly. . . . His soldiers were all around the tree. He walked away, and in five minutes the twelve uncles and the boy were dead—shot by his [Gessi's] orders."[51] Yet, while some heralded the destruction of al-Zubair's empire, at the same time, Collins argues, this destruction "disrupted the powerful commercial organizations whose experience and resources were essential at that time for the beginnings of a socio-economic change in Baḥr al-Ghazāl and the land beyond the watershed." Collins explains, "In place of a few large companies, those of al-Zubayr or 'Abd al-Ṣamad, there were now in the Congo and Central African Republic, a host of their subordinates acting as independent freebooters who, beyond the reach of Gessi's battalions, were determined to carve out for themselves petty states at Azande expense."[52] As a consequence, these developments prepared the political ground for more radical movements, not only within the Sudan, but also in the region at large.

The first of these movements was Rabiḥ Fadlallah's takeover of wide areas within Dar Kreish, Dar al-Kuti, and Wadai to establish his own empire. Rabiḥ was one of al-Zubair's most capable commanders. He was placed as the commanding officer of the bazinger corps, and under his command the unit became highly disciplined and well trained in the use of firearms. Rabiḥ and his bazinger played an important role in the defeat of Muḥammad al-Bilali, who attacked Deim al-Zubair in 1869 with troops supplied from Khartoum. Rabiḥ's bazinger also played a decisive role in the 1873–74 invasion of Darfur. Distrustful of Gessi, who was "surrounded by a retinue of Danāqla who were anxious to see Sulaymān and other leading Ja'aliyyin among his men eliminated,"[53] Rabiḥ broke away and headed south toward Dar Kreish with some seven to eight hundred bazinger and four hundred rifles. When Rabiḥ's forces invaded Darfur, in 1887, they recruited bazinger and settled down in Dar Kouti. By 1890, Rabiḥ had raised an army that exceeded five thousand men with over three thousand rifles. He became master of Bornu and later "declared himself a Mahdist and dressed his troops in the patched uniform of the *Ansār*. His followers and his troops became Muslims, and there is little doubt that they spread Sudanese influence throughout the Chad and Ubanghi Basin."[54]

The Southern Element in Mahdiyya

The second major development was the Mahdist revolt in the southern part of the Sudan that the young and inexperienced British governor of Baḥr al-Ghazāl, Frank Miller Lupton, faced. Fifteen months after the death of Sulayman, Gessi left for Khartoum, where he died. Lupton was appointed governor in his place. Lupton was now surrounded on all sides by rebellions against the Turko-Egyptian rule. He faced the Dinka and Nuer alliance from one side, the members of which objected to the Turkish rule, only to then face the Mahdists and their Shulluk allies, who overran Baḥr al-Ghazāl on the other side. The Mahdist revolution enticed different groups of the population and was able to connect also with "the *jallaba* who, by kinship and economic interests were drawn to the Mahdi's standard."[55]

The news of the complete annihilation of William Hicks Pasha's expedition against the Mahdi in the dense forest of Kasgale, thirty miles south of el-Obeid, electrified the entire country and convinced many that the end of Turkish rule in the Sudan was at hand. Out of seven thousand infantry, one thousand cavalry, and two thousand camp followers—including thirteen Europeans—only three hundred men of Hicks's army survived. Given this situation, Lupton's Egyptian deputy officer, Sāti Efendi, soon left for Khartoum, where he later deserted Lupton to join the Mahdists. In a moment of despair, Lupton wrote to Emin Pasha, the governor general of Equatoria, "I will fight to the last."[56] However, as Iain Smith explains, "Lupton's troops refused to fight and Lupton capitulated. In a last letter to Emin on 26 April he announced 'It is all up with me here, everyone has joined the Mahdi, and his army takes charge of the Mudireh [Province] the day after to-morrow. . . . Look out you; some 8,000 to 10,000 men are coming to you well armed.'"[57]

Moreover, the Mahdist revolution unified the Sudanese in the southern part of the country and elsewhere far beyond al-Zubair's trading, farming, and bazinger enterprises. Under Karam Allah Kurqusāwi, the Mahdist amir of Baḥr al-Ghazāl, the Dinka, the Nuer, the Shulluk, the jallaba, and the bazinger formed a united front. The groups' combined "motives transformed the Mahdiyya from a religious into a national political uprising that raged throughout the country."[58] But the Mahdist revolution itself created a double transformation in the mode of operation and in the Sudanese quest for independence. On the one hand, there was the consolidation of most of the Sudanese fighting forces into one powerful army. Gradually, most of the bazinger, their commanders, and other private armies, including al-Zubair's forces that did not follow Rabiḥ, joined the Mahdist revolution to form the main body of the *jihadiyya* army, in particular, as well as other parts of the Mahdist war machine. The careers of the main commanders, including Ḥamdan Abu 'Anja, al-Nur Angara, Zaki Ṭamal, Abu Garja, and 'Abdel Raḥman wad al-Nijumi, amply illustrated this process. On the other hand, there was a nagging feeling of discontent among the ranks of the Sudanese that continued to express itself since the early days of the invasion, penetrating the political and military zariba "enclosure," which a brutal slavery system had created and made remarkable successes in defeating that design militarily and ideologically. Thus, the Sudanese revolution, in all its constitutions, and not only the expressed religious one, was an imminent development. This was what, indeed, happened.

Politically, the mobilization against the Cairo's khedive regime harbored three fatal conditions. Although these three conditions had the most far-reaching consequences and were of great focal significance in the histories of Cairo, Omdurman, and Khartoum, they were contradictory in nature. Cairo of the khedive, which was crisis prone, would inevitably alarm the colonial powers, which were controlling it from the outside. First, the expanding revolutionary fervor in the Nile Valley warned the colonial forces of an imminent threat coming from the south. Faced by the rise of local and regional anticolonial nationalist and revolutionary movements in the Sudan and Egypt, London emerged, in a mysterious way, as the grantor of the fate of Cairo. Britain took that major crisis in Cairo as a pretext to step in and strengthen its internal control over Egyptian affairs.

The British colonialists saw the rise of that particular revolutionary fervor, in both Egypt and the Sudan, as an outcome of a host of conditions related to Cairo's khedive system of governance, which provoked an acceleration of a scheme of calamities that influenced all forms of discontent and escalated the different types of internal and external reactions.

Aḥmed 'Urabi led a rebellion from 1879 to 1882 that initiated the Egyptian nationalist reaction to Britain's renewed involvement in Egyptian affairs; however, Britain quickly crushed that rebellion. Muḥammad Aḥmed al-Mahdi's movement led the Sudanese in their revolution, which lasted from 1881 until 1885 and successfully advanced toward Khartoum, eventually to control the whole country. Both movements had distinct bearings on the fate of the two countries.

Aḥmed Pasha 'Urabi (1841–1911), an Egyptian (*fallāh*) army officer who later became a general, revolted in 1879 against the absolutist roles of the khedive and the European domination of Egypt, in what has come to be known as the 'Urabi revolt. Feeling that his throne was threatened, Khedive Tawfiq called on the Ottoman sultān 'Abdul Ḥamid II to put down the revolution, but the sultān hesitated to employ troops against Muslims who were opposing foreign interference. By contrast, the British and French governments were especially concerned that 'Urabi would default on Egypt's massive debt and might try to gain control of the Suez Canal. Both England and France dispatched warships to Egypt to intimidate 'Urabi and the Egyptian nationalists who supported him. In September 1872, a British army landed in Alexandria, but they were defeated at the battle of Kafr-el-Dawwar and failed to reach Cairo.

Ten years later, on September 13, 1882, another army, led by Sir Garnet Wolseley, landed at the Suez Canal and finally defeated 'Urabi's army at the battle of Tel el-Kebir. From there, the cavalry advanced on Cairo, which surrendered without firing a single shot, as did 'Urabi Pasha and the other nationalist leaders. Wolseley's army captured 'Urabi and sentenced him to death; however, his sentence was commuted, and 'Urabi was instead exiled to the British colony of Ceylon (now Sri Lanka). In 1901 he was allowed to return to Egypt. Egypt was not effectively transformed into an independent sovereign state until 1922. Two important developments in this state of affairs had an enduring and direct effect on both Cairo and Khartoum.

First, the anticolonial nationalists in colonized Cairo looked forward to the Mahdist-liberated Sudan to continue in its anticolonial march and liberate Egypt. All the while, the Mahdiyya's victory created the conditions that brought together tormented Britain (the colonizer) and terror-stricken official Cairo (the colonized) to work together in the recolonization of the Sudan.

Second, Britain and Egypt's recolonization of the Sudan and creation of the condominium, with its peculiar nature (see chapter 2), gave rise to differentiation within the newly created British mini-imperial system. The new system did not return the Nile Valley to Egyptian control; rather, it put almost the entire valley under the control of Britain.

In addition, it came with profound problems for the three countries. Specifically, the British imperial system in the Sudan, among other things, created a distinctively new colonial model, forcibly placed to control land and vital waterways. At this point, Britain, which had acquired the Nile Valley territory and access to land and sea, became the core state. Egypt, which was supposed to be codominus, was connected to that system as part of the semiperiphery of the British imperial system. As far as Egypt was concerned, "the Condominium was little more than having her face rubbed in the dirt by her British oppressors."[59] Egypt's manpower, as explained before, was used to fill the lower strata of employees—*ma'mur* (subordinate) and *na'ib ma'mur* (subordinate deputy)—as a cheaper, if not wholly efficient, way to staff the colonial administration and the system's division of labor. In that differentiated system, the Sudan was gradually incorporated as the periphery within a gradational form of accommodation and marginalization that was congruent with the new system's interests. The chapters that follow seek to address further how these processes of gradational forms of accommodation and marginalization participated in the creation of both the center or the core and the margins of the country.

Back to the Sudan Question

The last chapter ended with an exploration of how the Sudan question—within the developments that followed the failure of the 1924 revolution and the emergence of what could be described as the Omdurman factor—put Sudanese nationalism on the social and political map. This chapter too will end with a discussion of how Cairo—in its complex changing, multilayered, and constrained roles—contributed to that issue from the early days of the occupation of the Sudan, in 1898. Four important conclusions then follow.

First, official Cairo and its resources were manipulated to service the colonial state for the sake of cost savings. As Woodward reminds us, "Egypt had paid for the expedition and provided many of the troops; now she [Egypt] was being fobbed off with little more than a symbolic role in her former territories." Woodward continues, "Under the [condominium] agreement she had to continue to pay for Sudan while having no control over policy, and the cost appeared to grow rather than diminish, at least until Kitchener's arrival and the eventual ending of subvention in 1913."[60]

Second, the growing ranks of Cairo nationalists, who were critical of the entire political structures in the three countries and their new and old arrangements, saw the new British system as "one more step to cement Britain's position in the Nile valley."[61] Moreover, those complications of the new situation, targeting the regime and collaborators with the colonial system contrived cyclical and repetitive notions of violence. Boutros Ghali Pasha, the Egyptian prime minister who signed the condominium agreement with Lord Cromer, "was assassinated for his overt collaboration with the British."[62]

Third, by 1925 the northern part of the Sudan was integrated within the imperial division of labor through two major projects: first, the Gezira Scheme, the largest centrally managed farm in the world, was made operational; second, the Sudan railways, a government managed enterprise, were finally completed to transport Sudan's main products—cotton, gum arabic, sesame, and peanuts—to Britain, the core state. The establishment of the Gezira Scheme and the cotton it produced ultimately benefited the British textile industry, "which up to the end of the 19th century had occupied a paramount position in the world textile industry, [and] was at that time facing increasingly fierce competition from Germany and the United States."[63] The railways and the roads of the Sudan that were "built between 1899 and 1913 reflected military more than economic priority."[64] Later, this railway system was upgraded to connect the production areas in Gezira, through the Gezira Light Railway, Kordofan, and Kassala to Port Sudan, on the Red Sea. Hence, both projects were firmly situated within the colonial division of labor, and they both reflected "an expression and an extension of British power."[65]

Fourth, and finally, the rest of the Sudan was introduced to a systemic form of marginalization. If that aspect of colonial power were, by definition, true, then for that division of labor to be maintained and reproduced it would require viable strategies for change that could incorporate cooperation and interdependence within the system itself. Thus, in addition to the Egyptian personnel at the lower rungs of state employment, local reliable Sudanese intermediaries were employed between the local colonial administration and the rest of the population to maintain and run the system. Within that colonial scheme, a system of tribal rule was re-invented and restructured to overcome "the lack of personnel that every colonial power faced and the extreme difficulty in communicating over long distances."[66]

Another important feature of the complicated presence of Cairo within the condominium was that it continued to be a source of bitter divisions and conflict between all parties involved from the beginning. There was a deep rift between Lord Cromer, the British consul general in Egypt, and Wingate, the governor of the Sudan. As Peter Woodward explains, "Cromer saw Sudan as an adjunct of Egypt, once admonishing Wingate for 'a tendency to consider the Sudan as a separate and independent Government, more or less unconnected with Egypt.'"[67] That conflict was neither a difference in views nor an approach to governance; it "was the drift of Wingate's feeling for his own aggrandisement and his desire to limit the influence that Egyptians might be able to exercise in their former territory."[68] This difference remained alive, generating conflict until, in 1922, Egypt won its independence, only to take on deeper forms of conflict between the two former partners of the condominium.

On the other hand, although officially a condominium, the British had systematically pursued a policy of de-Egyptianization, excluding their codomini from all zones of governance and power sharing and keeping them out of senior positions in all parts of the government. Hence, continued Egyptian demands for restoration to genuine codominus status, as explained before, reflected what was to become known as the Sudan question, "which was to have different forms at different times and was to involve essentially the respective position of Egypt and Britain in the Sudan, and consequently wider relations between them, and the problem of the position of the Sudanese with regard to the future of the territory they inhabited."[69] The ever-growing polarities of the condominium's peculiar relationship and its conflict-riddled environment, both between its partners and within the dialectical forms of its actions and reactions, created four main currents and discourses of shared culture and representations of Sudanese nationalism. It was Cairo's divided self that played three different and contradictory roles within the domain of Sudanese national culture. Each of these three roles has had deep effects, contributing to the developing political Sudanese territory.

The first was the role of imperial Cairo, which continued to demand from Britain an arrangement that would "guarantee to Egypt her indisputable right of sovereignty over that country [the Sudan] and the control of the waters of the Nile."[70] After Egypt gained its independence, in 1922, the Egyptian constitution was promulgated, declaring Egypt a constitutional monarchy. Royal Cairo worked very hard to enshrine Egypt's control over the Sudan in its new constitution, which affirmed King Fouad "as the king of Egypt and the Sudan."[71] The draft constitution states, "Although the Sudan belongs to the Egyptian Kingdom, the constitution does not apply to it and a special administration will be provided."[72]

In all this language and both the clear and discreet intentions behind it, of course, appears one of official Cairo's tools, describing the many complicated issues contested in the British dispute with Egypt over the Sudan question. But Britain ascertained its position with the official Egyptian claim by threatening King Fouad.[73] The British warned Fouad that "unless he immediately withdrew his claim to the Sudan the British Government were determined to 'review at once, and radically, their recent declaration of Egyptian policy.'"[74] That is to say, Britain would recolonize Egypt. But, as before, Cairo's attitude toward the Sudan reflected both unity and diversity.

On the one hand, official Cairo and its ruling elite exhibited a form of unity, coming on the heels of the Egyptian Empire, which perceived the unity of the Nile Valley as maintaining that extended piece of real estate for its natural resources. As Hussein Zulfakar Sabry explains, while the Egyptian "Palace and Parties' Pashas intrigued for whatever scraps of influence which remained[, they] only thought of amassing wealth and luxury, oblivious to the bleak misery of the whole country."[75] On the other hand, national Cairo demonstrated a different and diverse growth of liberation, reformist, and Islamist movements with varying degrees of agreement on many issues with different sectors of the Sudanese on the tribulations of British designs in the two countries in particular and colonialism in general. In principle, however, all the new Egyptian movements—nationalist, Communist, and Islamist—in their common effort to establish an anticolonial move, developed discourses and visions that informed and empowered the institutions of public life in the two countries. Still, the practice, language, and context of the Egyptian hegemony over the Sudan became the essential staple that pinned together the new Egyptian political and social culture within its diverse and individual representations.

What generated a continuous feeling of frustration in the Sudan was the attitude of each of these Egyptian movements' self-image and conduct as the central directing agency and a "Big Brother" with regard to their Sudanese younger brethren in ideology. Simultaneously, these movements started to sprout in the Sudan through the increase in the numbers of Sudanese students in Egypt, the influence of some Egyptian employees in the Sudan, and the spread and influence of the Egyptian media. Thus, the old rivalries, antagonisms, and fissures among these movements in Egypt were transferred with their expansion south, only to plague and grow within the major fault lines over which emerging Sudanese leftist and Islamist movements were fighting among themselves and with each other. By 1924 it became clear that the Sudanese views and the strategies of different local power groups, with regard to the future relations with either one or both of the colonial parties over the Sudan, were not only different but were light-years apart.

Although all the emerging Sudanese power groups, in essence, aspired to an independent Sudan for the Sudanese, the vision and strategies of each of these groups was different, and they grew apart quickly. 'Ali 'Abdal Latif and Ḥussain Sharif, both of whom "supported the Idea of the Sudan for the Sudanese,"[76] reflected this idea in the discourses they initiated, which meant independence, for the first, while it "meant the continuation of British guardianship and the end of the Egyptian share in the Condominium."[77] As for the idea of the "unity of the Nile Valley, some of the [Sudanese] nationalists saw in Egypt the homeland of the Arab culture, and justified on this ground the union between the two countries, while others thought at uniting with Egypt as a way to obtain more rights for the Sudanese."[78]

In 1931, Yousif Mustafa al-Tinai captured the meaning of the mutual Sudanese and Egyptian strategic struggle against the British in his song "Fi al-foad tar'aho al-'inaya" (Grace will look after what is cherished by the heart), which is considered the most popular manifesto of the patriotic movement. In one of the verses al-Tinai says, *marfaīnnien ḍablan wa hazil shugo butn al-asad al-munazil* (two frail and skeletal wolves [the Sudan and Egypt] tore apart the belly of the hostile lion [Britain]). From the 1930s and through the 1940s and 1950s, the intellectual formulations of these trends gave each of the emerging Sudanese parties its coherence and force. The high end of these trends was manifest in the Umma Party and Ansār camp on one side while the other reflected itself in the Ashiqqa Party and the Khatmiyya camp. The British, the Egyptians, the Sudanese, and their respective states completely neglected the disenfranchised entities, including the southern population, the urban poor, and women. The small ideological parties, however, which included the Communist Party, the Republican Party, and the Islamist movements, continued to grow, however slow in pace. The Unlawful Association Act of 1924, which the state enacted before these parties emerged, expressly prohibited some of these organizations; however, they continued to grow as unlawful organizations. Within the new organization of society, the colonial state created the Advisory Council for the Northern Sudan. As Woodward explains, "advice, not legislation, was its task; and the southern Sudan was not ready for representation nor the Advisory Council an appropriate body to comment on that isolated and very different region."[79] The two processes of official and popular Cairo policies and attitudes toward the Sudan changed drastically after the 1952 military coup in Egypt, which General Muḥammad Naguib led.[80]

Naguib himself, who was born in Khartoum in 1901 to an Egyptian father, Yousif Naguib, and a Sudanese mother, Zohra Aḥmed 'Othman, was a representation of the unity of the Nile Valley. While his demise was another blow to dreams of the unity of the Nile Valley, it pushed the Sudanese consciousness toward a renewed feeling of disappointment toward Egyptians, similar to the embitterment felt by the 1924 revolutionaries, who had expected military support from Egypt. But this time the British acted differently. They did not intervene the way they had against Aḥmed 'Urabi in 1882. To all these effects, colonialism reduced itself, and, in 1956, the Sudanese found their push for complete independence much easier than they had in the past. Subsequent chapters will show how the major developments in the systems of amplification and representation of the center, as well as the visible and invisible margins, developed and continued to grow.

7

The Creation of the Center

What the Sudanese sometimes call, by way of euphemism, the center, the north, the south, the west, and the margin of their country, were all entities created within certain imagined spaces, populated by imagined and real human communities. Each of these spaces has been carrying differentiated labels—sketched in general assumptions—that vary, stockpile, and present certain demands, stigmas, and contested or uncontested self-gratifications based on a constructed self-image. Each of these spaces and the structural and social attributes of its inhabitants and its self-images were created by a host of conditions—all of which carried certain aspects of human intentions, and none of which could be impartial. Hence, the division of the Sudan, according to a system ranking its population according to this or that scheme of difference, was a fundamental province of colonial minds, the trifold experience of rejection, ambivalence, and imposition as well as the consequences of each of these colonial experiences.

In each of these cases, "the colonialist resorts to racism. It is significant that racism is part of colonialism throughout the world; and it is no coincidence. Racism sums up and symbolizes the fundamental relation which unites colonialist and colonized."[1] Moreover, the colonial state, as Partha Chatterjee maintains, "was not just the agency that brought the modular forms of the modern state to the colonies; it was also an agency that was destined never to fulfill the normalizing mission of the modern state because the premise of its power was a rule of colonial difference, namely, the preservation of the alienness of the ruling group."[2] Memmi, however, sheds more light on this complex relationship within the colonial experience: "the colonialist does not plan his future in terms of the colony, for he is there only temporarily and invests only what will bear fruit in his time. The true reason, the principal reason for most deficiencies is that the colonialist never planned to transform the colony into the image of his homeland, nor to remake the colonized in his own image! He cannot allow such an equation—it would destroy the principle of his privileges."[3]

The two types of colonialism the Sudan experienced—*al-Turkiyya al-sabiqa* (1821–75) and *al-Turkiyya al-lahigh* (1898–1956), as the Sudanese describe them—constituted a continuum of historical events that shared guiding differentialist ideologies. Each operated within its own historical and material circumstances. Together they contributed to the construction of the conditions that deeply affected the creation of the Sudanese center and the margins.

The Turko-Egyptian colonial system came with its own ideology of difference that turned the country into a hunting ground for slaves. The British colonial system of racial ranking transformed the cultural, religious, and social diversity of the country through an ideology that combined both overt (biological) and covert (differentialist) traits of racism that focused on both biological and cultural differences as well as called for natural preference for a specific cultural group or groups. Within such a combination of both forms of racism, the population was not only separated into superior and inferior categories, but it was also reduced, through an enforced system of closed and open districts within which every group was forced to reside and progress or regress quickly within its "own kind" and to stay separate from other social and human assemblages.

Within those closed and open district arrangements, the colonial state devised and enforced "acts of confinement, regulation, and supervision of the population [that] dawned suddenly. Wherever people looked, they were to be inspected, supervised, or instructed."[4] That is to say, that system of racism, which stigmatized the entire Sudanese population, decreed the mixing of cultures as most undesirable and, hence, supported a system of exclusion or closed districts as a continuous system of control. The following two chapters review the broad colonial strategies and the Sudanese counterstrategies that marked the creation of the center and the periphery.

Acts of Reorder, Confinement, Control, and Colonization

Within the British colonial reordering, confinement, and ranking of the population, the Sudanese were divided into Arab-Semitic people over

Hamites or Nubians, and Nubians over Sudanic and Nilotic peoples (Negroes). Sir Harold MacMichael, the identity management architect par excellence, as previously described, built on what the previous and existing colonial regimes proclaimed to be systems of difference. His conceptualization of an Islamic north and a negroid and pagan south was part of the segmentation of the country, which was later institutionalized within the colonial political and social classification and the reinvention of difference.

As argued by MacMichael, "the line of division, geographical, ethnical and cultural, between the predominantly Arab north and purely negroid south is well marked and obvious, and still, as we shall see, is potent as a political factor."[5] MacMichael came to this differentialist conclusion after he gave a broad generalization to the country and its people as "predominantly Arab and entirely Islamic in the north, and predominantly negroid and pagan in the south, but there are so many exceptions and qualifications to be made that the description would have only a partial value."[6] Nevertheless, MacMichael continues labeling as Azande some of those whom he described as a "highly educated, intelligent and progressive element" that came to being in towns and large villages, "aboriginal pagan stock" in the Nuba Mountains, a "primitive negroid . . . of whose origin is little known," and "quick-witted, musical brown folk of medium stature." For MacMichael, and the colonial mind as well, Africans were no ordinary children. They were destined to be perpetually—in the words of Christopher Fyfe—"'Peter Pan children who can never grow up, a child race.'"[7] But what makes MacMichael's conclusion important was that he is one of those people whom Maḥmood Mamdani describes as representatives of "the confluence of two institutions, scientific racism and scientific bureaucracy, as key to shaping"[8] colonial power.

At a more profound level, however, the Sudanese colonial experience added a third element by enacting such differentialist racism to constitute the cornerstone of the closed-district system and the formation of racial and religious zones. The colonial state's classification of the Sudan, administratively, into closed and open districts, and its formulation of its history for the reinvention of difference have had serious consequences for individuals, regions, women, the rural poor, and the entire population. The colonial system, in this sense, created "multispeed societies"; only one of them was connected to the newly constructed colonial minisystem mentioned before. Others—in the closed districts of race, gender, and rural poverty—were crowded together and separately outside the shopping window of that system of difference, observing those who were on display.

The built-up advantage that turned the colonialists' ideas and conclusions into a history, sociology, and anthropology of the country and turned what they believed to be its "immutable" elements into policies that were essential to the growth of the colonial state gave the British colonialists' discourse its special edge. This advantage was "built up" during the evolution of disciplines into discourses and the discourses into practices. This mode of production of knowledge, under the colonial institutional practice and polity, prejudiced the study of the past of all different groups by reconstructing the history of some groups in the country and denying other groups some or any history. Be that as it may, Immanuel Wallerstein gives, in an illustrious article, an insightful complement to the many attributes of the past. Wallerstein affirms that "pastness" is a central element in the socialization process of individuals and in the maintenance of group solidarity for the establishment of or challenge to social legitimation. This being the case, as Wallerstein maintains, pastness may become a tool that different entities can use against each other. "Pastness therefore is preeminently a moral phenomenon, therefore a political phenomenon, always a contemporary phenomenon."[9] Hence, it adds force to "a mode by which persons are persuaded to act in the present in ways they might not otherwise act;"[10] however, at the same time, "The real past, to be sure, is indeed inscribed in stone. The social past, how we understand this real past, on the other hand, is inscribed at best in soft clay."[11]

The social past was also an arena in which the colonized and the colonizer scrambled to affirm specific statements drawn "in soft clay." These forms of discourse appear to conflict when they are viewed from above—the colonialists' perspective—but they are complementary when they are viewed from below—within the Sudanese (the colonized) discourse. Here, the creation of the center is the synthesis of such contradictory principles, written in the historical past and reinterpreted to be inscribed in soft clay by different actors. The historian here, for both parties, is what Eric Hobsbawm describes as "the poppy-grower . . . to the heroin addicts: [he supplies] the essential raw material to the market."[12] In placing all these developments squarely within the context of power relations, the geographic center—northern Sudan—was endowed as the core of the colonial power structure. These parties were scrambling for the history of the place, while they were also competing to place each one's reading of the written and imagined pastness into the structure and the process of the development of the center. The discourses of both the colonized and the colonizer, with regard to the pastness of the center, might look both similar and dissimilar at the same time. The similarity of these discourses made the historical-cultural formation of the center more dynamic and ever developing, while its dissimilar aspects made it self-motivated, though riddled with conflict and discord, and poised to change.

These developments, as an event at the level of the construction of the center, are what Wallerstein describes as "peoplehood" (belonging to a people, which is more than an ethnicity but less than a nation) as they account for all the arrangements and processes that shaped the space the Sudanese people inhabited together. The historical-cultural formation of the center included several elements. First, the colonial racial reading of closeness and distance between inhabitants of the Sudanese space was perceived as different; however, the Sudanese peoples can easily be seen as examples of what Wallerstein would call "genetically continuous groups."[13] Second, according to that situation, the transformation of these groups into one nation, or their segregation into different entities, was shaped by a system of identity engineering, which a whole host of hegemonic and counterhegemonic entitlements governed. Third, the ranking of some parts of that human space was essentialized by bundling together and labeling marginalized groups within an internal foil of identities—southerners, Gharbawies (western Sudanese), Nuba, women, rural, and so forth—as a structural condition not only for the construction of difference but also for tagging all these groups as primitive and underdeveloped.

Finally, all that was contained within one local differentiated system, which was controlled from within by the constructed center as it gradually become entangled within its division of labor and subject to its system of control. At the same time, that system and its colonial state were controlled from without through an exploitive imperial core or center and its needs. These processes and the counterprocesses of resistance to local and imperial pressures within their historical-cultural formations in both the center and the different peripheries acted against the colonial system of control to reproduce a situation of considerable complexity.

The Historical, Economic, and Cultural Formation of the Center

The Sudanese center and its state core was constructed and grew as an ideology, which the colonial states framed, and "the historical-cultural formation,"[14] which captured the pastness and differentiated other constructed zones, shaped. Later, it constituted, and operated within, a life of its own. Symbols of racial representation and peoplehood were only the tip of the iceberg of a complex construction. The colonial knowledge, constraint, and exercise of power worked together, and sometimes separately, to write down a hegemonic construction of the past and to manufacture real and imagined communities of the state as subordinate layers. Further, the intricacy of the ideology of the center drew its system of representation by mediating sociopolitical relations, processes of accumulation, and progressive modes of elective affinity with and without different modes of resistance to that colonial state. This complex construction soon created its own worldview, while its apparatus, the state, continued to act as the sociopolitical maker that simultaneously determined and embodied old and new forms of representation and domination.

The British colonial experience in the Sudan was a creature that might be easy, but is sometimes difficult, to compare to any other similar or dissimilar colonial experience, no matter who the colonizing power was. The rivalry with and resistance to the colonial system, its differentialist racism, and the effects of what Mamdani described as the confluence of the scientific racism and scientific bureaucracy are what R. S. O'Fahey and other scholars of the Sudan observed: that the British colonialists "brought to the Sudan policies fashioned in India."[15] That could be, to a certain extent, true; however, it might not capture the whole picture of that experience. As Nicholas Dirks has recognized, "Colonial knowledge both enabled conquest and was produced by it; in certain important ways, knowledge was what colonialism was all about."[16] Conversely, the Sudanese themselves produced and codified their own form of knowledge and representation of the past. How these two processes collided and became amalgamated to create the ideology of the center lay in the foundation of that particular Sudanese experience, the historical-cultural formation of its ideology and the processes and structures that constituted its colonial state. In addition, the colonial experience in the Sudan possessed other critical dimensions that dispensed ways for individuals and groups to become "subjects" within and outside the colonial establishment and its decreed "iron cage" structure.

As John S. Furnivall has said, the colonial experience carries an association of both policy and practice. Hence, "if a survey of colonial policy reveals a fundamental identity in colonial relations, the study of colonial practice gives a first impression of diversity."[17] This aspect is not, in this instance, a merely unwarranted issue. Since aspects of policy and practice were inherent in the colonial experience, they might have continued making their unsettled presence felt not only in the Sudanese state but also in the construction of the Sudanese peoplehood and the zones designated to each group of them. That is to say, the Sudanese colonial experience, the building of its state, and the peoplehood of its inhabitants, was the pivot that engendered not only spatial division of labor but also the differential relational forms within various parts and peoples of the country and the progressive processes of marginalization of some of them.

Here, as MacMichael and the colonial discourse reflect, the most significant factors in the ideological and guiding principles of the administrative system in the management of identity, the reinvention of difference, and the formation of racial zones in the Sudan could be religion, foreignness, and conversion. What Peter van der Veer claims about the "long-standing colonial myth that Indian Muslims were originally a group of immigrants who had ruled over the great Indian masses,"[18] applies to MacMichael's claim "that the Muhammadan settlement in the Sudan caused a profound modification of the pre-existing native stock."[19] MacMichael continued, this modification "is apt to obscure the other equally important fact that long before the Islamic period Arabian races had been crossing over into Egypt and the Sudan."[20]

These three elements of foreignness—race, religion, and the assumption that Islam is an expanding conversion project—manifest a reflective theme in the perceived formation of what has been labeled as the north or the center in the Sudan as a peoplehood. The history of the center, according to MacMichael's account, is the history of the Arabs and Muslims, while the history of the "rest," or the periphery, is deemed to represent other peoplehoods composed of the "tribes." This negative code was broadened, becoming an all-embracing epistemology to a vast number of inhabitants of the periphery, including the Muslim tribes of Darfur, other tribes of the rural poor, and the "pagan" tribes of the rest. For most events, however, this racial experience of the outsider, or foreignness of the Arabs and Muslims, in its expressions and aims within the colonial discourse, diverges fundamentally from the experience of the rest—the southern and the western peoplehoods—who were considered indigenous. Here, the symbolic construction of each peoplehood and the field of subordination of each fall within two different and separate partnerships. First among these partnerships was a gemeinschaft, or a primitive community that could only be understood through Evans-Pritchard's Colonial Anthropology. Second was a gesellschaft, which was constructed through a history written in clay and archaeology, extracted from stone to fit the study of that standing myth of foreignness, and contributed to the symbolic construction of each community.

MacMichael and other colonial administrators-turned-scholars, like A. J. Arkell, reconstructed a discourse, a past, and a present for the Sudan. Their reasons for completing this reconstruction were not only to fit the standing construction, which claimed that immigrant Arabs and Muslims modified and ruled over the indigenous Sudanese population, but also to expand that discourse to a potentially longer time in antiquity.

Arkell argues that different foreign races, including ancient Egyptians, had continuously ruled over the Sudan.[21] The implication of this discourse emphasizes the deeper effects of the Sudanese experience with colonialism and its deeper consequences and aftereffects in shaping the state, on the one side, and Sudanese society, on the other. In this way, a new and different system of differentiation unfolded. As Veer explains, "the British replaced Muslims as just another ruling group coming from outside."[22] Britain and the British would rule and exercise power to maintain a Sudanese condition for which an outside or foreign domination has always been the norm. At the heart of such a colonial perspective and construction of self-image, Britain and the British were brought into being, and, in the Sudanese life, as in India, they were known "in an evolutionary perspective . . . as representatives of an enlightened civilization, [who] had to replace the Muslims, whose rule showed the signs of decline."[23] Hence, one of the fundamentals of the colonial administration's "burdens" and its "civilizing missions" was to protect the rest from the religious and cultural encroachments of the Arab and Muslim conversionist north or center. Similarly, it was also believed that it was the administration's "burden" to protect the north from Egyptian religious, cultural, and nationalist influences. Not only that, but the British colonialists in the Sudan continued to argue the opposite of every aspect the condominium partnership would entail. They tended to stick to the argument that the Sudan was lost to the Mahdists in 1885 because of the ineptitude of Turko-Egyptian rule.

Accordingly, the British community of the colonial state in the Sudan presented themselves as the decisive entity and the major reference, while Britain presented itself as the core state within the new system that ranked and ordered Egypt as the semiperiphery and the Sudan as the periphery. This ranking, its placement reasoning, and the exercise of power that followed reduced Egypt—the primary partner in the condominium—and the Egyptian role in the administration of the Sudan to an inferior status within the formation and running of the colonial state. The British harped on the idea that everything Egyptian must be inferior, not only to the British themselves, but also to what the British were doing in the Sudan. Some of the attacks on everything Egyptian that gained permanence were that the British-formed public education and expressive culture in the Sudan were considered superior in quality and prestige to Egyptian education and culture.

Since the early days of the colonial state in the Sudan, the British governor general, Francis Reginald Wingate, introduced and diligently followed a policy that extended, strengthened, and maintained an imperial order. This, in turn, sustained the British cultural and political power as superior and separated and debased what is non-British as inferior. For Wingate's "civilizing mission," the protection of the center from the negative influences of everything Egyptian was deemed incumbent upon him. Accordingly, "Wingate employed all the means at his disposal to stem the infiltration of Egyptian nationalist and pan-Islamic ideas into the Sudan."[24] In order to do that effectively, he devised a "special system of intelligence . . . to deal with this subtle [Egyptian] penetration. The intelligence department, whose headquarters were in Cairo, kept a close watch on developments in the Egyptian capital and warned its branch in Khartoum to take any necessary action."[25]

All these policies and procedures had a distinct bearing on the rise of the center, not only as part of the colonized Sudanese space, but also as a peculiar sphere during the colonial period. At the same time, colonial knowledge and power were exercised to divide the country into closed and open zones where that knowledge was more prejudiced against the Sudanese gemeinschaft, or what the colonialists deemed primitive communities. Nevertheless, functions of socially polarizing zones would be applied within the dictates of that "civilizing mission" to protect the periphery from the contagious influences of the center: Islamization and Arabization. All these developments had a distinct bearing on the rise of the center, its ideology, and practice because they penetrated, zoned, and dominated specific areas of the Sudanese space and shaped, to a great extent, its identity and peoplehood.

If history had that significant political potential in shaping the identification of the Sudanese human sociology and anthropology, religion had another role, equally important in the historical-cultural formation of the center. Colonized Islam, as I have explained, had created a hegemonic system that was enforced among the population as a new form of orthodox state religion. The colonial state's enforcement of a state religion through interventionism and a control system for the Muslim lifeworld was conducted as a function of reordering the Muslim zone and controlling the hierarchies of Muslim functionaries as state employees. In addition, this system of reordering "was an aspect of a colonial geography in which a colony is dramatically compartmentalized into an authoritative, European, modern space and a subordinated, traditional native space."[26] This system worked equally well with the creation of the center and the categorization of the Sudanese space into peoplehoods as Islam was correlated with foreignness and the Arab groups of the Sudanese center (the north). In another sense, it provided the colonialists with an orientalization aspect of the place, which can give an additional value to the legitimation and to the reality of the colonial state and its hierarchical system as the only justifiable system of the land. Nevertheless, the colonial state and its architects managed the issue of colonizing Islam in inconsistent ways.

First, they believed that orthodox Islam, or the "Azharite *'ulamā'* possessed the prestige needed to overcome the fanatical inclinations of popular Islam."[27] However, Azharite Islam came with expected and unexpected consequences as some of al-Azhar-trained 'ulamā' were rooted in the collective anticolonial spirits that Jamal el-Din al-Afghani and Muḥammad 'Abduh provoked. Until the 1919 independence movements, many of the al-Azhar 'ulamā' were involved in Egyptian politics, where they established strong connections with other secular nationalists. That caliber of 'ulamā', when it came to the Sudan, brought with it and promoted al-Nahda discourse about Islam and modernity and the Egyptian anticolonial antagonistic ideological currents. It is true, for example, that Sheikh Mustafa al-Maraghi, the Egyptian grand *qāḍi* of the Sudan (1908–15) "was described as leading a very modern life including eating with fork and knife and rode well-dressed horses. . . . A generation of qadis from Gordon College took to his lifestyle. They played polo, tennis, and soccer."[28] But it is also true that Sheikh al-Maraghi was one of the forerunners for reform and an ardent advocate of superior status for Islamic law and education.

Second, from the early days of rule by the condominium, Egyptian religious lawyers and disciples of Muḥammad 'Abduh, like Sheikh Muḥammad Shakir, Muḥammad Haroun, and Mustafa al-Maraghi, in addition to many more of 'Abduh's disciples, actively participated in laying the foundation for Arabic and shari'a studies at Gordon College. These scholars included Ahmed Hidiat, 'Abdel Raouf 'Abdelslam, Fouad al-Khatib, and 'Abdel Wahab al-Najar. In addition to those qudāt and scholars, some of the Egyptian nationalists and activists in the army, civil service, and education gave space to shared sentiments, oppositional impulses, and criticism of British rule, which grew with the ideologies of Sudanese nationalist opposition groups. So what Wingate feared most, that Egyptian nationalist and pan-Islamic ideas would enter the Sudan through the back door, came roaring in through the window of the policy of colonizing Islam.

Third, it might be true that colonized Islam and some of its qāḍi operatives "had a checkered history comprising resistance, hybridity, collaboration, and sly civility. . . . As graduates of the hub of colonial modernity (Khartoum's Gordon College), qudāt originated in a context of hybridity. In practicing sharia they had to meet colonial modernity half-way."[29] In doing so they did not escape the shackles of colonized Islam, which designated them as of inferior status and to a differentiated lower place within the state strata. Their distinctive native attire distinguished the shari'a qāḍis, and they were designated as having less power and prestige. It goes without saying, in the eyes of the colonialist, and, according to Sharkey, "in the eyes of the colonized," attire and in particular "Western clothes were markers of professional progress and achievement."[30] All that neither affirmed the colonial state's respect for Islam nor advanced the status of that version of Islam, which adopted a state religion. Saliḥ 'Abdel Gadir, a poet and one of the 1924 revolution leaders, expressed his bitterness and disrespect to the shari'a men with strong overtones that echoed throughout the country for generations:

Ala ya Hind quli aw ajize
rigal al-sharii adho kl maeze
ala liet al-liha sart hashishun
li talafahu khiul al-Engleeze.
Oh Hind, say or approve saying that the shari'a men have become like goats
I hoped beards were grass for the horses of the British to graze on.

The Formation of the Peoplehood of the Center: A White-Collar Salariat

The scramble for the Sudanese pastness was not limited to the colonial entities. The Sudanese communities of conversation themselves also scrambled for their pastness. Under the conditions that the colonial power dominated, its properties of hegemony, and its relations of inequalities, the Sudanese communities produced their reading of their own history as a prime contender for the colonial discourse. 'Abdullahi 'Abdul Raḥman, an early Gordon College graduate, told his audience in one of his very famous poems:

fa ḥaddith 'un bani al-Nielian 'anna bi
'alla al-Niel aw 'lla al-furati
bi 'anna nuntami ḥasaban wa nasaban ila mn fi al-Gazerati min roufati.
Tell about us to those [Arabs and Muslims] of the upper Nile or upper Euphrates
That we belong by origin and by marriage to those buried in the [Arabian] peninsula.

'Abdul Raḥman Shawqi, 'Abdullahi 'Abdul Raḥman, 'Abdullah Muḥammad 'Omer al-Banna, Ṣaliḥ Boutros (a Coptic Christian), and other poets of that generation created a "social organization of tradition," reading their poetry to a live audience at celebrations of the Prophet Muḥammad's birth (*Mawlid*) and other religious events. For 'Abdullahi 'Abdul Raḥman and his literary colleagues, pastness is a synthesis of two important dimensions of human experience. First, the enticement of the images, symbols, and articulateness of expression of high classical Arabic was to be presented as a significant part of the Sudanese intellectual landscape concerned in presenting the self in a language beyond the intellectual capacity of the colonizing Other. Second, giving meaning to existing experience in this way, the Sudanese community of conversation inspired and packaged history and pastness, in a context and stance superior to the human experience of the colonizer. That is, those poets developed and presented the notion of the local in a language that not only invited the vestiges of a venerated past human experience but also placed, restored, and introduced the colonized self as a renewed living extension to that past experience.

At the same time, this emerging discourse, by relating to the vicissitudes of such a high culture or civilization of an Arab origin and of Islam, minimizes the value of the dominating colonial culture and takes its discourse about the pastness of the place as recognition of that relationship and its self representations. In this sense, the Sudanese perceived the British discourse of the Muslim and Arab foreignness of the north with an elated mode of understanding that coincides with the wisdom of the Arabic verse, *al-fadul ma shahidat bihi al-a' da* (Good deeds are the ones attested to even by one's own enemies). Thus, all local expressions of pastness found their unity of meaning and different articulations, their imaginations and memories, within three provinces of meaning. Each of them contributed to the self-image of the center.

The first province relates to all early or recent rounds of confrontation that included Mahdist revolution, confronting the colonial invasion, and the different Sudanese resistance counters to the colonial entity as representations of an external reality. It is true that both Mahdism and neo-Mahdism have shaped a recurring phenomenon in the history and the present of the country; nevertheless, some considered them, in the emerging Sudanese community of the state, as a representation of the domain of an objectified ancien régime. The second province relates to members of that community of the state who approach the history and relationship to Islam and Arabism as working realities and moments of empowerment and glory that not only could confront the colonial themes of foreignness and inferiority but also could award a new, notable position to both Islam and Arabism, not Britain and the West, as the reference points.

The third province, within the proliferation of the apparatus of the colonial state and the degree of correspondence between being a member of the state's manufactured elite and a member of one of the Sudan peoplehoods, represented these emerging Sudanese communities of conversation, considering that they shared a nonconforming additional value with the colonizer—that is, a place within the domain of modernity. In *Kifah Jil*, Aḥmad Khair reasoned that his generation had aims similar to those of the European renaissance, which marked Europe's emergence from the Dark Ages into the light of "modern civilization." But Khair quickly qualified the kind of modernity about which he was talking. He argued that Egypt and the Arab east, at the turn of the twentieth century, followed a similar route under Jamal al-Din al-Afghani and his disciple Muḥammad 'Abduh, and that, in turn, shaped the liberal thinking of the Sudanese movement and its approach to modernity. Consequently, this compact with modernity came with its peculiar relations and serious consequences.

The first aspect of these peculiar relations and consequences was what developed out of the colonial system's ownership of the state as its means of production. More important is how that state developed a new mode of production that converted the entire new publicly educated Sudanese community into a salariat—white-collar workers who were "owned" by the state and for whose labor the colonial state paid. The reification of the production of this new group of Sudanese allotted them a peculiar status within the new division of labor. In one way, they were controlled, disciplined, and turned into an appendage of the state apparatus through a system that was enforced through hierarchies of rank, surveillance, and task supervision.

These processes of control and discipline were not elements of experience. They constituted an all-encompassing system, charged with daily coercive measures of evaluation. In one sense, one of the two faces of the Janus of this system of evaluation led to the gate of rewards that only the state could bestow on some privileged members of its workers, while tantalizing with or denying others such privileges. That is why that system of valuations pulls all those connected to that state apparatus and immerses them in its scheme of meaning and plausibility structures. The other face of the Janus led to the gates of alienation, as those members of the community of the state remained detached from the command of their product—but not the chains of their exploitation—the moment they left their offices and went home. That is how that system of valuation could push them out of the state's fields of power and prestige the moment any one of them was demoted or fired or retired. In order to have full command of their product, this community of the state had to try different possibilities to keep maintaining the same power both inside and outside the system.

Thus, this condition and its constitution of occupying conflicting positions within the system is what turned that white-collar salariat, or the members of the community of the state, into what Nandy and others have described as "colonialism's intimate enemies, making colonial rule a reality while hoping to see it undone."[31] In so doing they have to capture and "liberate" the state and themselves at the same time. This hope or desire developed into two forms of public politics, which as Charles Tilly explains, "almost always involve collective contention; rebellions, revolutions, social movements, demonstrations, general strikes, [and] contested electoral campaigns," which, in this case, illustrated "the irreducibly contentious forms of public politics."[32] Within these developments new conversation communities developed in organized civic and military associations. Among these associations, the community of the state, or the state-manufactured elite, emerged as an important development at the core of the new dominant society.

This society was transformed by gaining status and prestige through the "family-school dyad"[33] to simultaneously form the leadership of the political movement and the community of the state. All these reproductions, forms of resistance, and attempts to capture the state emerged from the internal reality of a colonized field of power. The picture that emerged out of this discourse—which made the center, within its two metropolitan cities of Omdurman (the residential city) and Khartoum (the workplace), the veritable platforms of political, social, religious, military, artistic, and other forms of discourse—relates to a new imagined Sudanese identity on a national scale.

The first attempt to capture the state through a combination of civil and violent means progressed within the revolutionary commission that ended with the defeat of the 1924 military action. As soon as these groups started establishing under- and above-ground political structures—like the League of Sudanese Union, the White Flag League, and syndicates—new and different expressions of resistance to colonial rule started to grow, and power groups began to emerge. "Shorn of the violence that existed from early resistance of the 1924 revolt," Woodward writes, "Sudan was becoming a highly political milieu in which the state was the common element endeavoring to shape collaborators while having to adapt to emerging realities to which it in fact was contributing."[34]

The second attempt to capture the state grew out of these dialectics between these white-collar workers as modes of continuities and differences toward resistance started to emerge after the defeat of the 1924 revolution. Members of the community of the state began to develop and upgrade effective ties that developed through reading groups into associations and later to stimulate them along the way with the sociopolitical relations of power and prestige, which the state bestowed on them as a growing class of white-collar workers of the state with a constrained symbolic capital. Enthusiastic as they were to lead most forms of social, cultural, and political expressions and conduct, the elite were equally ready to present themselves as a class for itself. The growth of the symbolic capital of this class gathered momentum through the effectiveness of the associations they built and sustained. These associations that grew out of the small clusters—groups like Abu Roaf and al-Fagr—turned into what Aḥmad Khair has described as an "'organized opinion through a representative organization entrusted with the demands of the country and supported by public opinion.'"[35] Apart from the reproduction of a new urban cultural and authoritative domination, this power elite engendered their own political identity, lifestyle, and practice that placed them as the preeminent agent in society. Having managed to win the battle of independence from the colonial powers, the Sudanese power elite instated themselves as the flagship of change in the country's social, cultural, and political processes. Acting from a seat of superiority with regard to the vast amount of the poor, marginalized, and illiterate population, they saw themselves as agents of social change who were destined to occupy a special position of authority and privilege. This social and cultural order has been imbued and legitimized through "the process whereby power relations are perceived not for what they objectively are but in a form which renders them legitimate in the eyes of the beholder."[36]

The universe of that pastness, and its double historicity, are included in both the Sudanese and the colonial narratives, which complement and contradict each other. However, they both, in one way or another, contributed to the development of a self-image of the center in a strange form of asymmetry in the production of the center and its ideology. This strange form of asymmetry emerged to feed this self-image of representation of the center and to work together with the colonial factor to make the image of that space demographically larger.

The Iron Arteries of the Center

The other moment in the development of the center was firmly connected to the new tools of communication and transportation. These tools were designed purposely as tools of control and exploitation that accompanied or planned and developed within the growth of the colonial state. One of the earliest tools in the service of control and centralization was the railway system. It was constructed as Sudan Military Railways, and, operating mainly as a major tool of the invasion, it was developed to support the tail of Kitchener's advancing army. In such a "vast, desert country, the railway facilitated the movement of troops and supplies and gave the Anglo-Egyptian army a tremendous advantage over the Mahdist forces."[37] In the strictest sense, the railway "was from the outset a priority for the Sudan's new rulers, occupying a key role in their strategy for internal security."[38] On the one hand, continued armed insurgencies and the spread of anticolonial movements in different parts of the country "forced the colonial administration to develop a transportation and communications infrastructure. The series of railways and roads built between 1899 and 1913 reflected military more than economic priority."[39] Even after 1913, and "until 1924, the Railway Battalion of the Egyptian Army provided most of the labor at its headquarters in Atbara and on the railway line."[40]

On the other hand, pressures from different industrial interests within the core state, Britain, such as the British Cotton Growing Association, to expedite the construction of a railway system in the Sudan and connect it to the Red Sea, materialized in the construction of Port Sudan harbor and in building a line connecting it to the hinterland. Along with the determination of the colonialists "to limit the Egyptian influences in the Sudan, the British decided to link Khartoum and the Nile region with the Red Sea coast."[41] Another purpose for building that line "was to make the Sudan less dependent on Egypt for transport, and to reduce the cost of transshipment by cutting the distance from Khartoum to the

Mediterranean."[42] By extending a line from Khartoum south to Sinnār and then later west through Gezira to el-Obeid, the gum arabic-producing center, another phase of the construction of the railway network was completed.

By upgrading the railway system to connect the production areas in Gezira, through al-Gezira Light Railway, Kordofan, and Kassala to Port Sudan on the Red Sea, the center was better interconnected than other parts of the country. The major, if not the only, colonial "developmental efforts were concentrated in an area resembling an inverted 'T' imposed on Sudan: composed of the valley of the Nile to the north of Khartoum, the Blue and White Nile areas immediately south of Khartoum, central Kordofan, and the southern part of Kassala province."[43] The establishment of this railway system was in itself a significant principle of order that spread and firmly controlled the center.

The army surrounded all the minicities of the colonial administration at the center, and they were connected to the railway line or river transportation port and other postal and telegram communication (see chapter 4). The introduction of the railway was behind the creation of two new cities: Port Sudan and 'Aṭbara and the integration of el-Obeid within the center.[44] The colonial authorities created the new town of 'Aṭbara in 1906, when the headquarters and the workshops of the Sudan railways were transferred from Wadi Ḥalfa to the new town. During its early days, the British and Egyptian military as well as a mix of foreigners dominated 'Aṭbara. According to the Sudan Government Railway annual report for 1914, summarized nicely by Aḥmad Sikainga, "the inhabitants of the railway cantonment numbered about 1,975. Of those, there were 85 British civilian personnel, 36 British troops, 132 Europeans, 731 Egyptian civilians, 653 soldiers of the Egyptian army battalion, 36 Syrians, 5 Indians, and 230 Sudanese, of whom 80 were former Mahdist soldiers."[45] The aftermath of the 1924 revolution and the removal of the Egyptian battalion, as well as a greater demand for labor, attracted more Sudanese to replace the Egyptian and foreign workers. The state of urgency and anxiety created by that development turned 'Aṭbara into the country's center of technical education, with its heart at "Gordon College and the Omdurman School for Stone Masons, founded in 1907."[46]

As a city owned by Sudan Railways, 'Aṭbara grew rapidly. The planning and layout of the place was a sociospatial representation of power relationships. It reflected the town's colonial character. Within its organization and management, "the railway line divided the town roughly into western and eastern zones. The native quarters were located east of the railway line, while the area west of the line was decidedly foreign."[47] The division, construction, and occupation of the space of the town marked an important aspect of its order and organization. That organization reflects the restructuring and ordering of social relations and the shaping of the subjective identities of the town's residents. Colonial 'Aṭbara's distinct hierarchies were reflected by the clear separation of the senior British officials' residential area, or bungalows, which were on the cool "bank of the Nile about half a mile west of the [railway] line."[48] The western side of the town enclosed the railway station, offices, and workshops in addition to the residential quarters that housed the British and Egyptian employees. Another technique of special management had created a new separation and marginalization of the Sudanese groups. The Sudanese residents of the old village of al-Dakhla were forced to move to the crowded eastern section of the town and on their land "the British quarter was built. It was the most opulent and exclusive part of Atbara, with beautiful bungalows, gardens, tennis courts, and clubs."[49] Closer to the center of the town's two worlds stood the market, where many merchants and Egyptian officials lived, creating a buffer zone between east and west.

To a great extent, that new development deeply transformed the common working experience and the lifestyle of the city's inhabitants. The life experience of thousands of immigrants from certain riverain farming communities had been transformed to fit the requirements of a new "modern" center for industry. They had to master many specific skills and techniques of workshops and offices as an entry into a new and different mode of production within an industrial culture. The dictates of that culture were to colonize the lifeworld of those groups and individuals through a militaristic and a bureaucratic discipline. In addition to all that, this system of colonization of the lifeworld of the 'Aṭbarawis was enshrined and enforced through a system of residential segregation that allocated them an inferior space, distinctly separate from the British district.

That new mode of production and its compact with modernity had given the 'Aṭbarawis entries into a new lifestyle, united the townspeople as urban 'Aṭbarawis, and provided a new sense of identity that entailed a clear break with their old way of life. At the same time, the accumulation of knowledge they collected about their collective demise and the boundaries of the collective power of their solidarity enticed them to work together and fight for issues like fairer wages and a better standard of living. The way this solidarity was structured marked the emergence of the trade union as a modern force introduced to Sudanese political and social life. A new structure of networks emerged, different but not necessarily parallel to the political parties, nor similar to the ṭarīqa, this last having brought together urban and rural groups in a loose coalition.

Members of the trade union, through collective bargaining and industrial action, could negotiate and achieve tangible results about issues that included wages, work rules, rules governing hiring, workers' benefits and promotions, workplace safety, and policies. Moreover, the trade unions and professional associations discovered that they had something to offer in the sociopolitical world of practice as organizing bodies for "a class for itself," both to their members and to the country at large as entities concerned about resistance to the colonial state. In this sense, and as citizens of the country, it would be very difficult for the working class as well as the professionals—within their objective relationships to other fields of power—to be reticent in presenting their interest as part of a generalized political action, rather than limiting them to narrow sectional disputes. Hence, to define and promote their political power and moral authority, these associations and trade unions had to position themselves between the other fields of power and the discourse that related to the foundational political necessity in the country. This was one of the lessons the 1924 revolution taught the emerging new forces in the Sudan.

Leaders such as 'Ali Aḥmed Ṣaliḥ and al-Tuhami Muḥammad 'Othman, both labor union organizers, provided early examples of the evolution of effective "modern" forms of resistance, including demonstrations and strikes. In addition, they provided new tools in the anticolonial struggle. Such a trait complemented and filled the center's social sphere with new organizations that both diversified it and added additional collective representation to its new fields of power. The blue-collar workers' organizations were to be found where the railway, riverain, postal, and telegraph arteries stretched. The impressive growth of blue-collar workers, who multiplied within the center's steel arteries in the major urban cities, extended the power of union headquarters in 'Aṭbara through the local union chapters. The fields of relationship at which the unions connected to the white-collar workers' political organizations was an important part of the Sudanese center society of politics. It was through the ideology that the Communist Party carried and the perception of its role as a vanguard organization, endowed with the task of leading the masses through a route of struggle and change, that the blue-collar workers allied and collided with white-collar workers' associations and later governments. For that reason, the trade unions and the professional associations, as well as the student unions and the army, and their fields of power became the primary focus and battleground for the Islamists and their sworn enemies, the Communists, as well as other political parties and regimes.

Holding the Center Together with a Bond of Cotton

Over and above all these processes that created the center, the Gezira Scheme "formed part of the larger colonial effort to establish a political order and constitute relations of authority."[50] By 1925 the colonial regime had turned a million acres between the Blue and the White Nile, which Sudanese pastoralists and farmers had previously inhabited, into the largest centrally managed irrigation farm in the world. The place is called al-Gezira. It is a flat triangular region of black soil south of where these two rivers meet, at the capital city of Khartoum. The scheme's total irrigated area during the colonial period grew to about one million acres. The Gezira Scheme has persisted under the same name, through various Sudanese government administrations and still exists today. The project, which was firmly situated within the division of labor of the colonial enterprise, in material form, represented more than the simple economic interest of that ruling entity and the imperial power that stood behind it. The colonial agricultural discourse was inseparable from the larger colonial discourse and the culture of power in general. This was especially true when it came to the establishment of the colonial program of the structural building of the center and the differentiation and marginalization of the rest.

Arthur Gaitskell, the first chairman and managing director of the Sudan Gezira Board, followed the foreignness discourse of his colonialist predecessors by describing "the northern Sudan, [as] a fringe of the Middle East and Mohammedan in civilization."[51] He later evoked General Charles Gordon's famous statement that "the Sudan is a useless possession, ever was so, and ever will be so."[52] However, the Sudan that he knew evoked "childhood impressions of the Old Testament and touched a chord of common heritage far back in his own nature." He added, "the place-names of the villages revealed the history," even admitting, "Most of them recalled the Semitic names of their founders or attributes to the Almighty. Wad Adam, Wad Jacoub, Wad Ibrahim, and such, recalled Adam, Jacob, and Abraham, while Abd el Rahman, Abd el Hakam and Barakat—the servant of the merciful, the servant of the Just One, and the place of blessing—added further to the biblical parallel."[53] Upon such perception of the country's history of the present, "a uniquely new system of agriculture was to descend."[54] Victoria Bernal argues that Gaitskell's "biblical references and use of the word *descend* almost lead one to believe that irrigated cotton schemes fell to Sudan from heaven rather than from the drawing board of British colonial officials, engineers, and assorted businessmen."[55]

Many points need to be made here on the significance of the Sudan and the Gezira Scheme for the colonial state and especially the British Empire. One important point is that the scheme did not emerge out of whole cloth. In fact, "the possibility of large-scale cotton cultivation had been realized as early as 1839, and the idea was toyed with throughout the nineteenth century."[56] This idea and the perception of the Sudan as space gained more importance as "the hierarchy of spaces by which the metropolitan center and, gradually, the metropolitan economy are seen as dependent upon an overseas system of territorial control, economic exploitation, and a socio-cultural vision; without these stability and prosperity at home . . . would not be possible."[57]

The colonization of the Sudan could be one of the prime examples in this respect, and the Gezira Scheme was one of the models of the manifestations of the colonial project. Here, the Sudan gained the highest significance to the strategy of the economic benefit and the welfare of the British Empire. As a space, "it formed an important link in the vision of a stretch of red on the map from the Cape [of Good Hope] to Cairo. Most importantly, it was an area which was essential to safeguarding the Suez Canal and the route to India. For these strategic reasons the Sudan had to be controlled by Britain, and was reconquered in 1898."[58] As an extension of British imperial power and its disciplinary methods, the Gezira project "presented an attempt not simply to remake or reform rural Sudanese society, but to *create* a (colonial) Sudanese society: a homogenous society of hardworking and disciplined peasants."[59] Moreover, and in a very different context, in spite of the economic purpose of the scheme, the Gezira Scheme "had a powerful lure for colonials quite apart from what it could produce."[60] It "captured British imaginations, being compared to the Panama Canal (Himsbury 1923) and even to the pyramids, in an article in the *Manchester Guardian* (Ransome 1925). The Gezira Scheme represented the triumph of modern civilization over nature and ignorant tradition, which in practice meant the imposition of colonial order on the Sudanese landscape and society."[61]

That colonial order provided a framework for how a new mode of regulation had to be devised to meet the requirements of Lancashire, the center of the British textile industry, whose effective demand for cotton had brought the Gezira Scheme into being. The fate of the Gezira Scheme was thus tied to the Lancashire textile industry. Here, a system was put into place in which the state, the scheme's administration, and the Sudanese could be placed within a universe centered around Lancaster. Just as the British colonial powers at home and abroad "considered Sudan especially suited for cotton production, they considered the rightful occupation and status of the Sudanese to be those of a peasant, regarding any Sudanese of stature with suspicion."[62] Hence, the colonial state created in al-Gezira a coercive system of administration built on a monopoly of institutionalized violence, which "resulted in one of the most hierarchical agrarian structures imaginable. The official structure of the Gezira Scheme was a rigid bureaucracy, with the tenant at the lowest level."[63] All this was secured under a distinctive system of military domination, which a military man, Arthur Gaitskell, who was described as the father of the "almighty Gezira Scheme," commanded.

The relations between the scheme's management and the tenants were of "absolute despotism." At the same time, "While the colonizers methodically created a subordinate and dependent population of farmers, the colonizers also represented and treated farmers as if they were free agents for certain purposes. Thus, in the official discourse of colonial authorities, tenants were 'partners' of the colonial government and the Sudan Plantations Syndicate."[64] The potential for such a condition to become shrouded in the strange idea of being a partner to the colonial regime reflected "the colonial fantasy that the Sudanese population (and other colonized peoples) as a whole willingly consented to British rule."[65] What was embedded in this partnership was the construction of a white-'arrāqi peasant worker,[66] whose lifeworld was totally colonized by and mortgaged to the scheme by a never-ending system of indentured servitude.

Each individual tenant had to sign the Tenancy Agreement and the Standard Conditions of Tenancy, contracts whose obligations materialized into a system of rollover indebtedness, which both individuals and the community of tenants were obligated to pay back. According to one of the terms of these contracts, "if the Tenant neglects or is careless in the cultivation of his crops the Syndicate shall have the right without the consent of the Tenant to take such steps as the Syndicate may consider proper for the safeguarding of the crops, and any expense incurred thereby shall be a debt from the Tenant to the Syndicate and may without his consent be deducted by the Syndicate from his share of the proceeds of the crops."[67] By contrast, the tenant "shall have no claim against the Syndicate for any compensation on account"[68] of neglectful or careless acts. The "construction of all tenants as a community whose profits and losses are pooled stands in contradiction to the economic individualism the British saw themselves as fostering."[69]

Located at the heart of the center, the scheme and its white-'arrāqi peasant workers were assigned a particular role to pull together and hold the centerpieces of that space, the country's economy, and its people with a cotton thread. Thus, without their consent, or even sharing the minimum of the power and prestige their labor provided their "partners," the people of Gezira were "incorporated into the global system and became consociates as well as contemporaries of the industrial capitalists of Lancashire." Later, for the potential for such a process to work better within the colonial system, "it was neither desirable nor feasible in the long-term that the Anglo-Egyptian administration should control the country solely by military means."[70] Quite to the contrary, "It was necessary to use the existing divisions within Sudanese society so as to tie the economic interests of sympathetic groups to the new, foreign administration, and construct a civil administration on this base."[71] But in practice this model came with inherent problems that constrained this relationship between the peasants and the administration as well as with the entire colonial system.

More than the other white- and blue-collar workers under the colonial system, the new white-'arrāqi peasant workers felt simultaneously alienated from their product and enslaved within the system. Gaitskell himself recorded the peasant's feelings as expressed in one of their sayings:

"The man on the East Bank [of the Blue Nile] is free like a nomad. The man on the West Bank is like a soldier in a camp." He added, "But curiously enough they did not necessarily dislike it."[72] Like other manufactured workers of the colonial state, the white-'arrāqi workers were another group of intimate enemies of the colonial state. The Gezira Scheme forced them to make the colonial state a reality, but they wished to see its system of enslavement gone. Like the white-, khaki-, and blue-collar workers, they discovered as well their organized collective efforts might help them as a group and might offer an added value to the sociopolitical world of practice. Hence, the emergence of these four groups of workers, together with the emergent rural and urban capitalist formations and their leadership, formed and maintained the parameters of the new center as a representation of the country.

The development of the ideology of the center within that system has developed a life of its own and its own hegemonic and counterhegemonic trends. This ideology of the center has shaped the minds of certain individuals and groups of the political society of the community of the state. Within this environment, members and groups of the community of the state, who continued to set themselves up as "moral subjects," have been nurtured and produced. Under these conditions, the state had the potential to deploy and utilize not only "the action of the subject" but also the "action that made the subject" (for example, public education, new types of work, and the system's overall structure). It could also impose all kinds of conditions and rules to create and maintain modes of existence and styles of life. Thus, the state shaped and finally created the center and the margins. The different circuits of exchange—whether political, social, economic, religious, or ideological—coupled with the modes and power of the exercise that created doctrines to maintain images of identities and modify the growth of communities' self-images.

8

The Creation of the Margin

The theme of the margin and of marginalization has an enduring hold on the contemporary Sudanese discourse. As a central concern for different Sudanese political and social groups and individuals, this theme spread like wildfire through scholarship, media, and everyday language. It developed its own proponents and practitioners. No one disagrees as to what the term and the theme mean, except, depending on the way it is articulated, marginalization might represent different actions or reactions loaded with unsettling predispositions. Within this sense, the margin theme and marginalization are dicey and multilayered concepts. To a large extent, marginalization is a shifting phenomenon, linked to a region, a peoplehood, an economic system, a political status, or a placement within a country and its total population.

In the Sudan, the margin theme is applied to the various regions of the country that continue to be marginalized from the main society. Their marginalization developed as a result of practices, zoning, certain policies, and programs that had the potential to contribute negatively to the needs of certain groups of people. Marginalization occurs also as a result of deliberately ignoring or denying some people the opportunity to fully participate in the society to which they belong. Defining and focusing the debate over the southern part of the country, a certain functional imperative arises. At the same time, the discourse of marginalization—its proliferation demands, rights, and entitlements—has expanded to include other areas in western Sudan, the Nuba Mountains, and the Blue Nile, as well as the eastern parts of the country. This represents only the visible forms of marginalization. Other, invisible forms of marginalization include women and the rural poor.

By way of euphemism and other forms of expression, the theme of marginalization—in all its different and uniform constitutive dimensions, such as underdevelopment—was part of the local, regional, and international debate. Now and again, as the Sudan's system of government changed, the different-minded people who formulated the debates and representations of marginalization brought with them other ideational, scholarly, and political platforms. Although this theme was never immune to totalizing discourses and contestations, nothing could be more totalizing than the colonial discourse that meant to organize, instruct, and colonize the country and the lifeworld of some or all of its different groups.

Many factors and inventions have created the Sudan; both in its objective reality, which lies within its geographical configurations, space-time factor, human veracity, and experiences, and in its subjective reality, which lies within its people's and other people's minds. Neither objective nor subjective reality claimed to have created any form of uniformization, except for their humanity and being "genetically continuous groups." However, certain internal and external aspects of power and discipline acted to regulate, control, and colonize the lifeworld of some or all of the Sudanese people. Using the powers of spatial control and discourse, the colonizing states produced maps in order to confine people to certain imaginary geographical zones. However, in the process, some deeper effects took hold. The invention of peoplehood emerged from the system of magnitude that operated and produced zones and margins in line with the colonial states' projects of control and order. The aim—and essence—of that order was to create margins and centers.

In this chapter I will address the creation of the margin and marginalization in order to demonstrate that the outcome of the formal and informal processes, or structural socioeconomic changes, which governed the Sudanese people's conduct, was subject to different colonial polarizing experiences of openness and closure. The dynamic relationship between openness and closure within the colonial system was the production of the regional confinements that the ruling colonial states labeled as the south, the east, and the west in addition to unlabeled invisible forms of marginalization. The structure and the differential chances of visibility and invisibility, together with discourses and the labels attached to each group, correspond, in turn, to what the colonial states made sense of, and attributed meaning to, as location, peoplehood, and representations of the margin and marginalization in relation to the north as the prime illustration of the center's core. At the heart of these labels and discourses lie the different forms of practice that one needs to examine in order to discover how and to what extent the colonizers labeled, characterized, practiced, and created a hegemonic language, exercised power, and how they eventually used up that power.

Identifying the Perspectives and Approaches of Marginality and Marginalization

'Ali Mazrui, a leading African social scientist, has raised the issue of marginality in the Sudan: "distinguished Arabic-speakers of the North, and distinguished southerners, have all been known to exaggerate the ethnic chasm which separates northerners from people of the South."[1] Many would agree with the British scholar Peter Woodward, who explained that this exaggeration "was to raise two very different images of Sudan as an Afro-Arab frontier that were sharply contested in 1968 and later. The first was that of Sudan as an Afro-Arab bridge able to show the way in which these two identities could be linked to each other. The second was Sudan as an example of the inability of these identities to live together in one country."[2]

Mazrui quoted the southern Sudanese politician Agrey Jāden, who asserted that the Sudan "falls sharply into two distinct areas, both in geographical area, ethnic group, and cultural systems. The Northern Sudan is occupied by a hybrid Arab race who are united by their common language, common culture and common religion; they look to the Arab world for their cultural and political inspiration. The people of the Southern Sudan, on the other hand, belong to the African ethnic group of East Africa."[3] Jāden continues his line of thought: "They not only differ from the hybrid Arab race in origin, arrangement and basic systems, but in all conceivable purposes. There is nothing in common between the various sections of the community; nobody of shared beliefs, no identity of interest, no local signs of unity and above all, the Sudan has failed to compose a single community."[4] Mazrui called these different Sudanese images a "dichotomous duality," and he went on to declare, "The Sudan is a paradigm case of an Afro-Arab dual identity."[5]

Currently, many scholars of the Sudan have taken the marginality thesis steps further to take different forms of political compositions and discourses void of the disadvantages that come with marginalization. At the same time, however, the marginality thesis remains foundational for at least four schools of thought that are prevalent in Sudanese scholarship.

First, the Sudanese scholar Francis Deng has led the study of the "dichotomous duality," or conflict of identities, in the Sudan, among Sudanese and Sudanist scholars. Deng has described the fault-finding order that emerges from such a situation: "Soon after my arrival as ambassador of the Sudan in Washington in 1974, a senior official at the state department asked me how, given a choice, I would want my country to be classified for administrative purposes. Should the Sudan be classified as a Middle Eastern or an African country, and within the continent should it be considered part of the Arab Muslim North or of sub-Saharan black Africa?"[6] Deng, who has contributed immensely to the field of Sudanese studies, responded to his interlocutor, "'Whichever category seems most obvious, I suggest that the Sudan be classified in the other.'"[7] In doing so, Deng perceived a Sudanese tendency, supporting the reasons for his choice with the statement, "'In that way, we expand our identity and benefit from both' [the Arab Muslim North and sub-Saharan black Africa]."[8] At the same time, according to the book publisher's remarks, Deng argues that the "north on south" violence is a "conflict of contrasting and seemingly incompatible identities in the Northern and Southern parts of the country. Identity is seen as a function of how people identify themselves and are identified by others in terms of race, ethnicity, culture, language, and religion."[9] Deng does explain, "The historical process that has separated the Arab Muslim North and the African South has its roots in the Arabization and Islamization of the North and in the resistance to those forces in the South."[10] Deng further asserts, "The assimilation processes favored the Arab religion and culture over the African race, religions, and cultures, which remained prevalent in the South."[11]

Another Sudanese scholar, Dustin Wai, expresses the Arab-African dichotomy even more emphatically than Deng: "In essence, it [the civil war] is a conflict of nationalism: one rooted in Africanism and the other in Arabism. It is not a mere case of ethnicity. The Northern Sudanese view themselves as Arabs and whether their Arabness is more by acquisition than heredity is of less importance. Whereas the Southern Sudanese feel themselves to be authentically Negroid Africans in every way."[12] Yet another Sudanese scholar, Malwal Leek, argues that one of the components of the war in the south could be related to an identity crisis: "'One component is that national culture is understood as Islamic and Arabic. This on the other hand has invited a response from those who have different cultural identities which are together described as African.'" Leek adds, "'There are also those who believe that they have acquired another cultural identity through the Christian religion adapted to the African way of life. These groups are resenting the definition of the national identity as Islamic and Arabic. Their resistance is expressed in various ways.'"[13]

Mansour Khalid, a scholar, writer, and politician—who served as a minister of youth, foreign affairs, and education during Ga'far Muhammad Nimeri's dictatorial rule (1969–85) and was a member of the government negotiating team in the Addis Ababa Agreement of 1972 and was a high-ranking northern member of the Sudan People's Liberation Movement (SPLM)—claims that the Sudanese conflict is about national self-identification: "It is a cultural problem which affects all Sudanese, from all regions, and which has disturbed the peace and unity of the Sudan for over 30 years. . . . For 30 years, and for reasons of myopia, ignorance, and unenlightened self-interest on the part of the Sudanese ruling elite, the Sudan's national identity has been obscured and distorted."[14]

Another Sudanese scholar-turned-politician, Sharif Ḥarir, leader and spokesperson of the SLA-Unity faction of the Darfur rebel group, claims, "Sudanese nationalism, in a strict sense, expressed only the riverain viewpoint because of the peculiar historical evolution which made both modern and traditional elites of the Sudan to be dominated by the northern sedentarized and riverain groups of, generally speaking, the northern provinces."[15] Ḥarir continues, "such dichotomized identities are again reduced to two main ones. These are that of Arabs (embedded in *Awlad Arab*) and that of non-Arabs carried sometimes to the extremes of *Zurga* (black) and *'Abid* (slaves)."[16] Further, "These prejudices have major political and economic consequences as they are, also, held by the power elite; for they, in many cases, define what is good for one or what one is supposed to be good at. As such they reflect, in a sense, the share each of these dichotomized identities could have in terms of power and economic well-being."[17]

Ann Lesch takes the identity crisis issue a step further. She argues that there is a "difficulty of achieving a consensus within the Sudan concerning its national identity. From that difficulty flows the problem of structuring a constitutional system that its diverse citizenry would view as legitimate."[18] Lesch explains, "Racial, linguistic, and religious categories have become the basis for crucially important power relationships that have resulted in the peoples who live in the northern and central Nile Valley wielding disproportionate political and economic power."[19] Lesch takes the same stand as other identity-crisis scholars who perceive the conflict in the context of an Afro-Arab dichotomy. She argues, "Those citizens' Arab-Islamic image of the Sudanese nation excludes citizens who reside on the geographic and/or ethnic margins: persons who define themselves as African rather than Arab, ethnically or linguistically." That includes "those who reside in the south[, who] generally adhere to Christianity or traditional African beliefs, whereas the ethnic minorities in the north are largely Muslim."[20] Accordingly, Lesch senses that the "marginalization [of these groups] has intensified as political, economic, and cultural power has remained concentrated in the hands of the Muslim Arab core and as the central government has intensified its drive to spread Islam and Arabic. In reaction, disaffection and revolts by the marginalized peoples have deepened and widened."[21]

'Abdullahi Aḥmed an-Na'im disagrees with the view of an Arab-Muslim and African-Christian dichotomy: "this portrayal vastly understates the complexity of the situation."[22] He adds that "students of religion, anthropology, politics, and related fields agree that there is no such thing as a single coherent Islamic or Arabic identity, much less a single coherent non-Islamic African identity."[23]

The late Moḥammed 'Omer Bashir, another leading Sudanese scholar in this field, argues, "While there is no small degree of diversity of people . . . it is generally accepted that culturally the country is divided into two broad regions: the north and the south. . . . Islam and Arabic have acted as unifying factors and contributed to the homogeneity of the north, whereas the south is a heterogeneous society."[24]

Second, for Norman O'Neill and Jay O'Brien, "the contemporary struggles in Sudan represent a struggle for control over its rich cultural heritage; its rulers counter-posing the glories of empire to mass traditions of resistance to oppression."[25] They further explain that this "battle for control over Sudan's cultural legacy has in many ways mystified both academic analysts and political strategists, who have tended to accept the sectarian religious form of much contemporary political contention and to miss the class interests which lie behind the overtly religious alliances which appear to shape the dominant political parties."[26] According to this school of thought, systems of domination and resistance movements both represent genuine elements of Sudan's complex cultural heritage within its contradicting patterns and historical moments.[27]

Third, another group of Sudanese scholars have contributed to what they call the jallaba hegemony. For this group of scholars, the jallaba—who were initially known as peddlers and mobile and nonmobile merchants—were transformed into a social group that controlled political, social, and economic life and eventually the state in the Sudan since its independence. Chief among this group of scholars is Fatima Babiker Mahmoud, who articulates a theoretical framework in this field in her book *The Sudanese Bourgeoisie: Vanguard of Development?*

In 1994, Dr. John Garang (1945–2005), leader of the Sudan People's Liberation Army (SPLA) and its political wing, the Sudan People's Liberation Movement (SPLM), gave the jallaba theory of hegemony a political dimension in his speech for the SPLA / SPLM national convention. Mansour Khalid tried to attribute the Sudan's problems to this jallaba mentality in his book *Al-nukhba al-sudania wa idman al-fashal* (The Sudanese Elite and the Infatuation with Failure). Later, Peter Nyot Kok reproduced the jallaba theory of hegemony in a wider context. Kok argues that several dynamics have caused "the crisis of governance, prevalence and recrudescence of armed conflict."[28] The first of these forces, according to Kok, is "the unwillingness and inability of the relevant social forces in the Sudan to forge a national democratic consensus on the fundamentals of state- and nation-building." The second is "the striving, by the forces of hegemony, to impose their vision of the state- and nation-building." The third and final dynamic is "the resistance to vision by marginalized people of the Sudan and their general struggle for justice, freedom, and cultural affirmation."[29]

Taisier Moḥamed 'Ali adds yet another dimension to the jallaba theory of hegemony: "For most Sudanese in the south (and growing numbers elsewhere), war and the use of force by the central government underscores northern tenacity to maintain age-old practices of pillage, exploitation and control practiced by Arab '*jellaba*' traders."[30] Building on that, 'Ali judges that the conflict is a result of the economic, political, and sociocultural values of the elite in the north.

Fourth, Douglas H. Johnson maintains, "The Sudan entered the twenty-first century mired in not one, but many civil wars. What had been seen in the 1980s as a war between North and South, Muslim against

Christian, 'Arab' against 'African,' has, after nearly two decades of hostilities, broken the bounds of any North-South conflict. Fighting has spread into theatres outside the southern Sudan and beyond the Sudan's borders."[31] Johnson aims to "examine some of the economic and political patterns which have affected the development and exercise of state power in the Sudan since at least the nineteenth century in an attempt to explain the process and consequences of regional underdevelopment, and the conjunction between perceptions of religion and race specific to this part of Africa."[32]

In their several articles and collaborations, which include *Islamism and Its Enemies in the Horn of Africa* and *The Phoenix State: Civil Society and the Future of Sudan*, Alex De Waal, A. H. Abdel Salam, and M. A. Moḥamed Saliḥ have brought together the historical antecedents and sociopolitical underpinnings of the violence as reflected in southern Sudan, the Nuba Mountains, and Darfur. In particular, Alex De Waal, a fellow of the Harvard Global Equity Initiative and the program director at the Social Science Research Council, has thoroughly investigated the root causes of the violence in Darfur.

These three contributory voices to the discourse on dual marginality represent an example of a long debate about what should be considered one particular people, the Sudanese, in their attempts to understand who they are, and this debate's incompleteness to grasp a coherent conclusion to their development in time and place. In some of its articulations, however, the debate reflects heavy ideological overtones that suggest a peculiar form of Sudanese exceptionalism. This exceptionalism proclaims the existence of different categories of Sudanese, frozen in time and place, and to each of these categories a permanent label is attached. None of these labels—Arab, African, southerner, northerner, westerner, easterner, riparian, zurga, jallaba—is value free. They are all complicated and each contains an inaccurate and questionable meaning. That is, such characterizations of each of these categories are debatable. But, on all levels, the most illusory and excessive aspect of such a debate is that it represents the wide space called the Sudan as consisting of different groups of people separated by firewalls who have populated it from the beginning of time and will continue to populate it until the end of time. For them, the Sudan is fossilized in time and place.

To complicate things more, outsiders have applied most, if not all, of these categories and labels, and, ambiguous as they are, each has serious consequences. One of these serious consequences is that most of these articulations elicit tacit assumptions about "original" underdevelopment. By ignoring the root causes of the development of the margin, these categories and labels either obscure or insinuate an "original" marginalization, which is almost similar to the curse of Ham or the notion of original sin. The idea of the original underdevelopment, whether imbedded in the curse of Ham or not, was well suited to the colonial ideological discourse and its *autoreferential* racism. Autoreferential racism, as explained before, is a type of racism in which the bearers of the prejudice, who exercise physical or symbolic violence, designate themselves as representatives of a superior race. Both the colonial ideological discourse and the kind of racism that was born of it were responsible for the policies and processes that led to the margin's social, political, and communicative construction.

Straddling the Margin

Ultimately the margin in itself is neither a modification of human nature nor a persistent human condition. The margin is not even a caste system into which people are born and in which they die. It is the creation of systematic processes of violence within the civil sphere that produced it.

The origins of the historical condition of marginalization go back to experiences, dating to different times, through which marginalized people internalize a whole host of processes. According to Edward Said, "Both [imperialism and colonialism] are supported and perhaps even impelled by impressive ideological formations that include notions that certain territories and people *require* and beseech domination, as well as forms of knowledge affiliated with domination."[33] Said continues, "the vocabulary of classic nineteenth-century . . . imperial culture is plentiful with words and concepts like 'inferior' or 'subject races,' 'subordinate peoples,' 'dependency,' 'expansion,' and 'authority.'"[34] Moreover, "Out of the imperial experiences, notions about culture were clarified, reinforced, criticized, or rejected."[35] The facts of these experiences and notions, however, entail "certain racist postures as *auto-referential*,"[36] leading to the construction of different imagined communities and districts that could be colonized and opened up to a different system of subjugation that included slavery (during the Turkiyya) or closed down to another form of subjugation (as during the British colonial period).

These two systems were exercised during both the rule of Muḥammad

'Ali (1805–49) and the British colonization of the Sudan (1898–1965). The rule of Muḥammad 'Ali and the British imperial colonization, although different in form and historical condition, both aimed at recuperating and assimilating into their "discourse[s] very old images of 'difference,' [which] is by no means a given state of affairs."[37]

The expression, practice, and extension of imperial power, along with the exercise of these forms of racism, produced what might be absent from Balibar's treatment. That is what I would call the formation of homoreferential racism. This impulse emerges when that particular practice of racism nominates some of those who were subjected to prejudice and colonization to see themselves as different from other groups within their same human milieu. Both colonial experiences were connected with processes by which the state's power "was stimulated by the growing influence of European technology, concepts and commerce, [which] had recently started to explore and to develop the economic and strategic possibilities of the Sudan."[38] There are four broad aspects of Muḥammad 'Ali's imperial colonial system of "open-districts experience" that converted the Sudan into differentiated spheres through an ideology and practice of systematic, though uneven, forms of violence and control.

By invading the Sudan, the first general aspect of that colonial experience endowed Muḥammad 'Ali with one of the largest empires in the history of Egypt—almost half the size of the European continent. Muḥammad 'Ali and his aides came to rule the country as "colonisers, to command obedience, to regulate the affairs of everyone at every level, and claimed a natural right to extract a surplus for the Egyptian treasury."[39] As explained before, Islam, Arabism, sovereignty, and the longstanding neighborly relations between the Sudan and Egypt did not save the country from invasion and colonization. An autoreferential form of racism drew new boundaries and relegated the Sudanese to an inferior status, which made them subject to invasion, colonization, and control. Under this form of racism, the Sudan was not only invaded but its "unknown mysterious parts" were "discovered," conquered, and opened to different forms of repression. Further, the Sudan was subject to "long-term plans of exploitation which went beyond the search for gold and the capture of slaves towards an emphasis on taxation and the export of agricultural and natural products. . . . The Sudanese, on the other hand, saw the Turkish administration and development efforts as instruments of oppression and injustice, and alien to most of their traditional religious, moral and cultural concepts."[40] An oppressive military regime in which "the real rulers were the Turkish central, provincial and district military governors" emphasized and carried out this enforced system of exploitation.[41] Against this background, the Sudan was considered a district, open to different forms of exploitation and an "enclosure" for other forms of oppression.

The second general element was one of the consequences of the open-district policy, which allowed the imperial Egyptian state to turn the southern part of the region into a hunting ground for slaves. The imperial state in Cairo and its auxiliary military system in Khartoum turned slave hunting into a function of the state. As stated earlier, Muḥammad 'Ali built a big war machine out of enslaved Sudanese to consolidate his power and expand his empire. Muḥammad 'Ali, who "had planned a new army, could not get any Turks or slaves from the Ottoman empire which had placed an embargo on the shipment of mercenaries or slaves to Egypt. He thought instead of developing a slave army from the Sudan."[42] Another reason for developing this slave army was that the wāli was not keen on conscripting the fellāheen of Egypt in the first place, "mainly because that would have meant moving productive labor from the agricultural sector which was the main source of revenue."[43]

The Sudanese, who were taken by the tens of thousands to the military training camps in Aswan, were placed under the *dīwān al-jihadiyya* (ministry of war), which was established in 1821. They were trained by "French officers who had served under Napoleon, and who brought with them French military discipline, promotion on merit, and desert drill."[44] These new "black Janissary units" were conditioned to serve as a lifetime fighting force whose barracks were their only homes. The open-district system, the slave hunt, and the creation of a slave army in Egypt constituted one of the biggest collective efforts to create conditions of systematic marginalization to all the areas which that practice of slavery affected.

The northern part of the country, which was open to different forms of exploitation and oppression, was opened for agricultural and commercial activities as well as heavy taxation (*tulba*). In the north people "sold their property to meet the demands for payment in cash."[45] Nevertheless, that part of the country experienced a relative growth in some of the urban centers compared to other marginalized areas in the south. Khartoum, which was established as a capital in 1830, grew faster than other parts as the center. At the same time, the rush for slaves and ivory stripped the southern part of the country of human and natural life. Khartoumers of all races contracted warrior-traders to ravage the entire region. What the Sudanese describe as *al-turkiyya al-sabiqa* (the first Turkiyya), in contrast to *al-turkiyya al-lahiqa* (British colonial rule), subjected each of the Sudan's regions to distinctive forms of violence, oppression, exploitation, and control. That experience planted and maintained different forms of resentment and anger that transcended generalities and generations.

The third general aspect was the open-district experience, which introduced Egyptians to a new and different country and a people that they knew little about. The invasion, colonization, and hegemonic discourse of Muḥammad 'Ali's imperial state provided the legitimating framework for the subjugation of the Sudanese in particular and other people within the empire, including the Egyptians, who were depicted as fellāheen. The stream of false consciousness within certain Egyptian social groups was instilled among the ranks of those who accepted, reasoned, and internalized the imperial discourse. Accordingly, it became inescapable for them not to expand it or liberate themselves as loyal agents of the empire or otherwise. The outcome of that was threefold.

Those who exercised their hegemony forgot that the same imperial regime subjugated them too. As the regime that employed them perceived the Sudan as a piece of a property, which Egypt owned, they accepted the premise of that argument and continued to look at relations between the two countries through that prism. Later the idea of the unity of the Nile Valley was accepted, without noticing the underlying problems that accompanied the imperial ideology behind it. Finally, they became the producers of a discourse that promoted the image of the Sudan as a primitive place and the Sudanese as savages. Hence, the imperial spirit, conquest, and colonization of the Sudan forever changed Egyptians who considered their transfer to governmental jobs in the Sudan as punishment, exile, or both.

Among the many important Egyptian personalities who traveled to and spent time in the Sudan for the purpose of discovery or employment were Muḥammad al-Tunisi, al-Binbashi (Colonel) Salim Qabutan, Rifā'ah Rāfi' aṭ-Ṭahṭāwī, 'Ali Mubarak, and at a later stage, Ibrahim Fawzi. For each of them, the Sudan was a place he had discovered, and each portrayed what he saw in the Sudan in a narrative that later influenced and framed the discourse about the Sudan.[46] The written observations and narratives of the five men, "when viewed together, reveal the interplay between personal experience and memory, popular myths, and the changing constructions of racial identity that occurred in Egyptian society after the official conquest of the Sudan."[47]

Rifā'ah's poem in which he describes his miserable situation in the Sudan represents a prime example of this discourse. It presents the Sudan as a "chain of references that produces the effect of the place."[48] He starts by saying that the Sudan is neither a place to his liking nor are its women his type. Later, he expresses his disgust with everything Sudanese. This includes not only disgust with their way of life but also some of the natural phenomena such as the *haboob*, or devil wind (*harmattan*). He then turns graphically racist when he says, *wa nisf al-qoum aktharhum whoush wa b 'ad al quom ashbah bi al-jamad*, meaning that the majority of the population are wild animals and some of the population is similar to stone. He continues: *wa lwola al-bāḍ min 'Arbin likano swadan fi sawadin fi sawadi*, meaning had not some Arabs been (among them) they could have been black in black in black.

As Powell explains, speaking of the above writers, except for Ibrahim Fawzi, "race is an important marker of difference for all four writers, who painstakingly noted racial differences in skin color, sexual behavior, and religious attitudes among the Sudanese."[49] Sometimes these writers were similar to other orientalist writers, who represent the place "as a set of references, a congeries of characteristics, that seems to have its origin in a quotation, or a fragment of a text, or a citation from someone's work on the Orient, or some bit of previous imagining, or an amalgam of all these."[50] As Powell contends, Egyptian orientalists "seem to have plucked these concepts from medieval literature about blacks and Sudanese, but more often they mixed stereotypes about blacks with new terminology about power and concepts of civilization translated from European texts."[51]

This discourse and its embedded autoreferential racism, as a reproduction of the imperial character, have been manifestly important in influencing the ideology of Egyptian nationalism. The discourse further made possible the distinction between the Sudanese and the Egyptians, which old media (verbal and print press) aroused early on, and new media (film at a later stage) continued to nurture.

Finally, the fourth general aspect were the consequences of Muḥammad 'Ali's conquest of opening the Sudanese space, followed by Salim Qubatan's expeditions far south, along the White Nile, to what Europeans considered a "discovery" of the unknown world. "Salim's expeditions had discovered therefore, not the sources of the Nile, but a route which seemed to open up vast possibilities."[52] Salim's unrelenting course of that exploratory journey to the "heart of darkness" turned the Nile into "a highway into tropical Africa."[53] The translation of Salim's journal into European languages and the details about that expedition, which Thibaut, d'Arnaud, and Werne narrated, all three of whom accompanied Salim through the "jungle," drew Europeans' attention to the fact that "the outside world suddenly discovered a navigable waterway stretching far into the unknown interior. During the following decades the southern Sudan by virtue of this discovery occupied a position of primary importance in the exploration and colonization of tropical Africa."[54]

The newly opened water route soon became the primary route for missionaries, merchants, and the devastation of the region by slave and ivory traders. Europeans and their agents' warrior-traders were able to break the Khartoum government over the monopoly of the ivory trade and to compete effectively with the Arab traders of Zanzibar. The new water route opened a new way for Christian and Islamic influences. Such an influence could be found among communities like "the Feroge, for example, [who] became Muslims. Some of the Southern chiefs adopted Arabic dress, names and customs and a pidgin form of Arabic began to spread."[55] According to Richard Gray, "It was rumored that a Protestant Bishop was intending to send missionaries to this virgin field, and since there was an obvious possibility that Islam might quickly spread over the area Pope Gregory XVI created the Vicariate Apostolic of Central Africa in 1846 and propaganda sent out a small reconnaissance party."[56] The missionaries found in the new waterway "a door through which they could reach the Christian Kingdom of Ethiopia where they planned to capture the Coptic Church."[57]

At the same time, the Sudanese resistance movement against the empire and its oppressive regime in Khartoum, which had started to gather momentum, brought together the Sudanese from northern and southern parts of the country. The Mahdist revolution had unified Sudanese in the northern and southern parts of the country and elsewhere (see chapter 6), far beyond the previous formations of resistance under al-Zubair's trading, farming, and bazinger enterprise, or any form of resistance since 1821. This was a new phenomenon. For the first time, a nationalist movement mobilized Sudanese groups and individuals across the social, regional, and religious spectrum and brought together all regions of marginalized Sudan for the social and political liberation of the country and maybe the entire Nile Valley.

Under Karam Allah Kurqusāwi, the Mahdist amir of Baḥr al-Ghazāl, the Dinka, the Nuer, the Shulluk, the jallaba, and the bazinger were mobilized as one united front that "transformed the Mahdiyya from a religious into a national political uprising that raged throughout the country."[58] The Mahdist revolution itself was a double transformation in the mode of operation in the Sudanese quest for independence, which was driven by a deeper feeling of nationalism and patriotism as an ideology.

On the one hand, for the first time there was the consolidation of all different fighting forces in the Sudan into one powerful army. Gradually, most of the bazinger, their commanders, and other private armies, including al-Zubair's forces, particularly those who did not follow Rabiḥ Fadlallah, joined the Mahdist revolution, forming the leadership and the main body of the *jihadiyya* army in particular and other parts of the Mahdist war machine. The seizure of power in the southern part of the country by Kurkusāwi and his associates from the south finally demolished the zariba forever, introduced a new form of repair to the social sphere, and paved the way for the revolution's success.

On the other hand, there was a never-ending feeling of discontent among the ranks of Sudanese that had continued to express itself since the early days of the invasion. That discontent united the Sudanese and demolished the political and military "enclosure," which a brutal regime had created, making remarkable successes in defeating that system, militarily and ideologically. Thus, the Sudanese revolution, in all its constitutions, went a step outside the role structures of the religiopolitical association and its expressed orientation. It was an imminent multidirectional development in the country, embodied not only in a singular social change but also in accomplishing one particular task.

Omdurman, the newly built capital and the seat of the Mahdist state, witnessed different forms of representation, which wad Sa'd described as *al-jira al-'ammana khiera* (the neighborhood in which we all relished its virtuous wealth). Wad Sa'd provided another model of reference, which the society began to favor and which attested to a kind of progress in the repair of the social sphere. Joseph Ohrwalder described al-Khalifa 'Abdullahi's forms of state entertainment as performed in the mosque: "Sometimes just before midnight he [the khalifa] will again enter the mosque, and will summon the poets to sing his praises. He delights in music, and keeps a number of Dar Fertit and Niam Niam singers, who accompany themselves on the rubaba (a sort of native guitar), and their strange and weird melodies delight the Khalifa's soul."[59] That type of music that delighted the khalifa and annoyed Ohrwalder had an appeal among the population of Omdurman: "These native musicians have a sort of school of music, in which they practise all day; but they never seem to learn anything new."[60] Rather than the musicians, it was Ohrwalder who never seems to have learned anything new. But there were even more generative continuities than what he saw that were not associated with the regime's policies. That indicated that Omdurman was a new and diverse social space, representing broad groups of people from different parts of the country who were coming together through the exercise of different forms of socialization.

Moreover, what could be significant here was the anti-imperial program of nationalism within the different parts of the Nile Valley from one side and the Niger Nile on the other—the link between the central and Nilotic Sudan—and the degree of transformation that came with it in both the Sudan and Egypt. The rise of a particular revolutionary fervor in both Egypt and the Sudan has to be seen as an outcome of a whole host of conditions. These conditions are related to the nature of Cairo of the khedive's system of governance, which provoked an acceleration of a scheme of calamities. These conditions influenced all forms of discontent and accelerated the pace of different types of internal and external reactions. At the same time, this revolutionary fervor did not mediate elements within each region independently; it mediated between revolutionary elements within the entire Nile Valley.

Although Britain crushed the rebellion that Aḥmed 'Urabi led from 1879 until 1882, which had initiated the Egyptian revolutionary action, the revolutionary impulse stayed alive and continued to permeate the Egyptian private sphere. Simultaneously, the Sudanese revolution (1881–85), which Muḥammad Aḥmed al-Mahdi commanded, advanced successfully toward Khartoum. During this time, the Egyptian revolutionaries communicated with the Sudanese, encouraging the Sudanese to continue their advance toward Egypt and promising to support them. Both movements had distinct internal and external bearings on the fate and a new form of direct action, by different systems of inter- and intra-social repair not only within each country, but also within the Nile Valley and the Niger Valley at large. The most important aspect of this development was that all the revolutionary groups in the region started to get closer to each other.

The Mahdist revolution acted as a magnet that attracted them all together. The anticolonial, or revolutionary, nationalists, in colonized Egypt looked forward to the Mahdist revolution, which liberated the Sudan to continue its anticolonial march north and liberate Egypt as well. West African revolutionaries, such as Mohamed al-Dadari and his Fulani followers, already joined the long Mahdist march as early as 1882. Simultaneously, Ḥayatu bin Sāid, the great-grandson of 'Uthman Dan Fadio, became a significant supporter of the Mahdist revolution in West Africa. Ḥayatu, al-Dadari, and Muḥammad Aḥmed al-Mahdi exchanged some correspondence, and later Ḥayatu, whom al-Mahdi appointed as his agent (*'āmil*) for western Sudan, fought with Rabiḥ Fadlallah under the banner of al-Mahdi in West Africa. Again, and in a similar fashion as in Egypt, the British encroachment checked the revolutionary activities in West Africa, especially in Nigeria, where the colonialists were most concerned about a Mahdist revival.

But the Mahdiyya victory should be considered an event that led to dire consequences. The self-motivating attitudes of other actors in the region, who joined or encouraged the Mahdist movement, created the conditions that united tormented Britain (the colonizer) with terror-stricken official Cairo. This unity allowed the two forces to work together to counter the revolution, recolonize the Sudan, and mutilate the revolutionary body that brought the Nile and Niger together. Hence, the colonial movement's success was not only a defeat to the Mahdist state; by checking the expansion of an emerging civil space, it also delivered a powerful blow to the social movement that brought the Sudanese together, the Nile Valley closer, and brought the Niger-Nile space into a new condition, discourse, social and jihadist solidarity, and sociopolitical life for the first time. Only by understanding the depth and breadth of this colonial moment and the progression of its regime can one begin to understand the basis of how the margin was recreated and maintained through the closed and open districts and disciplinary practices of the new colonial system.

The British Open- and Closed-District Policies and Practice

Britain and Egypt's recolonization of the Sudan, as well as the creation of the condominium, with its peculiar nature, as already explained, gave rise to a differentiation within the newly created British mini-imperial system. The newly created system did not return the Nile Valley to Egyptian control; rather, it put almost the entire valley under Britain's control. In addition, it came with profound problems, affecting all three countries: Britain, Egypt, and the Sudan.

Specifically, the British imperial system of rule in the Sudan, among other things, created a distinctively new colonial model, which was forcibly placed to control land, vital waterways, and map space. At this point, Britain, which had acquired the Nile Valley and access to land and sea, became the core state. Egypt, which was supposed to be codominus, but which Britain had colonized, was connected to that system as part of the British imperial system's semiperiphery.

The Sudan was a designated periphery zone, with an inferior status. Within that periphery, certain areas, primarily the southern part of the country, which Lord Cromer described as "consisting of 'large tracts of useless territory' with no value 'for the official mind of British Imperialism . . . ' to which it would be 'difficult and costly to administer properly,'"[61] were assigned an even more inferior status: the periphery of the periphery. Hence, the creation of such difference, inherent in the colonial pathology, manifested and intensified itself in policies that joined the autoreferential racism together with selective forms of affinity, which created a complex situation that could be described as a complex system of control, exploitation, and creation of peoplehoods.

First, both the Egyptian and British imperial autoreferential forms of racism, as the condominium authorities expressed them, drew new boundaries and assigned the southern part of the Sudan a more inferior status, making it subject to control through a planned and well-guarded system of closure through neglect. For the colonial state, that part of the country was a space where "at least three million people, primitive, unclothed, pagan, and tremendously virile, keep very much to themselves. And virility is the keynote. A man cannot hold his place if he is weak; and the women live, not in the out-of-date seclusion of Sudanic Islam, but in pristine open vigour."[62] J. S. R. Duncan argued, "the British attitudes toward the south were permeated with a racist view of their mission in the southern Sudan."[63] As a representation of that form of racism, Duncan quoted a British administrator who stated that "the task in the north was simple compared with that in the south. The northern Sudanese at least knew what administration was, and they were civilized in some degree. The primitive southerners . . . were quite untamed, and a handful of British officers, with a few soldiers, went off into the unknown to gain the confidence of such people as they might meet."[64] As for the colonial-state enterprise, which was based on an economy of domination and subjugation, the southern part of the country was "too far from Sudanese or Egyptian ports and lacked adequate transport to make colonial economic exploitation profitable."As for the state, the southern part of the country "assumed greater importance mainly because through it flows the White Nile. It was then realised that the Nile constituted the only highway from the North into East Africa. Secondly, it was evident that the waters of the White Nile were of great importance to Egypt. The later future development would depend on the supply of water." Hence, controlling that space was of great consequence in controlling Egypt.[65]

Second, the open system of control in the north was different from that in the south. The open system of control was organized through the creation of white- and blue-collar, and white-'arrāqi state-manufactured workers as a mode of production to service the state's means of production and services that included the state itself, its transportation and communication systems, and the Gezira Scheme. Hence, the colonial state gained wealth not only by having a monopoly on the productive forces, but also by controlling the country through the application of this type of labor to the country's human and natural resources. On the other hand, the closed system of control, which was created before the 1929 Closed Districts Act, was based on closing the southern part of the country to all forms of economic, political, educational, or social activity in or with other parts of the country or even the world. Furthermore, as the resources of the north were extracted to benefit the colonial system's core state first and provide subsistence to its satellite state at Khartoum—the center—the margin was left to deal with progressive forms of marginalization and underdevelopment. Both cases, as different as they might appear, represent the main source of marginalization and underdevelopment, or the creation of the margin, which the very same processes that generated the economic wealth of the colonial core state and that its capitalist system generated and sustained.

This system of control demanded the simultaneous incorporation of other institutions such as the colonized church, colonized anthropology, and the colonial state to put this system of closure into effect as an incident of state power. The south, Darfur, and the Nuba Mountains, together with other parts of the country, were not that easy to control (see chapter 3). In the face of different violent forms of resistance, the colonial state followed different cost-effective means of control. One of these means was to transform the social system into primordial communities. That is, to pursue a "civilizing mission" in reverse, within which a system of control is devised to turn "tribalism, once seen as the focal point of native resistance" to "now be looked upon as an efficient mode of native control"[66]—a system of colonizing the lifeworld of the population from the outside through what Mamdani describes as decentralized despotism. Within this process of control, "many anthropological studies by Evans-Pritchard and others of the London School of Oriental and African Studies during the '20s and '30s were conducted to spy on and help the British administration to control the native population of the south."[67] This remains true for colonial anthropology in its relationship to state power as well as other forms of colonial knowledge.

The colonial state, as Nicholas B. Dirks maintains, "is seen as a theater for state experimentation, where historiography, documentation, certification, and representation were all state modalities that transformed knowledge into power."[68] This might go some way to explain the complicated relationship between the colonial state and the church.

At the beginning of colonial rule some British administrators opposed missionary work for the protection of the primordial communities. Colonel Jackson, who acted for the governor general during his absence, wrote to Lord Cromer in 1900 that, "a black when converted becomes a scamp, loafer, scoundrel and liar whereas they are now happy, contented, honest and vice unknown . . . from the time missionaries enter their country these tribes will disappear."[69] The Sudan "had been nominally included in the Anglican diocese of Jerusalem since 1899. However, Bishop Blyth of Jerusalem was warned not to ' . . . exercise active episcopal functions in that country.'"[70] The archbishop of Canterbury criticized the Sudan's government policy, accusing "the Sudan administration of infringement on principles of religious liberty and acting contrary to policies of 'a country guided by Christian principles.'"[71] The missionary society also reacted strongly against the Sudanese government's policy: "Christianity had been the religion of the people in the Sudan for centuries and the reconquest provided the chance for its replanting in a region which originally belonged to it."[72] But Wingate did not surrender to these pressures until he "was certain of his own authority over church affairs." The colonized church, like the colonized mosque, under Wingate was one of the departments of the state.

When Wingate put his efforts toward the construction of Khartoum Cathedral, he claimed that it would "'more than anything else, prove to the Oriental mind the permanent nature of our occupation.'" From one side Wingate noticed that "the whole of Baḥr al-Ghazāl was threatened by Islamic influence," and that there are "hundreds of Moslems each of whom by the very nature of his religion appeals to the blacks very much more than the Christian religion can." Wingate thought that "if therefore, we are to succeed in Christianizing these Southern tribes, it can only be done by very much greater missionary activity than exist at present and I can perfectly encourage and facilitate such missionary work."[73]

Moreover, the colonial state organized and supervised the activities of the entire church and divided the areas south of the tenth parallel into three zones: the Austrian mission, the American Presbyterians, and the Church Missionary Society (CMS). As long as the state would colonize the church, and both church and state were keen to "insulate the non-Muslim areas of the Sudan from the political stirring in the north," the state was willing to allow the church to take part in the education of the country's southern regions. Thus, "the government refrained from opening schools, even in cases where there was a genuine demand for education, on the grounds of lack of finance and fear of Islam."[74]

Hence, what stands out is that, without any exception, church education in southern Sudan, in its poor quality and isolation from the country's main educational system, served to increase the marginalization of that part of the country. Moreover, while the public education system in the northern part of the country was employment oriented, the educational system in the south was oriented toward "the spread of Christianity and the prevention of the southward spread of Islam." These two different stances became the bases of the transformation in the fields of power and in the growth of conditions that influenced conditions of cultural and political production and different nationalist impulses, especially among the older generations. All this is to say that the creation of the margin was a complex process that grew, increased, and was maintained with the invention of certain mechanisms that the state created and nurtured.

Conclusion

"Hurrah Mahdism finished," cabled a jubilant Francis Reginald Wingate to his wife on November 24, 1899. However, Wingate lived in the Sudan as one of the long-reigning rulers of the country for long enough to discover that was merely wishful thinking. Kitchener, Wingate, and their army could justifiably say that they successfully defeated the Mahdist army that day at what was considered by them the final battle of Omdurman on September 2. That day also marked the first day of the displacement of a Sudanese independent imperial state by a different, peculiar, alien one. However, the cracks in the structure of that British imperial state and its system were opened through the persistent Sudanese resistance to that state design and its order. The cracks were not wide enough for the colonial regime to crumble, but nevertheless they opened the way for the Khatmiyya and Mahdism, in their new guises, together with other Sudanese resistance groups that were hostile to the new environment and its oppressive regime to emerge while undergoing different forms of transformation.

The new construction of neo-Mahdism and neo-Khatmiyya began by way of adhering to faith-based practices of community. Gradually, however, the spirit of that community and the ṭarīqa invested in the work ethic of each group was behind the emergence of a rural agricultural form of capitalism around Sayyid 'Abdel Raḥman al-Mahdi and a merchant form of capitalism around Sayyid 'Ali al-Mirghani. This emergence gave rise to a number of opposing regimes of meaning, practice, and incongruent elements of power relations within the Sudanese sociopolitical sphere. Each of these developments was oriented and identified by its own discourse.

While the state used its hegemonic and military power and structural violence to write down the basic principles of creating a center and marginalized zones, the emerging Sudanese entities and their communities of conversation continued to utilize and mobilize their resources and frame their discourses to meet the challenge of the age. Hence, the colonial period not only embodied but also produced—in its comprehensive form of life—ideology and experience, not only to counter but also to restrain these opposing regimes. The colonial experience here takes the period from 1898 to 1956 as an epoch and the state as a structure, and they both continue to reproduce their discontents and their system of opposition to each other as colonization, which is, in its very essence, "a 'reinvention of difference' and not an act of cultural uniformity."[1]

Hence, the reinvention of difference remains one of the main functions of the colonial state and its system of categorization of open and closed districts, its inherent stimulus to totalitarianism, and its reliance on violence as a mode of operation.

The reinvention of difference, which had the force of state hegemonic power and its tools of mass destruction, imposed unprecedented transactions of control, discipline, exploitation, and coercive restrictions. The initial framework in which all that was happening enforced, through the state's centralized power, a regulatory system based on the creation of peoplehoods, and an uneven distribution system of division of labor, rewards, and a residue of the aftereffects of regulatory systems of a previous colonial experience during the Turkiyya (1821–85). The resultant developments that have come out of that experience continued to have very specific consequences for the entire population. The colonial state had the capacity to create different and unequal groups of "peoples." Its different attempts to control them separately included the following: first, by causing new groups to coalesce—such as white-, khaki-, blue-collar, and white-'arrāqi workers—through the creation of new types of work and workers whose lifeworld was colonized by the state; second, by pushing other groups of the population en masse to the fringes of progressive underdevelopment. Both strategies remain within the colonial state's pattern of promotions "associated with the axial division of labour."[2] In the historical-cultural formation of both the center and the margin, the colonial racial reading of closeness and distance between inhabitants of the Sudanese space was perceived within a differentialist racism and a discourse that categorizes people as different, even though they can easily be seen as "genetically continuous groups." Within all that, and according to that situation, a system of identity engineering—which a whole host of hegemonic and counterhegemonic discourses, entitlements, and exercises of power governed—would shape the transformation of these groups into a single nation or their segregation into different entities. The ranking of some parts and the classification of groups of that human space was essentialized by bundling together and labeling marginalized groups within an internal foil of identities as a structural condition; not only for the construction of difference, but also for tagging all these groups as primitive, heathen, and nondeveloped. These, together with other tags, such as Arabs, Muslims, and fanatics, all come with their ideological stigmas and racist bearings. On the one hand, the closure or opening of each part of the country within different spatial orders and regulatory practices for controlling both parts of the country together with the human groups that dwell in them were responsible for the creation of both the center and the margin. On the other hand, the expressions, the practices, and the extension of both imperial powers, along with the exercise of their forms of racism, were responsible for forming a homoreferential impulse. This impulse emerged when some of those who were subjected to prejudice and colonization were nominated by their oppressors, who caused them to see themselves as different from some groups who were within their same human milieu.

Viewed from the standpoint of the growth of the colonial state and its multidimensional formation, each of these constructions has continued to evolve with a life of its own, contained within one local differentiated system. This system was controlled from the constructed center, which interacted with the operations of the colonial state.

But the colonial state, since its first day and through time, took shape and had been struggling so hard against hostile groups resisting its order and intimate enemies that it produced and nurtured. Within the developments of each of these entities the growth and concentration of accord, cooperation, and conflict between each was accompanied by the production of the means of social, cultural, economic, and political discourses that typified the Sudanese experience.

The collective strategies, the advantage each of these emerging entities gained and how they were able to cultivate power as proprietors of social, economic, and cultural capital, and how they were able to bring that to the social space, made it possible for the Sudanese people to say in 1956 to the British community of the state:

> *ya ghareeb baladk. yalla lai baladk. lamlim 'idadc wa soug māak wladak.*[3]
> O stranger, go home. Go to your home. Collect your household and take your son with you.

And willy-nilly, the British did so. But they generously left behind their household, the state, and their adopted children of the state, who became its surrogate mother.

However, in entering the new Sudanese social world, the colonizing process in its center point—that is, the state—emerged as a centralized violent governing entity with a total monopoly on all the means of physical and symbolic violence and a brand of authority by which the conduct of the population is governed, disciplined, and coerced. Through this governing system, the state continued to be the "major manufacturer of inequality," racial engineering, and social stratification on a grandiose scale.

Five major developments in the structures emerged or transformed under the colonial state. These developments continued to breed as conveyers of violence in the cross-generational transfer of affairs and regime productions as they also continued to constitute the performance of the national state and its social order. First, with the introduction of mass public education, the new forms of division of labor, and to a certain extent church-based education, throughout the colonial state's lifetime and after, new forms of labor with different titles emerged. These new forms of labor, with their close relationship to the state, produced the state's organic and nonorganic intellectuals as well as a new sense of citizenship and characteristics of other, different political formations and demands. These developments combined and divided five different communities of conversations, discourses, and ambitions to hold the state together. The first includes regular and civil service personnel (white-collar workers). The second group includes members of trade union organizations (blue-collar workers). The third group (khaki-collar workers) includes the military as well as regular forces. The fourth group refers to the private khaki-collar workers, who include the Christian guerrilla forces and insurgency organizers and leadership in the south. In addition, the colonial distribution of labor brought a fifth and new peasant community of (white-'arrāqi workers).

Second, and at the same time, the state continued to maintain itself as an economic enterprise. That enterprise included not only a hegemonic system of domination and exploitation but also the capacity to organize all aspects and forms of labor and to reproduce as well all of a dominant ideology's constitutions. This self-sustaining, hegemonic enterprise bestowed upon the state a powerful social status, prestigious entitlements of control ambition, and, most notably, the power to recognize and reward some while denying others, according to their real or visible distance from the state. At the same time, the state continued to govern by exercising all the same tools, which induced feelings of trepidation in some and gave others reason for repulsion with the state government. In all that, the production of the social character and the creation of that state—as an objective and objectified entity with all the attributes and dynamics of a dominant and all-embracing power—placed it as a distinct sociopolitical and economic field. Thus, the state emerged and continued to cast itself as a fetish or a new deity, with its own worshippers, priests, and prophets, who identified themselves as such, especially within the community of the state. Within its historical growth, the colonial community of the state represented the genetic mother that constructed, produced, and nurtured it. Gradually, members of the Sudanese community of the state inherited that state as its surrogate mother. These arrangements, within their permanence and the solidarity of the sociopolitical relationships, emerged and persisted within the state's growth and fields of power. Moreover, power groups have continued to reproduce different approaches for how to control the state and direct its power either to serve the interest of this, that, or the other group or to incapacitate the life experience of a competing or ruling entity. Each of these approaches worked through specific programs and different institutions, such as the political party, the trade union, and both the national and the private army, to either control the state from within or to influence its scheme of action from without.

Third, with the state's growth and the subsequent proliferation of its institutions during the colonial period, parallel forms of urban and rural capitalistic enterprises grew outside the state's sphere of action. One by one, these enterprises grew and embodied a capacity of organizations within the social sphere, which continued to influence and nurture the foundation of a good number of distinctive formations and contingent social, economic, and political attributions and representations. Each of the emerging rural and urban capitalist formations—through accepted wisdom and experimentation—created around itself a self-regulating political institution. Each of these political institutions embodied, in structure, a duality of representations: the Ansār and their Umma Party, and the Khatmiyya and its Unionist Party.

The rebirth of the Ansār resulted, in the first place, from the transformation of the neo-Mahdist fields of power. In the second place, the Ansār was reborn as an enduring religiopolitical group, which restored the image of the Mahdiyya and its social-capital-in-circulation. Thus, it brought together social groups within the Umma Party as a political entity with an ideology that the relationship of these groups to that social-capital-in-circulation inspired.

The neo-Khatmiyya and its rebirth in the Sudanese social sphere provided another model of reference and aversion to the colonial order. This aversion is best exemplified in the example of Sayyid 'Ali al-Mirghani, who persistently and patiently succeeded, not only to counter the colonial policy toward Sufi Islam, but also to restore the state's recognition of al-Khatmiyya ṭarīqa as a legitimate socioreligious practice that openly recruited and converted followers. This development provided the Sudanese social sphere with a narrow window of opportunity to repair and restore itself as other ṭuruq proliferated in the open within each one's appropriate field of power and civil space.

Simultaneously, the structural change that came with public education brought with it political organizations that included Islamists, Communists, other types of leftists, and pan-Arabists in the northern part of the country, while church education produced most of the southern political elite. Each of these political groups and organizations committed itself to certain exclusivist ideologies that followed or propositioned a doctrinaire order for the state, modernity, and society. Further, each group entertained self-assurances that only their group represented a self-contained model of political representation. By virtue of their upbringing, these different political schools and their representations among the community of the state developed a self-image that claimed that, although they might be a minority in terms of numbers, they were a majority in terms of status. Hence, they either openly rejected or discreetly undermined the rules and the results of the democratic game. As long as the democratic game put down the Umma Party or their other "sectarian" rivals, the Unionist Party would maintain an advantageous position.

Fourth, the primary opposition between the different ideological schools and their varied political affiliations reflected a self-image and underlaid, to a certain degree, a lifestyle and selective affinities that grounded each of those ideological schools and the political affiliations they each produced. This primary opposition reflected its secondary opposition within the political discourse as well as rivalry and antagonism that reflects a degree of status-inconsistency. At the same time, within the minority political representational discourses, neither the Islamists nor the leftists saw themselves in that way. These representational discourses embodied, from one side, a reductionist impulse as they describe the majority parties and their selective affinities as *taqlidi* (traditional), *ṭaifi* (sectarian), *rajii* (reactionary), or *muhafiz* (conservative). They all share the view that these parties and the social groups that support them were part of an old, static order that was inimical to social and political progress and that had to go. At the same time, the attitude of these minority groups toward each other was less benign than one might imagine. The modes of reductionism in which these parties were interlocked have paved the way for a remorseless and never-ending war of attrition between the Islamists (with all of their different feathers), the Communists, and the regional leftists. The main political parties and their religious and social associations in their totalizing discourses perceived these minority parties as *tanzimat 'aqa idiyya* (ideological organizations) either born out of alien *musturada* (exported ideologies) or as a product of the rejection of the mainstream associations. In retrospect, we have seen, within the last five decades, both sides living in a "state of suspended extinction." That is, each side has been turned, by the other, into an object that should be eliminated through the state apparatus of coercion or through private violence. Both state and private violence grew stronger over time, especially during military rule, when the ruling elite and their rivals continually resorted to different sorts of armed violence. Moreover, these modes of reductionism and the mutual hostilities have generated the most enduring and consequential political and cultural wars, with aims of not only humiliating the Other, but also of eliminating them completely, whenever possible. Within such an environment, public debate becomes unconducive to reason and civility. All too often, a military coup, which progresses into a dictatorial rule, has silenced public debate and, with it, has stifled any possibility for reason or civility. It is not surprising, therefore, that this state of affairs continued to enlist military aid to resolve political conflicts. This process of coercing opponents through military rule forced most, if not all, political organizations to take turns in acting as clandestine organizations, receiving harsh treatment from different regimes. And through either coup or violence, each group transformed its "othering" impulses and past negative feelings or hostilities into an organized form of subjugation of the dreaded Other. Behind every military coup in the Sudan—successful or abortive—has been a civilian political party or a group of conspirators. All the while, groups of civilian as well as military collaborators took part in every military regime. Hence, the self-fulfilling prophecy about the Islamists as *jihaz fashisti* (a fascist apparatus) as their Communist enemies used to describe them, has become both the living example and the enduring legacy of their rule during their republic, especially between 1989 and 1999. But the experience of the Islamist with power stands as one of the most violent experiences in the history of the country. It engendered disastrous situations to the country as a whole and to them as a political entity. Within these situations, the social world of Islamism, its moral value, and the knowledge at its disposal has completely eroded and sunk into oblivion as its practitioners wrestled with its ambiguities, fought helplessly with other power groups, combatted fiercely with the state, and clashed ferociously among themselves as they turned Islam into a billboard for their violence.

Fifth, and finally, was the development that resulted from both the violent and the nonviolent actions of those peoples who found themselves marginalized. Although the contingency of marginalization is also evident in all its variations, in addition to marginalized regions, invisible marginalized groups also include the rural and urban poor, women, and followers of oppositional ideologies. But the rise of resentment and different forms of expression of grievances in the periphery—which the centralized state has never fully understood and has continued to portray as a rebellion that needed to be dealt with firmly—turned violence into a main topic of conversation. Attempts at enforcing compulsion—as a way of adding sufficient devotion to the higher national ideals of unity and conformity—as well as the presentation of the state—as a grand form of disciplinary actions, including military power—ensured the state's continued existence and demonstrated its overarching power. Operations of counterviolent expressions, by those who felt excluded or marginalized, have become the preferred modus operandi to ensure recognition. The collective attributes of that form of exercise of state power and the counterpower over that state has drained human and material resources, and they became an added value to progressive forms of the development of underdevelopment. But this phenomenon involved a causal relationship between the state's reactions to the violent and nonviolent dissension and demands of the emerging geographies of marginalization and the poverty-enhanced ruralization of urban centers. Rural dislocated poor, who fled marginalization and its discontents of war, famine, and poverty, left behind a disrupted way of life and tried to find protection in urban areas in which resources were continuously exhausted and are now incredibly scarce. The same process that created ruralization underpinned the urban centers as oppressive regimes that drove away workers, professionals, and artisans by the thousands, encouraging them, instead, to seek employment in oil-rich Arab countries in particular and other countries in general.

All this is to say that for all the development of this complex situation and for a considerable period of time the Sudanese civil society has been deferred. But the question remains, until when? The Sudanese can only succeed if they can see now, in this unhappy hour, that their long and complex experiences of failure and success do point to matters of considerable weight. These things can also enable them to draw upon a deep repertoire to make sense of a history of experiences, values, and complex inheritances. All this has yielded a variety of responses that shaped their lifeworld and endeavored to constrain their social sphere. These have been combined with violent actions and reactions, which the state, along with the enterprises the Sudanese involved themselves in, caused either to further certain agendas or to use the state's military and other coercive power to subjugate each other. Yet they can see past the thin line separating things; they have the potential to reconstruct a civil society. They can "see emerging from the outer shadows of these 'zones of waiting' unprecedented"[4] social life within which they can create a space where active and peaceful engagement is vital over the long term. The Sudanese could achieve this by building up their inner resources to construct their state within their all-encompassing self-definition.

Epilogue

A Missed Opportunity

A referendum took place in the southern part of the Sudan from January 9 to 15, 2011, on the future status of the southern region whether to remain part of a united Sudan or secede as a separate country. The referendum was one of the consequences of the 2005 Naivasha or Comprehensive Peace Agreement (CPA) between the Islamist ruling National Congress Party (NCP) and the Sudan People's Liberation Movement/Army (SPLM/A). The agreement called for a six-year interim period, during which the NCP and SPLM would share control of a government of national unity and work together to make unity for the southern Sudanese an attractive option. On February 7, 2011, the final result of the referendum was published with 98.83 percent voting in favor of independence despite centuries of coexistence within the same country.

The magnitude of perils of fragmentation facing the entire country and the opportunity to be liberated from the clutches of the old Sudan and its inherited state were both viable. However, like all events of scale, a historic moment had made itself available for the Sudanese people to grasp and rebuild a new nation and a state. Had the Naivasha agreement been taken as the starting point for reconstructing a new Sudan where civil society could be revitalized and the state rebuilt by changing the environment of public discourse to accommodate and adapt to the inner resources, the historical resentments, and the self-definition of a new Sudan, these and other conditions could have produced a new social contract out of the collective aspiration of the Sudanese people for a good society. This could have also provided for the needed and meaningful subversion of the vicious circles of totalitarian rule and paved the way for the reconstruction of a new state built on citizenry, justice, de-marginalization, inclusive social and political life, and a solid foundation for the repair of the social sphere. The Sudan could have provided a new model for creating a nationality, a state, and a country.

Unfortunately, things went toward secession. Was there a missed opportunity? Yes; however, the wind of change is blowing all over the Middle East and Africa. The street's cry for freedom is *al-Sha'b yurid isqāt al-Nizām* [The people need to end the regime]. The Sudanese, who are more experienced in leading successful civil disobedience movements against dictatorial rule, in 1964 and 1985, might do it for the third time and liberate themselves from all the different, inherited, and current forms of tyranny and totalitarianism of the state. Then, perhaps, there will be a new opportunity for building a new Sudan.

Appendix

AGREEMENT between Her Britannic Majesty's Government and the Government of His Highness the Khedive of Egypt, relative to the future administration of the Sudan.

Whereas certain provinces in the Sudan which were in rebellion against the authority of His Highness the Khedive have now been reconquered by the joint military and financial efforts of Her Britannic Majesty's Government and the Government of His Highness the Khedive;

And whereas it has become necessary to decide upon a system for the administration of and for the making of laws for the said reconquered provinces, under which due allowance may be made for the backward and unsettled condition of large portions thereof, and for the varying requirements of different localities;

And whereas it is desired to give effect to the claims which have accrued to Her Britannic Majesty's Government by right of conquest, to share in the present settlement and future working and development of the said system of administration and legislation;

And whereas it is conceived that for many purposes Wadi Halfa and Suakin may be most effectively administered in conjunction with the reconquered provinces to which they are respectively adjacent;

Now, it is hereby agreed and declared by and between the Undersigned, duly authorized for that purpose, as follows:

Art. I. The word 'Sudan' in this Agreement means all the territories South of the 22nd parallel of latitude, which:

1. Have never been evacuated by Egyptian troops since the year 1882; or

2. Which, having before the late rebellion in the Sudan been administered by the Government of His Highness the Khedive, were temporarily lost to Egypt, and have been reconquered by Her Majesty's Government and the Egyptian Government, acting in concert; or

3. Which may hereafter be reconquered by the two Governments acting in concert.

Art. II. The British and Egyptian flags shall be used together, both on land and water, throughout the Sudan, except in the town of Suakin, in which locality the Egyptian flag alone shall be used.

Art. III. The supreme military and civil command in the Sudan shall be vested in one officer, termed the 'Governor-General of the Sudan' He shall be appointed by Khedivial Decree on the recommendation' of Her Britannic Majesty's Government, and shall be removed only by Khedivial Decree, with the consent of Her Britannic Majesty's Government.

Art. IV. Laws, as also Orders and Regulations with the full force of law, for the good government of the Sudan, and for regulating the holding, disposal, and devolution of property of every kind therein situate, may from time to time be made, altered, or abrogated by Proclamation of the Governor-General. Such Laws, Orders and Regulations may apply to the whole or any named part of the Sudan, and may, either explicitly or by necessary implication, alter or abrogate any existing Law or Regulation.

All such Proclamations shall be forthwith notified to Her Britannic Majesty's Agent and Consul-General in Cairo, and to the President of the Council of Ministers of His Highness the Khedive.

Art. V. No Egyptian Law, Decree, Ministerial Arrete, or other enactment hereafter to be made or promulgated shall apply to the Sudan or any part thereof, save in so far as the same shall be applied by Proclamation of the Governor-General in manner hereinbefore provided.

Art. VI. In the definition by Proclamation of the conditions under which Europeans, of whatever nationality, shall be at liberty to trade with or reside in the Sudan, or to hold property within its limits, no special privileges shall be accorded to the subjects of any one or more Power.

Art. VII. Import duties on entering the Sudan shall not be payable on goods coming from Egyptian territory. Such duties may, however, be levied on goods coming from elsewhere than Egyptian territory, but in the case of goods entering the Sudan at Suakin, or any other port on the Red Sea Littoral, they shall not exceed the corresponding duties for the time being leviable on goods entering Egypt from abroad. Duties may be levied on goods leaving the Sudan, at such rates as may from time to time be prescribed by Proclamation.

Art. VIII. The jurisdiction of the Mixed Tribunals shall not extend, nor be recognized for any purpose whatsoever, in any part of the Sudan, except in the town of Suakin.

Art. IX. Until, and save so far as it shall be otherwise determined, by Proclamation, the Sudan, with the exception of the town of Suakin, shall be and remain under martial law.

Art. X. No Consuls, Vice-Consuls, or Consular Agents shall be accredited in respect of nor allowed to reside in the Sudan, without the previous consent of Her Britannic Majesty's Government.

Art. XI. The importation of slaves into the Sudan, as also their exportation, is absolutely prohibited. Provision shall be made by Proclamation for the enforcement of this Regulation.

Art. XII. It is agreed between the two Governments that special attention shall be paid to the enforcement of the Brussels Act of the 2nd July 1890, in respect to the import, sale, and manufacture of fire-arms and their munitions, and distilled or spirituous liquors.

Done in Cairo, the 19th January, 1899.

(Signed) BOUTROS GHALI—CROMER.

Notes

Preface

1. Giddens, *Nation-State*, 11.

2. Robert Fossaert, quoted in Young, *African Colonial State*, 221.

3. Ibid.

4. Said, *Culture and Imperialism*, xxii.

5. Hobson, *Imperialism*, v.

6. Hobsbawm, "Globalization," 224.

7. Ibid.

8. Helms, *Ulysses' Sail*, 9.

9. Hansen and Stepputat, "States of Imagination," 19.

10. Ibid., 1.

11. O'Neill, "Class and Politics," 25.

12. Mamdani, *Good Muslim*, 52.

13. When the Sudan was reconquered by a joint Anglo-Egyptian campaign, the two occupying governments "created a hybrid form of government, hitherto unknown to international jurisprudence," and Cromer himself admitted that "it was to some extent the child of opportunism." Cromer, *Modern Egypt*, 2:114. Egypt, as Woodward explains, "had paid for the expedition and provided many of the troops; now she was being fobbed off with little more than a symbolic role in her former territories." Woodward, *Sudan*, 15. For the British, and according to the condominium agreement, the Sudan was under the responsibility of the Foreign Office in London rather than the Colonial Office.

14. Horatio Kitchener was born in Ireland in 1850 and died in 1916. He was educated at the Royal Military Academy and entered the Royal Engineers in 1871. In 1892 he become commander in chief (*sirdar*) of the Egyptian army and commanded the reconquest of the Sudan, which took more than two years: 1896. After defeating the Sudanese army at the battle of Karari he was named Lord Kitchener of Khartoum and the first governor general of the Anglo-Egyptian Sudan.

15. Sir Reginald Wingate was born in Scotland in 1861 and died in 1953. He was a British general and imperial administrator, principal founder of the colonial state, and governor general of the Anglo-Egyptian Sudan until 1916. He

succeeded Kitchener as governor general of the Sudan and sirdar of the Egyptian army in 1899.

16. Evelyn Baring (1841–1917), first earl of Cromer, was a British statesman, diplomat, and colonial administrator. He was British controller general in Egypt in 1879 and later agent and consul general in Egypt from 1883 to 1907. Lord Cromer was the author of the condominium agreement that in 1898 he and Boutros Ghali signed as the Agreement for the Administration of the Sudan.

17. Rudolf Karl, baron von Slatin, was born in 1857, at Ober St. Veit, near Vienna, and died in 1932. An Austrian soldier in the service of England in the Sudan, he became famous for his stay in the Sudan during the Mahdists' rule (1883–99). He converted to Islam and renamed himself Abdelgadir in order to improve morale among his Sudanese troops. He was governor of Darfur Province before being captured and held prisoner by the Mahdists. He escaped after eleven years and served Lord Kitchener in the reconquest of the Sudan against the Mahdists. His nearly forty years in the Sudan and his knowledge of the country, its people, and language proved to be invaluable for the establishment of the colonial state in the Sudan.

18. The *'arrāqi* is a knee-length Sudanese garment. This term *white-'arrāqi* is used here to refer to an emerging category of peasant workers connected to the Gezira Scheme on par with blue-collar railway workers, white-collar government workers, and khaki-collar army workers.

19. Abdel Ghaffar Moḥamed Aḥmed, "Management of Crisis."

20. Tocqueville, *Democracy in America,* 2:129.

21. Alexander, *Civil Sphere,* 9.

Chapter 1. The Sociopolitical Construction of a Country

1. These names include Kush (or Cush), Nubia, Yam, Ta-Seti, Kerma, Meroe, and Ethiopia. During the Christian period other names, such as Nubatia, Mukurra, and Alwa, were applied. These names all carry implications of color, race, or geographical place.

2. Spaulding, *Heroic Age,* xvii.

3. Ibid., xviii.

4. Ibid., xviii–xix.

5. Muḥammad 'Ali Pasha (1769–1849) was the Ottoman wāli, or governor general, of Egypt (1805–49) and is often recognized as the founder of Muḥammad 'Ali's family dynasty, which extended its rule in Egypt until 1952. Muḥammad 'Ali is often cited as the builder of modern Egypt. He extended his power over the Sudan in 1821 to seek strategic raw materials such as gold and ivory for his treasury, to expand his empire, and to acquire slaves for his army. The Turko-Egyptian administration (known as the Turkiyya) ruled the country till 1885.

6. Powell, *Different Shade,* 27.

7. Sayyid-Marsot, *Egypt in the Reign,* 197.

8. 'Abdel-Raḥim, "Arabism, Africanism," 237.

9. Fluehr-Lobban, "Race in the Nile Valley," 207–36.

10. Homer, *Odyssey*, 1.

11. Homer, *Iliad*, 70.

12. The Greek historian Herodotus was one of the first "Europeans" to write about Ethiopia during his travels on the Nile. In approximately 430 BCE Herodotus visited Egypt, and although he never made it as far south as Meroe, he was told by Egyptian locals about the existence of the Merotic kingdom and its people, whose "customs . . . differ[ed] greatly from the rest of mankind." He describes Meroe as the mother city of the other Ethiopians.

13. Herodotus, *The Histories*.

14. Diodorus, *Works*, 103–5.

15. Ibn Khaldun, *Muqaddimah*, 1:171.

16. Ibid., 1:60.

17. "Bilad al-Sudan," in Chambers and Chambers, *Encyclopaedia*.

18. Isma'il Pasha (1830–95), grandson of Muḥammad 'Ali, was wāli and later the first khedive of Egypt and the Sudan from 1863 until he was removed from office. In May 1879 the British Empire and France began pressuring the Ottoman sulṭān 'Abdul Ḥamid II to depose Isma'il Pasha, and this was done on June 26, 1879. After the Aḥmed 'Urabi Revolt of 1882, Britain invaded Egypt in support of Isma'il's eldest son Tewfik Pasha and continued occupying the country for decades.

19. 'Abdel-Raḥim, "Arabism, Africanism," 237.

20. Ibid.

21. Ṭayeb, "Abyssinian Hijrah," 159–64.

22. Snowden, *Blacks in Antiquity*, 176.

23. Ibid.

24. Miller, *Blank Darkness*, 25.

25. Fluehr-Lobban, "Race in the Nile Valley," 141.

26. Du Bois, *Reader*, 625.

27. 'Antara was an Arab poet and a legendary warrior of the pre-Islamic period. He was born to an Arab chief from the tribe of 'Abs and an Abyssinian slave woman called Zabiba. Ever since ancient times, 'Antara's story has been the subject of a series of tales, folk stories, and films. A recurring part of his story relates to heroism and freedom. According to the story, 'Antara's 'Abs tribe was raided by another tribe. When 'Antara was called on by his father to charge, he replied, "'Antara is a slave, and the slave does not know how to charge. He only knows how to milk camels and bind their udders." His father said, "Charge and you are free."

28. 'Antara, *Sharh al-Mu'allaqāt*.

29. Qur'an, Surat al-Rum (the Romans), 30:22.

30. The general consensus among both scholars and ordinary Muslims is that the name of this observance comes from *'ashoura*, Arabic for tenth. It represents the tenth day of Muḥarram, the first month of the Muslim hejira calendar. Among the Shī'a, the day marks one of history's most important events: the martyrdom of al-Ḥussein, grandson of the Prophet Muḥammad, in what is now Kerbala, Iraq,

in 61 AH (680 CE). For centuries most Shi'a around the world have taken part in rituals of collective atonement through lamentation and self-mutilation. This latter is articulated through several types of group practices, such as self-inflicted wounds or rhythmic self-flagellation with iron chains. These acts symbolize the larger Shī'a community's everlasting connection to al-Ḥussein's suffering, and the enduring shame they feel for failing to aid al-Ḥussein in his battle against Yazid ibn Mu'awiyah (646–83). Yazid was the second caliph of the Umayyad dynasty, and—to the Shī'a mind—the unlawful claimant to the legitimate leadership of the Muslim community.

31. Powell, "Silence of the Slaves," xxv.

32. Hunwick, "Same but Different," ix.

33. Mazrui, *Africa's International Relations,* 130.

34. Hunwick, "Same but Different," ix.

35. Sartre, *Anti-Semite and Jew.*

36. Wai, "African-Arab Relations," 9.

37. Ibid.

38. Ibid.

39. Sulṭān Muḥammad Tirab was the seventh Fur sulṭān. In 1787 he moved east, conquering and extending his sultanate to the Nile and annexing the rich Kordofan region.

40. Bādi II Abu Duqn, in his attempts to expand his sultanate, defeated the Fur and took control of much of the Kordofan region.

41. Muḥammad Aḥmed Ibn 'Abd Allah al-Mahdi (1844–85) led a successful war of liberation from Turko-Egyptian rule in the Sudan. His rebellion was a movement for both religious and political reform. He captured Khartoum, where General Gordon, the last British Turkish governor, was killed in 1885. Muḥammad Aḥmed died in the same year, to be succeeded by his second in command, 'Abdullahi Ibn Muḥammad, better known as 'Abdullahi al-Ta'ishi (1846–99). 'Abdullahi was named khalifa (successor) by al-Mahdi in 1881. The country remained independent until 1898.

42. Robinson, *Muslim Societies,* 27.

43. Robertson, "Globalization," 25–44.

44. Spaulding, "Precolonial Islam," 120.

45. Ibid.

46. Quoted from 'Abdullahi Ibrahim, *al-Sra'a*, 52–53.

47. Shibeika, "Expansionist Movement," 142–55.

48. Trémaux, *Voyages*, 92.

49. Moorehead, *Blue Nile,* 168–69.

50. Niblock, *Class and Power*, 2.

51. Ibid.

52. Kapeteijns and Spaulding, "Pre-colonial Trade," 70.

53. Abu-Lughod, *Before European Hegemony,* 26.

54. Adams, *Nubia.*

55. Kapeteijns and Spaulding, "Pre-colonial Trade," 70.

56. Burckhardt, *Travels in Nubia,* 286.

57. Ibid.

58. Ibid.

59. Kapeteijns and Spaulding, "Pre-colonial Trade," 38.

60. Krump, "Sudanese Travels," 1.

61. Ibid.

62. Hunwick, *Timbuktu.*

63. Roberts, *Warriors, Merchants,* 21.

64. Krump, "Sudanese Travels," 1.

65. Lovejoy, *Transformations in Slavery,* 33.

66. Faulkner, *Rome,* xi.

67. Ibid.

68. El-Bushra, "Towns in the Sudan," 63–70.

69. Browne, *Travels in Africa.*

70. Pallme, *Travels in Kordofan.*

71. O'Fahey and Spaulding, *Kingdoms of the Sudan,* 79.

72. Sikainga, *Slaves into Workers,* 13.

73. McHugh, *Holymen,* 10.

74. Veer, *Religious Nationalism,* 11.

75. Ibid.

76. Weber, *The Protestant Ethic,* 181. McHugh, *Holymen,* 10–11.

77. O'Voll, "Eastern Sudan," 154.

78. Sikainga, *Slaves into Workers,* 32.

79. Geertz, *Old Societies,* 109.

80. The subtitle of *The Black Book* (*al-kitab al-aswad*) is *Imbalance of Power and Wealth in Sudan.* It appeared first in 2000. The authors are given as "Seekers of Truth and Justice." There is no reference to its place of publication. According to the authors, the book describes the level of injustice inflicted on the western Sudan by successive governments, secular and theocratic, democratic and autocratic, since the independence of the country, in 1956. Khalil Ibrahim, the leader of the Movement for Justice and Equality, claimed that he wrote *The Black Book.*

81. Mark Duffield, pers. comm.

Chapter 2. Constructing New Identities

1. Young, *African Colonial State,* 43.

2. Young, "Colonial State and Post-Colonial Crisis," 3–6.

3. Woodward, *Sudan,* 15.

4. Ibid.

5. Zulfo, *Karari,* 125.

6. For more information about the Sudanese units that formed one-third of the invading army, see Sikainga, *Slaves into Workers,* 58–59, 63–65.

7. Ibid., 63.

8. Balamon, *People and Economics,* 42.

9. Emmert, *Churchill on Empire,* 104.

10. *Nation* 70, 132.

11. Churchill, *River War,* quoted in Daly, *Empire on the Nile,* 3.

12. Ibid. Omdurman was the capital of the Mahdist state. The battle of Karari was fought in the hilly regions outside the city, so the battle often takes the name of the capital itself.

13. Daly, *Empire on the Nile,* 3.

14. For the full text of the Condominium Agreement for the Administration of the Sudan, see the appendix.

15. See appendix.

16. See appendix.

17. Deng and Daly, *Bonds of Silk,* 6.

18. Peter Woodward, pers. comm.

19. See appendix.

20. Cromer, *Modern Egypt,* 2:119.

21. Daly, *Empire on the Nile,* 18.

22. Boddy, *Civilizing Women,* 22.

23. Macaulay, *Works,* 8:122.

24. Daly, *Empire on the Nile,* 18.

25. Macaulay, *Works,* 8:117.

26. Said, *Orientalism,* 3.

27. Boddy, *Civilizing Women,* 24.

28. Said, *Orientalism,* 31.

29. Roland Wingate, *Wingate of the Sudan,* 82.

30. Ibid., 259.

31. Young, *African Colonial State,* 78.

32. Ibid.

33. Daly, *Empire on the Nile,* 62.

34. Roland Wingate, *Wingate of the Sudan,* 129.

35. Warburg, *Sudan under Wingate,* 49.

36. Daly, *Empire on the Nile,* 87.

37. Ibid., 89.

38. Sconyers, "Servant or Saboteur?" 42.

39. Quoted in Daly, *Empire on the Nile,* 82.

40. Ibid., 83.

41. Ibid.

42. Ibid., 83–84.

43. Roland Wingate, *Wingate of the Sudan,* 134.

44. Ibid.

45. Ibid., 135.

46. Daly, *Empire on the Nile,* 87.

47. One British officer interviewed by Low was "a veteran of thirty-seven, who held high office under the Sudan Government, had no esteem for the New Civilian, and imparted to me unfavourable opinions of this young gentleman. 'I am not a university man,' said this unbeliever, 'so perhaps you can tell me what they

do learn at Oxford and Cambridge that can be of the smallest use to anybody? When we get them out here we have to begin teaching them the simplest things, which we stupid British officers learnt before we left Sandhurst. . . . We have to teach them book-keeping, office accounts, map measuring, how to docket papers and draw up reports, the elements of land-surveying; surely these are things that their schoolmasters might have taught them before they sent them out to us. Of course, they know all there is to know about Latin and Greek. . . . They can play cricket, I believe; but that isn't much use in a country where there's no turf. They had much better teach them to ride decently, and to shoot, and give them some military drill, which, you know, we have to put them through when they have come out. It seems to me that their real education only begins when we take them in hand." Low, *Egypt in Transition,* 90–91, emphasis in original.

48. Roland Wingate, *Wingate of the Sudan,* 133.
49. Sharkey, *Living with Colonialism,* 68.
50. Boddy, *Civilizing Women,* 23–24.
51. Sharkey, *Living with Colonialism,* 68.
52. Boddy, *Civilizing Women,* 69–70.
53. Sharkey, *Living with Colonialism,* 68.
54. Young, *African Colonial State,* 4.
55. Warburg, *Sudan under Wingate,* 19.
56. Boddy, *Civilizing Women,* 24.
57. Young, *African Colonial State,* 110.
58. Ibid.
59. Ibid., 110–11.
60. Warburg, *Sudan under Wingate,* 95.
61. Ibid.
62. Daly, *Empire on the Nile,* 63.
63. Ibid.
64. Khalil, "Legal System," 629.
65. Warburg, *Sudan under Wingate,* 50.
66. Berman, "Ethnicity, Patronage," 314.
67. Ibid., 315.
68. Ibid.
69. Mamdani, *Citizen and Subject,* chs. 2–3.
70. Hobsbawm and Ranger, *Invention of Tradition,* 9.
71. Cohn, "Representing Authority," 168.
72. Ibid.
73. Boddy, *Civilizing Women,* 32.
74. Johnston, *Colonization of Africa,* 91.
75. Ibid.
76. Davis, "Colonial Period," 384.
77. Amin, "Underdevelopment and Dependence," 118.
78. MacMichael, *Sudan,* 17.
79. Ibid., 16.

80. Ibid.
81. Mamdani, *Victims Become Killers,* 76.
82. Nandy, *Exiled at Home,* iv.
83. Ibid.
84. Nandy, *Intimate Enemy,* 10.
85. Francis, "Domestication of the Male?" 639.
86. Boddy, *Civilizing Women,* 76.
87. Hansen and Stepputat, "States of Imagination," 16–17.
88. Bernal, "Colonial Moral Economy," 451.
89. Balamon, *People and Economics,* 46.
90. Boddy, *Civilizing Women,* 76.
91. Bernal, "Colonial Moral Economy," 448.
92. Davis, "Colonial Period," 393.

Chapter 3. The Malignant Tumor of the Colonial State

1. The *juba,* or *jibba,* is a patched homemade garment worn by the Mahdi's followers (Ansār), depicted by Victorian Britain as dervishes. It was a symbol of piety and poverty.
2. Cursing religion, or *sabb al-din,* was one of the signs of these alarming developments that came with the invasion and its new order. In response, "cursing the Cross" (*sabb al-Ṣalieb*) became widespread among the population of urban areas.
3. Tignor, introduction, 5.
4. 'Abd al-Raḥman al-Jabarti is the foremost Egyptian Muslim historian and chronicler of events, especially of Napoléon Bonaparte's invasion and occupation of Egypt (1798–1801). His major works that chronicle the French occupation of Egypt include his first, *Tarikh muddat al-Faransis bi Misr* (History of the French Presence in Egypt), which covers the first six months of the French colonial period. His second work, *Muzhir al-taqdis bi dhahab dawlat al-Faransis* (Demonstrations of Godliness in the Demise of the French State), is a detailed chronicle of daily events during the French occupation of Egypt that reflects a unique combination of historical narration and observations about French organization of administrative matters, the battles and the flight of the Mamluks (the native Egyptian rulers) to Upper Egypt, the Revolt of Cairo, and the author's complete rejection of the French occupation of Egypt. His third principal work, *Ajaib al-athar fi al-tarajim wa al-akhbar* (Astounding Records from Biographies and Events), known in English simply as *Al-Jabarti's History of Egypt,* was banned by Muḥammad 'Ali Pasha and was not published as a complete work until 1879.
5. Tripp, *Islam,* 15.
6. McHugh, *Holymen,* 89.
7. Zulfo, *Karari,* 238.
8. Ibid., 242.
9. Ibid., 242–43.
10. Ibid., 246.
11. Quoted in Daly, *Empire on the Nile,* 11.

12. Roland Wingate, *Wingate of the Sudan,* 126.

13. Quoted in Ḥassan Ibrahim, *Sayyid 'Abd al-Raḥman,* 32.

14. Karsani, "Establishment of Neo-Mahdism," 394.

15. Juergensmeyer, *New Cold War?,* 156.

16. Woodward, *Sudan,* 25.

17. Beshir, *Southern Sudan,* 19.

18. Johnson, *Root Causes,* 11.

19. Daly, *Empire on the Nile,* 130.

20. Ibid.

21. Ibid.

22. Theobald, *'Ali Dinar,* 30.

23. Zulfo, *Karari,* 242.

24. British colonel William Hicks, known as Hicks Pasha (1830–83). He led an expedition from Khartoum to Kordofan to put down al-Mahdi's rebellion in 1883. His force, about 11,500 men, was made up mainly of Egyptian regulars. His army was ambushed in the forest at Kashgil, thirty miles south of Obeid. Hicks and his entire force, with the exception of five hundred men who fled back to Khartoum, were killed.

25. Theobald, *'Ali Dinar,* 41.

26. de Waal, "Counter-Insurgency on the Cheap." Daly, *Empire on the Nile,* 178.

27. Ibid., 180.

28. *Faki* (or *fiki*) is a Sudanese colloquial term applied to persons with no organized education of the Qur'an or religious sciences, but who are known for their piety and knowledge of certain aspects of religion.

29. Karsani, "Neo-Mahdism," 388.

30. Quoted in ibid., 390.

31. Quoted in ibid., 390.

32. James Currie to Slatin, July 4, 1908, FO/431/50, quoted in Warburg, *Sudan under Wingate,* 102.

33. Duffield, *Maiurno,* 18.

34. Mahdi, *Jihad,* 137.

35. Ibrahim, *Sayyid 'Abd al-Raḥman,* 71.

36. Ibid.

37. Daly, *Empire on the Nile,* 167.

38. Ibid.

39. Quoted in Ibrahim, *Sayyid 'Abd al-Raḥman,* 73. Nandy, *Intimate Enemy,* 3.

40. Quoted in Ibrahim, *Sayyid 'Abd al-Raḥman,* 95.

41. Ibid., 95–96.

42. *Jihad fi sabiel al-istiqlal.* Sayyid 'Abd al-Raḥman dictated the book to 'Abd al-Raḥim al-Amin, Bashir Moḥmed Said, and Zain al-'Abdin Ḥussein, and it was edited by his grandson al-Sadiq al-Mahdi.

43. Ibrahim, *Sayyid 'Abd al-Raḥman,* 74.

44. Mahdi, *Jihad,* 22.

45. Shahi, "Noah's Ark," 16.

46. Daly, *Empire on the Nile,* 122.

47. Asst. CS to intelligence officer, August 15, 1901, intel 2/32/339, quoted in Daly, *Empire on the Nile*, 122.

48. Salomon, *Undoing the Mahdiyya*, 19.

49. Daly, *Empire on the Nile*, 122.

50. Zald, "Theological Crucibles," 320.

51. Ibid., 322.

52. Ibid., 323.

53. Ibid.

54. Ibid.

55. Woodward, *Sudan*, 24.

56. Sikainga, *Slaves into Workers*, 142–43.

57. Woodward, "Footsteps of Gordon," 47.

58. Woodward, *Sudan*, 25.

59. Ibid.

60. Lange, *Lineages of Despotism*, 4.

61. Burleigh, *Khartoum Campaign*, 51.

62. Young, *African Colonial State*, 95.

63. Ibid., 139.

64. Dirks, *Colonialism and Culture*, 7.

Chapter 4. A Tale of Three Cities: Khartoum

1. Said, *Orientalism*, 9.

2. Nandy, *Intimate Enemy*, 6.

3. Ibid.

4. Foucault, *Ethics*, 16–49.

5. Young, *African Colonial State*, 218.

6. Giddens, *Historical Materialism*, 7.

7. Boddy, *Civilizing Women*, 14.

8. Ibid.

9. Daly, *Images of Empire*, 104.

10. Ibid.

11. Ibid.

12. Boddy, *Civilizing Women*, 22.

13. Ibid.

14. Daly, *Images of Empire*, 232.

15. Ibid., 233.

16. Ḥamdan, "Structure of Khartoum," 28.

17. Ibid.

18. Myers, "Intellectual of Empire," 5.

19. Ḥamdan, "Structure of Khartoum," 28.

20. Ibid., 29–30.

21. Boddy, *Civilizing Women*, 22.

22. Ḥamdan, "Structure of Khartoum," 21–40.

23. Habitat Group, "Khartoum," 21.

24. Home, *Planting and Planning*, 8.

25. Metcalf, *Imperial Vision,* 7.
26. Said, *Orientalism,* 55.
27. Young, *African Colonial State,* 78.
28. Said, *Orientalism,* 31.
29. Currie, "Educational Experiment," 361.
30. Quoted in King Edward, *Lord Kitchener,* 88.
31. Currie, "Educational Experiment," 363.
32. Boddy, *Civilizing Women,* 83.
33. Ibid.
34. Quoted in ibid.
35. Ibid., 84.
36. Kenny, "Climate, Race, and Imperial Authority," 695.
37. Quoted in King Edward, *Lord Kitchener,* 90.
38. Nur, *Qisas wa khawatir,* 35.
39. Ibid.
40. Frederick Lugard (1858–1945), British soldier, administrator, and prominent Victorian colonial practitioner, served in East Africa, West Africa, and Hong Kong. His name is especially associated with Nigeria, where he became high commissioner of the Protectorate of Northern Nigeria (1900–1906), governor, and governor general (1912–19). Lugard's major work, *The Dual Mandate in British Tropical Africa,* is the manifesto of indirect rule in colonial Africa. He outlines the reasons and methods that should be employed as reciprocal principles in the colonization of Africa by Britain. His justifications of the "benign nature" of British colonialism included spreading Christianity and ending barbarism.
41. Nur, *Qisas wa khawatir,* 34.
42. Babiker, "Khartoum," 17.
43. Ibid.
44. Yeoh, *Contesting Space,* 11.
45. Thiong'o, *Decolonising the Mind,* 3.
46. Ibid.
47. Maj.-Gen. Sir George Frederick Gorringe (1868–1945) was nicknamed Bloody Orange for his rude behavior. He was commissioned in the Royal Engineers in 1888 and made his reputation in the Sudan. His first experience of active service was in the Dongola expedition (1896), while attached to the Egyptian army. In addition to the palace and Gordon Memorial College, he built the government offices at Wad Medani and Singa and the Sudan Club in Khartoum.
48. Peel, *Binding of the Nile,* 214–15.
49. Ibid., 214.
50. Sharkey, *Living with Colonialism,* 43.
51. Ibid.
52. Kitchener, quoted in King Edward, *Lord Kitchener,* 88.
53. Cohn, *Colonialism,* 10.
54. Ibid.
55. Mamdani, *Saviors and Survivors,* 56.
56. Boddy, *Civilizing Women,* 25.

57. Colvin, *Making of Modern Egypt*, 372.
58. Warburg, *Sudan under Wingate*, 95.
59. Kitchener, quoted in ibid.
60. Warburg, ibid.
61. Quoted in Daly, *Empire of the Nile*, 122.
62. Ibid.
63. Ibid.
64. Khalil, "Legal System," 629.
65. Warburg, *Sudan under Wingate*, 50.
66. Salih, *Al-sahfa al-sudaniyya*, 192.
67. Sharkey, "Century in Print," 531.

Chapter 5. A Tale of Three Cities: Omdurman

1. Boddy, *Civilizing Women*, 22.
2. Ziegler, *Omdurman*, 60.
3. Ibid.
4. Ohrwalder, *Ten Years' Captivity*, 206.
5. Holt, "Sudanese Mahdia," 276–90.
6. Ohrwalder, *Ten Years' Captivity*, 206.
7. Ibid.
8. Ziegler, *Omdurman*, 60.
9. Barthes, "Semiology and Urbanism," 168.
10. Deemer, "Umm Durmān," 12.
11. For more details about the long march and the transit encampments, see Isma'il 'Abd al-Qadir al-Kordofani, *al-mustahdi bi sirat al-Imam al-Mahdi*.
12. F. R. Wingate, *Mahdiism*, 227.
13. Deemer, "Umm Durmān," 12.
14. Zulfo, *Karari*, 32.
15. Ibid.
16. Ziegler, *Omdurman*, 60.
17. F. R. Wingate, *Mahdiism*, 283.
18. Ohrwalder, *Ten Years' Captivity*, 277–78.
19. Ibid.
20. Deemer, "Umm Durmān," 569.
21. Ibid.
22. Bedri, *Memoirs*, 144.
23. Ibid.
24. Slatin, *Fire and Sword*, 172.
25. Muḥammad Aḥmed al-Mahdi started the plan for building the fourth mosque, and his successor, al-Khalifa 'Abdullahi, completed it. It was considered the fourth mosque, after the Mecca, Medina, and al-Aqsa mosques. Wad Sa'd described the mosque in his poem *al-Masjid al-Rabi 'i al-Mahdi Imamu 'uomaru al lai taqua Allah adamuh* (The Fourth Mosque al-Mahdi Is Its Imam; Its Attendants Sustained It by Allah's Piety).

26. F. R. Wingate, *Mahdism*, 486.
27. Kordofani, *S'adat al-mustahdi*, 392–93.
28. Neufeld, *Prisoner of the Khalifa*, 99.
29. Ohrwalder, *Ten Years' Captivity*, 208.
30. Abu Shouk and Bjørkelo, *Public Treasury*, xii.
31. Zulfo, *Karari*, 36.
32. Abu Shouk and Bjørkelo, *Public Treasury*, xiv.
33. Ibid.
34. Ibid.
35. Ohrwalder, *Ten Years' Captivity*, 282.
36. Ibid.
37. Ibid.
38. Ibid.
39. Daly, "Omdurman and Fashoda," 21.
40. Steevens, *With Kitchener*, 300.
41. Ziegler, *Omdurman*, 194.
42. Kramer, "Holy City," 256.
43. Daly, *Empire on the Nile*, 11.
44. 'Abdullahi Ibrahim, *Manichaean Delirium*, 83.
45. Ibid.
46. Cohn, *Colonialism*, 48.
47. Horkheimer, *Dialectic of Enlightenment*, 15.
48. Nandy, *Intimate Enemy*, v.
49. Bakhiet, *Al-idara al-biritania*, 74.
50. Bakhiet, "British Administration."
51. Kurita, *'Ali 'Abd al-Latif*.
52. Vezzadini, "1924 Revolution."
53. Beshir, *Revolution and Nationalism*, 87.
54. Vezzadini, "1924 Revolution," 327.
55. Beshir, *Revolution and Nationalism*, 75.
56. Ibid.
57. Vezzadini, "1924 Revolution," 327.
58. Ibid.
59. Beshir, *Revolution and Nationalism*, 102.
60. Ibid.
61. Quoted in Bakhiet, "British Administration," 94.
62. Ibid.
63. Ibid.
64. Abbas, *Sudan Question*, 60.
65. Ibid.
66. Woodward, *Sudan*, 69.
67. Ibid.
68. Niblock, *Class and Power*, 181.
69. Sharkey, *Living with Colonialism*, 39.
70. Woodward, *Sudan*, 58.

Chapter 6. A Tale of Three Cities: Cairo

1. Sayyid-Marsot, *Egypt in the Reign*, 206.
2. Helms, *Ulysses' Sail*, 101.
3. Powell, *Different Shade*, 6.
4. Ibid.
5. Quoted in Holt, "Sultan Selim," 21.
6. Sayyid-Marsot, *Egypt in the Reign*, 59.
7. Powell, *Different Shade*, 7.
8. Meillassoux, *Anthropology of Slavery*, 67.
9. Sikainga, *Slaves into Workers*, 8.
10. Meillassoux, *Anthropology of Slavery*, 75.
11. Sikainga, *Slaves into Workers*, 16.
12. Ibid.
13. Mire, "Al-Zubayr Pasha," 107.
14. Ibid.
15. Ibid.
16. Shukri, *Misr wa al-Sudan*, 85.
17. R. Collins, "Sudanese Factors," 160.
18. Johnson, "Recruitment and Entrapment," 162.
19. Ibid.
20. Cordell, *Dar al-Kuti*.
21. Schweinfurth, *Heart of Africa*, 229.
22. Ibid.
23. Ibid.
24. Johnson, "Recruitment and Entrapment," 162–73.
25. Lovejoy, *Transformations in Slavery*, 276.
26. Ibid., 282.
27. Johnson, "Recruitment and Entrapment," 162–73.
28. Ibid.
29. Bjørkelo, *Prelude to the Mahdiyya*, 129.
30. Ibid.
31. Mire, "Al-Zubayr Pasha," 101.
32. Ibid.
33. Shaw, "Zebehr Pasha," 333–49, 568–85, 658–82.
34. Ibid.
35. Ibid.
36. Ibid.
37. Polanyi, *Great Transformation*, 60.
38. Shaw, "Zebehr Pasha," 333–49, 568–85, 658–82.
39. Ewald, *Soldiers, Traders*, 172.
40. Ibid.
41. Ibid.
42. Pallme, *Travels in Kordofan*, 13.
43. Cordell, *Dar al-Kuti*, 18.

44. Ibid.

45. Pallme, *Travels in Kordofan*, 13.

46. Cordell, *Dar al-Kuti*, 18.

47. Slatin, *Fire and Sword*, 50.

48. Hake, *Chinese Gordon*, 179.

49. Lang, *Story of General Gordon*, 74. Shaw, "Zebehr Pasha," 333–49, 568–85, 658–82.

50. Ibid.

51. Ibid.

52. R. Collins, "Sudanese Factors," 163.

53. Ḥajj, "Ḥayātu B. Sa'īd," 132.

54. R. Collins, "Sudanese Factors," 156.

55. Ibid.

56. Quoted in Smith, *Emin Pasha*, 20.

57. Ibid., 20–21.

58. Ruay, *Politics of Two Sudans*, 159.

59. Woodward, *Sudan*, 16.

60. Ibid., 17.

61. Ibid., 16.

62. Ibid., 15.

63. Niblock, *Class and Power*, 11.

64. C. Collins, *Colonialism*, 6.

65. Bernal, "Colonial Moral Economy," 451.

66. Mamdani, *Citizen and Subject*, 73.

67. Woodward, *Sudan*, 16.

68. Ibid.

69. Ibid., 44.

70. Abbas, *Sudan Question*, 61.

71. Ibid.

72. Ibid.

73. Aḥmed Fouad I (1868–1936) was the first ruler of independent Egypt. During his reign (1917–36) as the ninth sovereign of the line of Muḥammad 'Ali, Egypt changed from a British colony to become a full-fledged and independent kingdom. His title changed from sulṭān to king of Egypt and the Sudan, sovereign of Nubia, Kordofan, and Darfur. He was the first Egyptian royal to substitute the title of king for sulṭān when Egypt gained its independence, in 1922. Two years later, the 1924 revolution officers cheered King Fouad.

74. Abbas, *Sudan Question*, 61.

75. Ṣabry, *Sovereignty for Sudan*, 1.

76. Vezzadini, "1924 Revolution," 143.

77. Ibid.

78. Ibid.

79. Woodward, *Sudan*, 73.

80. Muḥammad Naguib (1901–84) was born, educated, and grew up in the Sudan. General Naguib was the leader of the military coup of 1952 in Egypt,

which deposed King Farouq and ended the rule of the Muḥammad 'Ali dynasty in Egypt and the Sudan. Upon the declaration of Egypt as a republic, in June 1953, he became the country's first president. An acrimonious but brief power struggle broke out between him and Gamal 'Abdel Nasser for leadership and control of the military and how to rule the country. Nasser managed to force Naguib to resign from the presidency of Egypt in November 1954. After he was removed from office, he was subject to house arrest for eighteen years until President Anwar el-Sādāt released him in 1972.

Chapter 7. The Creation of the Center

1. Memmi, *Colonizer and Colonized,* 69–70.
2. Chatterjee, *Nation and Its Fragments,* 10.
3. Memmi, *Colonizer and Colonized,* 69.
4. Mitchell, *Colonising Egypt,* 34.
5. MacMichael, *Sudan,* 17.
6. Ibid.
7. Mamdani, *Citizen and Subject,* 4.
8. Ibid.
9. Wallerstein, "Construction of Peoplehood," 78.
10. Ibid.
11. Ibid.
12. Hobsbawm and Kertzer, "Ethnicity and Nationalism," 3–13.
13. Wallerstein, "Construction of Peoplehood," 78.
14. David Baronov developed the concept of "historical-cultural formations" to study and incorporate large-scale cultural processes alongside economic and political processes across the capitalist world system. The concept of historical-cultural formations is more fully developed in his recent book *The African Transformation of Western Medicine and the Dynamics of Global Cultural Exchange.*
15. O'Fahey, "Islam and Ethnicity," 259.
16. Dirks, foreword to Cohn, *Colonialism,* ix.
17. Furnivall, *Colonial Policy,* 8.
18. Veer, *Religious Nationalism,* 26.
19. MacMichael, *History of the Arabs,* 3.
20. Ibid.
21. Arkell, *History of the Sudan.*
22. Veer, *Religious Nationalism,* 26.
23. Ibid.
24. Warburg, *Sudan under Wingate,* 19.
25. Ibid.
26. Ibrahim, *Manichaean Delirium,* 6.
27. Warburg, *Islam, Sectarianism,* 59.
28. Ibrahim, *Manichaean Delirium,* 21.
29. Ibid.
30. Sharkey, *Living with Colonialism,* 50.

31. Ibid.
32. Tilly, *Politics of Collective Violence*, 30.
33. Balibar and Wallerstein, *Race, Nation, Class*, 102.
34. Woodward, *Sudan*, 54.
35. Quoted in Beshir, *Revolution and Nationalism*, 132–33.
36. Bourdieu and Passeron, *Reproduction in Education*, iii.
37. Sikainga, *City of Steel*, 26.
38. Cross, "British Attitudes," 223.
39. C. Collins, *Colonialism and Class Struggle*, 6.
40. Sikainga, *Slaves into Workers*, 135.
41. Sikainga, *City of Steel*, 26.
42. Ibid.
43. Niblock, *Class and Power*, 49.
44. For more information about the creation and development of 'Aṭbara, see Sikainga, *City of Steel*.
45. Ibid., 33.
46. Sikainga, *Slaves into Workers*, 136.
47. Sikainga, *City of Steel*, 35.
48. Ibid.
49. Ibid., 66.
50. Bernal, "Colonial Moral Economy," 448.
51. Gaitskell, *Gezira*, 25.
52. Ibid.
53. Ibid.
54. Ibid.
55. Bernal, "Colonial Moral Economy," 449.
56. Barnett, *Gezira Scheme*, 4.
57. Said, *Culture and Imperialism*, 58.
58. Barnett, *Gezira Scheme*, 4.
59. Ibid., emphasis in original.
60. Bernal, "Colonial Moral Economy," 450.
61. Ibid., 451.
62. Ibid., 459.
63. Ibid., 462.
64. Ibid., 463.
65. Ibid., 462.
66. See note 18 in the preface.
67. Contract between the Tenant and the Sudan Gezira Board, quoted in Barnett, *Gezira Scheme*, 92.
68. Ibid.
69. Ibid.
70. Barnett and 'Abdelkarim, *Sudan*, 4.
71. Ibid.
72. Gaitskell, *Gezira*, 156.

Chapter 8. The Creation of the Margin

1. Mazrui, "Multiple Marginality," 248.
2. Woodward, "Multiple Marginality Multiplied," 5.
3. Quoted in Mazrui, "Multiple Marginality," 243.
4. Ibid.
5. Ibid., 244.
6. Deng, *War of Visions*, 2.
7. Ibid.
8. Ibid.
9. Ibid., 580.
10. Ibid., 9.
11. Ibid.
12. Quoted in Idris, *Sudan's Civil War*, 25.
13. Quoted in Deng, *War of Visions*, 443–44.
14. Khalid, "External Factors," 109–10.
15. Ḥarir, "Recycling the Past," 36.
16. Ibid., 37.
17. Ibid.
18. Lesch, *Sudan*, 3.
19. Ibid.
20. Ibid.
21. Ibid.
22. Na'im, "National Unity," 71.
23. Ibid.
24. Quoted in Deng, *War of Visions*, 26.
25. O'Neill and O'Brian, *Economy and Class*, 6.
26. Ibid.
27. Ibid.
28. Kok, *Governance and Conflict*, 11.
29. Ibid.
30. 'Ali, foreword, ii.
31. Johnson, *Root Causes*, xi.
32. Ibid., xii.
33. Said, *Culture and Imperialism*, 9, emphasis in original.
34. Ibid.
35. Ibid.
36. Balibar and Wallerstein, *Race, Nation, Class*, 39, emphasis in original.
37. Ibid.
38. Gray, *History of the Southern Sudan*, 1.
39. Bjørkelo, *Prelude to the Mahdiyya*, 34.
40. Ibid., 35.
41. Ibid.
42. Sayyid-Marsot, *Egypt in the Reign*, 205.

43. Fahmy, *All the Pasha's Men*, 86.
44. Gray, *History of the Southern Sudan*, 3.
45. Bjørkelo, *Prelude to the Mahdiyya*, 84.
46. For more detailed information about these five personalities and their contribution to the Egyptian discourse about the Sudan, see Powell, *Different Shade*.
47. Ibid., 29.
48. Mitchell, *Colonising Egypt*, 31.
49. Powell, *Different Shade*, 30.
50. Said, *Orientalism*, 177.
51. Powell, *Different Shade*, 30.
52. Gray, *History of the Southern Sudan*, 19.
53. Ibid.
54. Ibid., 1.
55. Beshir, *Southern Sudan*, 13.
56. Gray, *History of the Southern Sudan*, 23.
57. Beshir, *Southern Sudan*, 13.
58. Ruay, *Politics of Two Sudans*, 159.
59. Ohrwalder, *Ten Years' Captivity*, 301.
60. Ibid.
61. Beshir, *Southern Sudan*, 18.
62. Duncan, *Sudan*, 4–5.
63. Ibid.
64. Ibid.
65. Ibid.
66. Mamdani, *Citizen and Subject*, 93.
67. Duncan, *Sudan*.
68. Dirks, foreword, xi.
69. Quoted in Beshir, *Southern Sudan*, 25.
70. Warburg, *Sudan under Wingate*, 109.
71. Beshir, *Southern Sudan*, 26.
72. Ibid.
73. Quoted in Warburg, *Sudan under Wingate*, 111.
74. Ibid., 121.

Conclusion

1. Bayart, *Global Subjects*, 148.
2. Balibar and Wallerstein, *Race, Nation, Class*, 80.
3. A very popular patriotic song after WWII by Ḥassan Khalifa al-'Aṭbarawi.
4. Bayart, *Global Subjects*, 268.

Bibliography

Abbas, Mekki. *The Sudan Question: The Dispute over the Anglo-Egyptian Condominium, 1884–1951*. New York: Praeger, 1952.

'Abdel-Raḥim, Muddathir. "Arabism, Africanism, and Self-Identification in the Sudan." In *Sudan in Africa, Studies Presented to the First International Conference Sponsored by the Sudan Research Unit, February 1968*, edited by Yusuf Fadl Hassan. Khartoum: Khartoum University Press, 1971.

Abdel Salam, A. H., and Alex De Waal. *The Phoenix State: Civil Society and the Future of Sudan*. Lawrenceville, N.J.: Red Sea Press, 2001.

Abu-Lughod, Janet L. *Before European Hegemony: The World System A.D. 1250–1350*. Oxford: Oxford University Press, 1991.

Abu Shouk, Ahmad Ibrahim, and Anders J. Bjørkelo. *The Public Treasury of the Muslims: Monthly Budgets of the Mahdist State in the Sudan, 1897*. Leiden: Brill, 1996.

Adams, William Y. *Nubia: Corridor to Africa*. Princeton: Princeton University Press, 1977.

Alexander, Jeffrey C. *The Civil Sphere*. Oxford: Oxford University Press, 2006.

'Ali, Taisier Moḥamed. Foreword to *Sudan's Civil War: Slavery, Race, and Formational Identities* by Amir H. Idris. Queenston, Ont.: Edwin Mellen, 2001.

Amin, Samir. "Underdevelopment and Dependence in Black Africa: Historical Origin." *Journal of Peace Research* 9, no. 2 (1972): 105–20.

'Antara, Mu'alaqat 'Antara. *Sharh al-Mu'allaqāt al-Sab'aa*. Edited by Al-Zawzani. Beirut: Dar Beyrouth, 1980.

Arkell, Anthony John. *A History of the Sudan: From the Earliest Times to 1821*. London: Athlone Press, 1961.

Babiker, Bushra. "Khartoum: Past, Present and the Prospects for the Future." *Durham Middle East Papers* (1997). http://eprints.dur.ac.uk/archive/00000136/01/Babiker.pdf.

Bakhiet, Ja'far Moḥamed 'Ali. *Al-idara al-biritania wa al-haraka al-watania fi al-Sudan 1919–1939*. Translated by Henry Riad. Beirut: Dar al-Thaqāfa, 1973.

———. "British Administration and Sudanese Nationalism, 1919–1939." PhD diss., Cambridge University, 1966.

Balamon, G. Ayoub. *The People and Economics in the Sudan, 1884 to 1956*. Cambridge, Mass.: Harvard University Center for Population Studies, 1981.

Balibar, Etienne. "Racism and Nationalism." In *Race, Nation, Class: Ambiguous Identities*, edited by Balibar and Immanuel Wallerstein. London: Verso, 1991.

Balibar, Etienne, and Immanuel Wallerstein. *Race, Nation, Class: Ambiguous Identities*. London: Verso, 1991.

Barnett, Tony. *The Gezira Scheme: An Illusion of Development*. London: Frank Cass, 1977.

Barnett, Tony, and Abbas 'Abdelkarim. *Sudan: The Gezira Scheme and Agricultural Transition*. London: Frank Cass, 1991.

Baronov, David. *The African Transformation of Western Medicine and the Dynamics of Global Cultural Exchange*. Philadelphia: Temple University Press, 2008.

Barthes, Roland. *The Pleasure of the Text*. New York: Hill and Wang, 1975.

Bayart, Jean-Francois. *Global Subjects: A Political Critique of Globalization*. Cambridge: Polity Press, 2008.

———. *The Illusion of Cultural Identity*. Chicago: University of Chicago Press, 2005.

———. *The State in Africa: The Politics of the Belly*. 2nd ed. Cambridge: Polity, 2009.

Bedri, Babikr. *The Memoirs of Babikr Bedri*. Translated by Yousef Bedri and George Scott. New York: Oxford University Press, 1969.

Berman, Bruce J. "Ethnicity, Patronage and the African State: The Politics of Uncivil Nationalism." *African Affairs* 97, no. 388 (July 1998): 305–341

Bernal, Victoria. "Colonial Moral Economy and the Discipline of Development: The Gezira Scheme and 'Modern' Sudan." *Cultural Anthropology* 12, no. 4 (November 1997): 31.

Beshir, Moḥamed 'Omer. *Revolution and Nationalism in the Sudan*. London: Rex Colling, 1974

———. *The Southern Sudan: Background to Conflict*. New York: Praeger, 1968.

Bjørkelo, Anders. *Prelude to the Mahdiyya: Peasants and Traders in the Shendi Region, 1821–1885*. Cambridge: Cambridge University Press, 1989.

Boddy, Janice. *Civilizing Women: British Crusades in Colonial Sudan*. Princeton: Princeton University Press, 2007.

Bourdieu, Pierre. *Outline of a Theory of Practice*. Translated by Richard Nice. Edited by Ernest Gellner, Jack Goody, Stephen Gudeman, Michael Herzfeld, and Jonathan Parry. Cambridge Studies in Social and Cultural Anthropology. Cambridge: Cambridge University Press, 1977.

Bourdieu, Pierre, and Jean-Claude Passeron. *Reproduction in Education, Society and Culture*. 2nd ed. London: Sage, 1990.

Browne, W. G. *Travels in Africa, Egypt, and Syria, from the Year 1792 to 1798*. London: Printed for T. Cadell and W. Davies, 1806.

Burckhardt, John Lewis. *Travels in Nubia*. London: John Murray Publications, 1819.

Burleigh, Bennet. *Khartoum Campaign, 1898: or, the Re-Conquest of the Soudan*. London: Chapman and Hall, 1899.

Bushra, el-Sayed el-. "Towns in the Sudan in the Eighteenth and Early Nineteenth Centuries." *Sudan Notes and Records* 52 (1971): 7.

Chambers, William, and Robert Chambers. *Chambers's Encyclopaedia World Survey*. Oxford: Pergamon, 1966.

Chatterjee, Partha. *The Nation and Its Fragments: Colonial and Postcolonial Histories*. Princeton: Princeton University Press, 2007.

Churchill, Winston. *The River War: An Account of the Reconquest of the Sudan*. London: Eyre and Spottiswoode, 1951.

Cohn, Bernard S. *Colonialism and Its Forms of Knowledge: The British in India*. Princeton: Princeton University Press, 1996.

———. "Representing Authority in Victorian India." In *The Invention of Tradition*, edited by Eric Hobsbawn and Terence Ranger. London: Cambridge University Press, 2009.

Collins, Carole. *Colonialism and Class Struggle in Sudan*. Cambridge, Mass.: Middle East Research and Information Project, 1976.

Collins, R. O. "Sudanese Factors in the History of the Congo and Central West Africa in the Nineteenth Century." In *Sudan in Africa: Studies Presented to the First International Conference Sponsored by the Sudan Research Unit, February 1968*, edited by Yusuf Fadl Hasan. Khartoum: Khartoum University Press, 1971.

Colvin, Sir Auckland. *The Making of Modern Egypt*. London: Seeley, 1906.

Cordell, Dennis D. *Dar al-Kuti and the Last Years of the Trans-Saharan Slave Trade*. Madison: University of Wisconsin Press, 1985.

Cromer, Evelyn Baring, Earl of. *Modern Egypt*. 2 vols. New York: Macmillan, 1909.

Cross, Peter. "British Attitudes to Sudanese Labour: The Foreign Office Records as Sources for Social History." *British Journal of Middle Eastern Studies* 24, no. 2 (November 1997): 217–60.

Currie, James. "The Educational Experiment in the Anglo-Egyptian Sudan 1900–1933. Part I." *Journal of the Royal African Society* 33, no. 133 (October 1934): 10.

Daly, M. W. *Darfur's Sorrow: A History of Destruction and Genocide*. Cambridge: Cambridge University Press, 2007.

———. *Empire on the Nile: The Anglo-Egyptian Sudan, 1898–1934*. London: Cambridge University Press, 1986.

———. *Images of Empire: Photographic Sources of the British in the Sudan*. Leiden: Brill, 2005.

———. "Omdurman and Fashoda, 1898: Edited and Annotated Letters of F. R. Wingate." Bulletin, *British Society for Middle Eastern Studies* 10, no. 1 (1983): 16.

Davis, R. Hunt. "Interpreting the Colonial Period in African History." *African Affairs* 72, no. 289 (October 1973): 17.

Deemer, James (Khalid) Davidson. "Umm Durmān during the Mahdiyya." PhD diss., Harvard University, 1988.

Deng, Francis M. *War of Visions: Conflict of Identities in the Sudan*. Washington D.C.: Brookings Institution, 1995.

Deng, Francis M., and M. W. Daly. *Bonds of Silk: The Human Factor in the British Administration of the Sudan*. East Lansing: Michigan State University Press, 1989.

Deng, Francis Mading, and Prosser Gifford, eds. *The Search for Peace and Unity in the Sudan*. Washington, D.C.: Wilson Center Press, 1987.

de Waal, Alex. "Counter-Insurgency on the Cheap." *London Review of Books*, 26, no. 15 (August 2004): 25–27.

———. *Islamism and Its Enemies in the Horn of Africa*. Bloomington: Indiana University Press, 2004.

Diodorus Siculus. *Works*. Translated by C. H. Oldfather. Cambridge, Mass.: Harvard University Press, 1935.

Dirks, Nicholas B., ed. *Colonialism and Culture*. Comparative Studies in Society and History. Ann Arbor: University of Michigan Press, 1992.

———. Foreword to *Colonialism and Its Forms of Knowledge: The British in India*, edited by Bernard S. Cohn. Princeton: Princeton University Press, 1996.

Du Bois, W. E. B. *The Oxford W. E. B. Du Bois Reader*. Edited by Eric J. Sundquist. New York: Oxford University Press, 1996.

Duffield, Mark. *Maiurno: Capitalism and Rural Life in Sudan*. London: Ithaca Press, 1981.

Duncan, J. S. R. *The Sudan: A Record of Achievement*. Edinburgh: William Blackwood, 1952.

Emmert, Kirk. *Winston S. Churchill on Empire*. Durham: Carolina Academic Press, 1989.

Ewald, Janet J. *Soldiers, Traders, and Slaves: State Formation and Economic Transformation in the Greater Nile Valley, 1700–1885*. Madison: University of Wisconsin Press, 1990.

Fahmy, Khaled. *All the Pasha's Men: Mehmed Ali, His Army, and the Making of Modern Egypt*. Cambridge: Cambridge University Press, 1997.

Faulkner, Neil. *Rome: Empire of the Eagles, 735 BC–AD 476*. Harlow: Pearson Longman, 2008.

Fluehr-Lobban, Carolyn. "A Critical Anthropological Review of Race in the Nile Valley." In *Race and Identity in the Nile Valley: Ancient and Modern Perspectives*, edited by Fluehr-Lobban and Kharyssa Rhodes. Trenton, N.J.: Africa World Press, 2004.

Foucault, Michel. *Ethics: Subjectivity and Truth*. Translated by Robert Hurley. Edited by Paul Rabinow. Vol. 1, *The Essential Works of Michel Foucault*. New York: New Press, 1997.

Francis, Martin. "The Domestication of the Male? Recent Research on Nineteenth- and Twentieth-Century British Masculinity." *Historical Journal* 45, no. 3 (September 2002): 637–52.

Furnivall, John S. *Colonial Policy and Practice: A Comparative Study of Burma and Netherlands India*. New York: New York University Press, 1956.

Gaitskell, Arthur. *Gezira: A Story of Development in the Sudan*. London: Faber and Faber, 1959.

Geertz, Clifford. *Old Societies and New States*. New York: Free Press, 1963.

Giddens, Anthony. *A Contemporary Critique of Historical Materialism*. Stanford: Stanford University Press, 1995.

———. *The Nation-State and Violence*. Cambridge: Polity Press, 1985.

Gifford, Prosser, and William Roger Louis. "The Colonial State and Post-colonial Crisis." In *Decolonization and African Independence: The Transfers of Power, 1960–1980,* edited by Prosser and Louis. New Haven: Yale University Press, 1988.

Gramsci, Antonio. *Selections from the Prison Notebooks*. New York: International Publishers, 1971.

Gray, Richard. *A History of the Southern Sudan, 1839–1889*. London: Oxford University Press, 1961.

Habitat Group, ed. *Khartoum: A Profile of Urban Housing*. Zurich: School of Architecture, 1995.

Ḥajj, Muhammad Ahmad al-. "Ḥayātu B. Sa'īd: A Revolutionary Mahdist in the Western Sudan." In *Sudan in Africa: Studies Presented to the First International Conference Sponsored by the Sudan Research Unit, February 1968*, edited by Yusuf Fadl Hasan. Khartoum: Khartoum University Press, 1985.

Hake, Alfred Egmont. *The Story of Chinese Gordon*. New York: R. Worthington, 1884.

Ḥamdan, G. "The Growth and Functional Structure of Khartoum." *Geographical Review* 50, no. 1 (January 1960): 19.

Hansen, Thomas Blom, and Finn Stepputat. "States of Imagination." Introduction to *States of Imagination: Ethnographic Explorations of the Postcolonial State,* edited by Hansen and Stepputat. Durham: Duke University Press, 2001.

Ḥarir, Sharif. "Recycling the Past in the Sudan: An Overview of Political Decay." In *Short-Cut to Decay: The Case of the Sudan,* edited by Ḥarir and Terje Tvedt, 10–67. Uppsala: Nordiska Afrikaininstitutet (Scandinavian Institute of African Studies), 1994.

Helms, Mary W. *Ulysses' Sail: An Ethnographic Odyssey of Power, Knowledge, and Geographical Distance*. Princeton: Princeton University Press, 1988.

Herodotus. *The History of Herodotus*. Edited by George Rawlinson, Sir Henry Rawlinson, and Sir J. G. Wilkinson. 4 vols. New York: D. Appleton and Company, 1866–70.

Hobsbawm, Eric. "Globalization in the Age of Empire." In *Understanding Business: Markets,* edited by Vivek Sunjeta. London: Routledge, 2000.

Hobsbawm, Eric, and Terence O. Ranger, eds. *The Invention of Tradition*. 12th ed. London: Cambridge University Press, 2009.

Hobsbawm, Eric, and David J. Kertzer. "Ethnicity and Nationalism in Europe Today." *Anthropology Today* 8, no. 1 (February 1992): 6.

Hobson, John A. *Imperialism, A Study*. New York: Gordon Press, 1975.

Holt, P. M. "The Sudanese Mahdia and the Outside World: 1881–91." *Bulletin of the School of Oriental and African Studies, University of London* 21, no. 1/3 (1958): 14.

———. "Sultan Selim I and the Sudan." *Journal of African History* 8, no. 1 (1967): 4.

Home, Robert K. *Of Planting and Planning: The Making of British Colonial Cities*. London: Routledge, 1996.

Homer. *The Iliad*. Translated by Richard Lattimore. Chicago: University of Chicago Press, 1951.

———. *The Odyssey*. Translated by Walter Shewring. New York: Oxford University Press, 1986.

Horkheimer, Max, and Theodor W. Adorno. *Dialectic of Enlightenment*. New York: Continuum, 1993.

Hunter, James Davidson. *Culture Wars: The Struggle to Define America*. New York: Basic Books, 1991.

Hunwick, John. *Timbuktu and Songhay: Al-sa'di's T'rīkh al-Sudan down to 1613 and Other Contemporary Documents*. Leiden: Brill, 1999.

Hunwick, John, and Eve Troutt Powell, eds. *The African Diaspora in the Mediterranean Lands of Islam*. Princeton: Markus Weiner Publishers, 2002.

———. "The Same but Different: Africans in Slavery in the Mediterranean Muslim World." Introduction to *The African Diaspora in the Mediterranean Lands of Islam*, edited by Hunwick and Eve Troutt Powell. Princeton: Markus Weiner, 2002.

———. *Timbuktu and the Songhay Empire: Al-Sa'di's* Ta'rīkh al-Sudan *Down to 1613 and Other Contemporary Documents*. Leiden: Brill, 1999.

Ibn Khaldun. *The Muqaddimah: An Introduction to History*. Translated by Franz Rosenthal. Edited by N. J. Dawood. Princeton: Princeton University Press, 1969.

Ibrahim, 'Abdullahi Ali. *Manichaean Delirium: Decolonizing the Judiciary and Islamic Renewal in the Sudan*. Princeton: Princeton University Press, 1996.

———. *Al-ṣirā'a bayna al-Mahdi wa-al-'Ulamā'*. Khartoum: University of Khartoum, Sudan Research Unit, 1968.

Ibrahim, Ḥassan Ahmed. *Sayyid 'Abd al-Raḥman al-Mahdi: A Study of Neo-Mahdism in the Sudan, 1899–1956*. Leiden: Brill, 2004.

Idris, Amir H. *Sudan's Civil War: Slavery, Race, and Formational Identities*. Lewiston, N.Y.: Edwin Mellen Press, 2001.

Johnson, Douglas H. "Recruitment and Entrapment in Private Slave Armies: The Structure of the Zara'ib in Southern Sudan." *Slavery and Abolition: A Journal of Slave and Post-slave Studies* 13, no. 1 (1992): 162–73.

———. *The Root Causes of Sudan's Civil Wars*. Bloomington: Indiana University Press, 2003.

Johnston, Sir Harry Hamilton. *A History of the Colonization of Africa by Alien Races*. Cambridge: University Press, 1899.

Juergensmeyer, Mark. *The New Cold War? Religious Nationalism Confronts the Secular State*. Berkeley: University of California Press, 1993.

Kapeteijns, Lidwein, and Jay Spaulding. "Pre-colonial Trade between States in Eastern Sudan c. 1700–c. 1900." In *Economy and Class in Sudan*, edited by Norman O'Neill and Jay O'Brien. Aldershot, UK: Avebury, 1988.

Karsani, Awad al-Sid al-. "The Establishment of Neo-Mahdism in the Western Sudan, 1920–1936." *African Affairs* 86, no. 344 (July 1987): 19.

Kenny, J. T. "Climate, Race, and Imperial Authority: The Symbolic Landscape of the British Hill Station in India." *Annals of the Association of American Geographers*, 85 (December 1995): 694–714.

Khair, Aḥmad. *Kifah Jil* (A Generation's Struggle). Khartoum, Sudan: al-Dar al-Sudania, 1980.

Khalid, Mansour. "The External Factors in the Sudanese Conflict." In *The Search for Peace and Unity in the Sudan*, edited by Francis Mading Deng and Prosser Gifford. Washington D.C.: Wilson Center Press, 1987.

———. *Al-nukhba al-sudania wa idman al-fashal* (The Sudanese Elite and the Infatuation with Failure). Cairo: Dar al-amin, 1993.

Khalil, M. I. "The Legal System of the Sudan." *International and Comparative Law Quarterly* 20, no. 4 (October 1971): 20.

King Edward the Seventh. *Lord Kitchener of Khartoum: A Biography*. London: James Nisbet and Company, 1914.

Kipling, Rudyard. *The Five Nations*. New York: Doubleday, 1903.

Kok, Peter Nyot. *Governance and Conflict in the Sudan, 1985–1995: Analysis, Evaluation and Documentation*. Hamburg: Deutsches Orient-Institut, 1996.

Kordofani, Isma'il 'Abd al-Qadir al-. *S'ādat al-mustahdi bi sirat al-Imam al-Mahdi*. Khartoum: al-Majlis al-Qawmi li Rayat al-Adab wa al-Finon, 1972.

Kramer, Robert. "Holy City on the Nile: Omdurman, 1885–1898." PhD diss., Northwestern University, 1991.

Krump, Theodoro. "The Sudanese Travels of Theodoro Krump." Translated by Jay Spaulding, 2001. http://www.kean.edu/~jspauldi/krump2home.html.

Kurita, Yoshiko. *'Ali 'Abd al-Latif wa thawrat 1924: Bahth fi masadir al-thawra al-sudaniyya*. Translated by Majdi al-Na'im. Cairo: Markaz al-Dirasat al-Sudaniyya, 1997.

Lang, Jeanie. *Story of General Gordon*. London: T. C. and E. C. Jack, 1900.

Lange, Matthew. *Lineages of Despotism and Development: British Colonialism and State Power*. Chicago: University of Chicago Press, 2009.

Lesch, Anne Mosely. *The Sudan: Contested National Identities*. Bloomington: Indiana University Press, 1998.

Lovejoy, Paul E. *Transformations in Slavery: A History of Slavery in Africa*. Cambridge: Cambridge University Press, 2000.

Low, Sidney. *Egypt in Transition*. New York: Macmillan, 1914.

Macaulay, Thomas Babington. *The Works of Lord Macaulay Complete*. Edited by Lady Trevelyan. 8 vols. London: Longmans, Green, 1879.

MacMichael, Harold. *A History of the Arabs in the Sudan; and Some Account of the People Who Preceded Them and of Tribes Inhabiting Darfur*. 1922. Reprint, New York: Barnes and Noble, 1967.

———. *The Sudan*. London: Ernest Benn Limited, 1954.

Mahdi, al-Sadiq al-, ed. *Jihad fi sabiel al-istiglal* (Jihad for Independence). Khartoum: Matbaat al-Tamadon al-Maḥdūda, 1986.

Mahmoud, Fatima Babiker. *The Sudanese Bourgeoisie: Vanguard of Development?* London: Zed Books, 1984.

Mamdani, Maḥmood. *Citizen and Subject: Contemporary Africa and the Legacy of Late Colonialism*. Princeton: Princeton University Press, 1996.

———. *Good Muslim, Bad Muslim: America, the Cold War, and the Roots of Terror.* New York: Pantheon Books, 2004.

———. *Saviors and Survivors: Darfur, Politics, and the War on Terror.* New York Pantheon Books, 2009.

———. *When Victims Become Killers: Colonialism, Nativism, and Genocide in Rwanda.* Princeton: Princeton University Press, 2001.

Marx, Karl. *Capital: A Critical Analysis of Capitalist Production*. Translated by Samuel Moore and Edward Averling. Edited by Frederick Engels. 2 vols. New York: Humbolt Publishers, 1890.

Mazrui, Ali A. *Africa's International Relations: The Diplomacy of Dependency and Change*. London: Heinemann, 1977.

———. "The Multiple Marginality of the Sudan." In *Sudan in Africa: Studies Presented to the First International Conference Sponsored by the Sudan Research Unit, February 1968,* edited by Yousif Fadul Hassan. Khartoum: Khartoum University Press, 1971.

McHugh, Neil. *Holymen of the Blue Nile: The Making of an Arab-Islamic Community in the Nilotic Sudan, 1500–1850*. Evanston: Northwestern University Press, 1994.

Meillassoux, Claude. *The Anthropology of Slavery: The Womb of Iron and Gold.* Chicago: University of Chicago Press, 1991.

Memmi, Albert. *The Colonizer and the Colonized*. Boston: Beacon Press, 1991.

Metcalf, Thomas R. *An Imperial Vision: Indian Architecture and Britain's Raj.* Berkeley: University of California Press, 1989.

Miller, Christopher L. *Blank Darkness: Africanist Discourse in French*. Chicago: University of Chicago Press, 1985.

Mire, Lawrence. "Al-Zubayr Pasha and the Zariba Based Slave Trade in the Bahr al-Ghazal, 1855–1879." In *Slaves and Slavery in Muslim Africa,* vol. 2, *The Servile Estate,* edited by John Ralph Willis. London: Routledge, 1986.

Mitchell, Timothy. *Colonising Egypt.* Cambridge Middle East Library. New York: Cambridge University Press, 1988.

Mohamed Ahmed, 'Abdel Ghaffar. "Management of Crisis in the Sudan: Alternative Models for Action." *Centre for Development Studies of the University of Bergen,* Proceeding of the Bergen Forum, February 23–24, 1989.

Moorehead, Alan. *The Blue Nile*. New York: Harper and Row, 1962.

Myers, Garth Andrew. "Intellectual of Empire: Eric Dutton and Hegemony in British Africa." *Annals of the Association of American Geographers* 88, no. 1 (March 1998): 27.

Na'im, 'Abdullahi Aḥmed an-. "National Unity and the Diversity of Identities." In *The Search for Peace and Unity in the Sudan,* edited by Francis M. Deng and Prosser Gifford. Washington, D.C.: Wilson Center Press, 1987.

Nandy, Ashis. *Exiled at Home: Comprising, At the Edge of Psychology, The Intimate Enemy, Creating a Nationality*. Delhi: Oxford University Press, 1998.

———. *The Intimate Enemy: Loss and Recovery of Self under Colonialism*. Delhi: Oxford University Press, 1998.

Niblock, Tim. *Class and Power in Sudan: The Dynamics of Sudanese Politics, 1898–1985*. Albany: State University of New York Press, 1987.

Nur, Mo'awia Muḥammad. *Qisas wa khawatir*. Khartoum: Khartoum University Press, n.d.

O'Fahey, R. S. "Islam and Ethnicity in the Sudan." *Journal of Religion in Africa* 26, no. 3 (1996): 258–67.

O'Fahey, R. S., and J. L. Spaulding. *Kingdoms of the Sudan*. Studies in African History, no. 9. London: Methuen, 1974.

Ohrwalder, Joseph, and Sir Francis Reginald Wingate. *Ten Years' Captivity in the Mahdi's Camp, 1882–1892: From the Original Manuscripts of Father Joseph Ohrwalder*. 9th ed. London: Sampson Low, Marston and Company, 1893.

O'Neill, Norman. "Class and Politics in the Modern History of Sudan." In *Economy and Class in Sudan*, edited by O'Neill and Jay O'Brien. Avebury, UK: Aldershot, 1988.

O'Neill, Norman, and Jay O'Brien. *Economy and Class in Sudan*. Avebury, UK: Aldershot, 1988.

Pallme, Ignatius. *Travels in Kordofan: Embracing a Description of That Province of Egypt, and of Some of the Bordering Countries, with a Review of the Present State of the Commerce in Those Countries, of the Habits and Customs of the Inhabitants, as Also an Account of the Slave-Hunts Taking Place under the Government of Mehemed Ali*. London: J. Madden and Company, 1844.

Peel, Sidney. *The Binding of the Nile and the New Soudan*. London: Edward Arnold, 1904.

Polanyi, Karl. *The Great Transformation: The Political and Economic Origins of Our Time*. Boston: Beacon Press, 2001.

Powell, Eve M. Troutt. *A Different Shade of Colonialism: Egypt, Great Britain, and the Mastery of the Sudan*. Berkeley: University of California Press, 2003.

———. "The Silence of the Slaves." Introduction to *The African Diaspora in the Mediterranean Lands of Islam*, edited by John Hunwick and Powell. Princeton: Markus Weiner Publishers, 2002.

Roberts, Richard L. *Warriors, Merchants, and Slaves: The State and the Economy in the Middle Niger Valley, 1700–1914*. Stanford: Stanford University Press, 1987.

Robertson, Roland. "Globalization: Time-Space and Homogeneity-Heterogeneity." In *Global Modernities*, edited by Mike Featherstone, Scott Lash, and Roland Robertson. London: Sage Publications, 1995.

Robinson, David. *Muslim Societies in African History*. New York: Cambridge University Press, 2004.

Ruay, Deng D. Akol. *The Politics of Two Sudans: The South and the North, 1821–1969*. Uppsala: Nordiska Afrikainstitutet, 1994.

Sabry, Hussein Zulfakar. *Sovereignty for Sudan*. London: Ithaca Press, 1982.

Sa'dī, Abderrahman al-. *Ta'rīkh al-Sudan*.

Said, Edward W. *Culture and Imperialism*. New York: Random House, 1993.

———. *Orientalism*. New York: Vintage Books, 1979.

Salih, Mahjoub Mohamed. *Al-sahfa al-sudaniyya fi nisf qurn*. Khartoum: University of Khartoum Press, 1971.

Salomon, Noah. *Undoing the Mahdiyya: British Colonialism as Religious Reform in Anglo-Egyptian Sudan, 1898–1914*. Chicago: University of Chicago, Martin Marty Center, 2004.

Sartre, Jean-Paul. *Anti-Semite and Jew: An Exploration of the Etiology of Hate*. New York: Schocken Books, 1995.

Sayyid-Marsot, Afaf Lutfi. *Egypt in the Reign of Muḥammad 'Ali*. Cambridge: Cambridge University Press, 1984.

Schweinfurth, Georg August. *The Heart of Africa: Three Years' Travels and Adventures in the Unexplored Regions of Central Africa from 1868 to 1871*. Translated by Ellen E. Frewer. Chicago: Afro-Am Press, 1969.

Sconyers, David. "Servant or Saboteur? The Sudan Political Service during the Crucial Decade: 1946–1956." Bulletin, *British Society for Middle Eastern Studies* 14, no. 1 (1987): 42–51.

Shahi, Ahmed al-. "A Noah's Ark: The Continuity of the Khatmiyya Order in Northern Sudan." *British Society for Middle Eastern Studies* 8, no. 1 (1981): 16.

Sharkey, Heather J. "A Century in Print: Arabic Journalism and Nationalism in Sudan: 1899–1999." *International Journal of Middle East Studies* 31, no. 31 (November 1999): 18.

———. *Living with Colonialism: Nationalism and Culture in the Anglo-Egyptian Sudan*. Berkeley: University of California Press, 2003.

Shaw, Flora L. "The Story of Zebehr Pasha, as Told by Himself." *Contemporary Review* 52 (1887).

Shibeika, Mekki. "The Expansionist Movement of Khedive Ismail to the Lakes." In *Sudan in Africa, Studies Presented to the First International Conference Sponsored by the Sudan Research Unit, February 1968*, edited by Yusuf Fadl Hasan. Khartoum: Khartoum University Press, 1971.

Shukri, Muhammad Fouad. *Misr wa al-Sudan: Tarikh wahdat Wadi al-Nil al-siyasiya fi al-qarn al-tas'i 'ashar, 1820–1899*. Cairo: Dar al-Ma'arif, 1963.

Sikainga, Aḥmad Alawad. *City of Steel and Fire: A Social History of Atbara, Sudan's Railway Town, 1906–1984*. Portsmouth, N.H.: Heinemann, 2002.

———. *Slaves into Workers: Emancipation and Labor in Colonial Sudan*. Austin: University of Texas Press, 1996.

Slatin, Rudolf Carl. *Fire and Sword in the Sudan: A Personal Narrative of Fighting and Serving the Dervishes 1879–1895*. Translated by F. R. Wingate. London: Edward Arnold, 1903.

Smith, Iain R. *The Emin Pasha Relief Expedition, 1886–1890*. Oxford: Clarendon Press, 1972.

Snowden, Frank M. *Blacks in Antiquity: Ethiopians in the Greco-Roman Experience*. Cambridge, Mass.: Belknap Press of Harvard University Press, 1970.

Spaulding, Jay. *The Heroic Age in Sinnār*. Trenton, N.J.: Red Sea Press, 2007.

———. "Precolonial Islam in the Eastern Sudan." In *The History of Islam in Africa,* edited by Nehemia Levtzion and Randall L. Pouwels. Athens: Ohio University Press, 2000.

Steevens, George Warrington. *With Kitchener to Khartoum*. Edinburgh: W. Blackwood, 1909.

Ṭayeb, 'Abdullah el-. "On the Abyssinian Hijrah." *Sudan Notes and Records* 2, no. 2 (1998): 5.

Theobald, A. B. *'Ali Dinar: Last Sultan of Darfur, 1889–1916*. London: Longmans, Green, 1965.

Thiong'o, Ngũgi Wa. *Decolonising the Mind: The Politics of Language in African Literature*. London: James Currey, 1986.

Tignor, Robert L. Introduction to *Napoleon in Egypt: Al-Jabarti's Chronicle of the French Occupation, 1798,* by 'Abd al-Raḥman al-Jabarti. Princeton: Markus Wiener, 1993.

Tilly, Charles. *The Politics of Collective Violence*. Cambridge: Cambridge University Press, 2003.

Tocqueville, Alexis de. *Democracy in America*. Translated by Arthur Goldhammer. Library of America, no. 147. New York: Penguin Putnam, 2004.

Trémaux, Pierre. *Voyages to Eastern Sudan and to Septentrionale Africa (1847–1854).* Translated by Richard A. Lobban Jr., Tissaigna N'Dem, and Bénédicte Chupin. Cairo: Al-Fatima Printing House, 2005.

Tripp, Charles. *Islam and the Moral Economy: The Challenge of Capitalism*. Cambridge: Cambridge University Press, 2006.

Veer, Peter van der. *Religious Nationalism: Hindus and Muslims in India*. Berkeley: University of California Press, 1994.

Vezzadini, Elena. "The 1924 Revolution: Hegemony, Resistance, and Nationalism in the Colonial Sudan." PhD thesis, University of Bergen, 2007.

Voll, John O. "The Eastern Sudan, 1822 to the Present." In *The History of Islam in Africa,* edited by Nehemia Levtzion and Randall L. Pouwels, 153–67. Athens: Ohio University Press, 2000.

Wai, Dustan M. *The African-Arab Conflict in the Sudan*. New York: Africana Publishing, 1981.

———. "African-Arab Relations: From Slavery to Petro-Jihad." *Issue: A Journal of Opinion* (African Studies Association) 13 (1984): 4.

Wallerstein, Immanuel. "The Construction of Peoplehood: Racism, Nationalism, Ethnicity." In *Race, Nation, Class: Ambiguous Identities,* edited by Etienne Balibar and Wallerstein. London: Verso, 1991.

Warburg, Gabriel. *Islam, Sectarianism and Politics in Sudan since the Mahdiyya*. London: Hurst, 2003.

———. *The Sudan under Wingate: Administration in the Anglo-Egyptian Sudan, 1899–1916*. London: Frank Cass, 1971.

Weber, Max. *The Protestant Ethic and the Spirit of Capitalism*. New York: Courier Dover Publications, 2003.

Wingate, Francis Reginald. *Mahdism and the Egyptian Sudan: Being an Account of the*

Rise and Progress of Mahdism, and the Subsequent Events in the Sudan to Present Time. London: Macmillan, 1891.

Wingate, Roland. *Wingate of the Sudan: The Life and Times of General Sir Reginald Wingate, Maker of the Anglo-Egyptian Sudan*. London: John Murray, 1955.

Wilson, Salim [Chatashil Masha Katish]. *I Was A Slave*. London: Stanley Paul, 1939.

Woodward, Peter. "In the Footsteps of Gordon: The Sudan Government and the Rise of Sayyid Sir 'Abd al-Raḥman al-Mahdi, 1915–1935." *African Affairs* 84, no. 334 (January 1985): 12.

———. "The Multiple Marginality Multiplied." *Sudan Studies Association Newsletter* 22, no. 3 (2003): 4–8.

———. *Sudan, 1898–1989: The Unstable State*. Boulder: Lynne Rienner, 1990.

Yeoh, Brenda S. A. *Contesting Space: Power Relations and the Urban Built Environment in Colonial Singapore*. New York: Oxford University Press, 1996.

Young, Crawford. *The African Colonial State in Comparative Perspective*. New Haven: Yale University Press, 1994.

———. "The Colonial State and Post-colonial Crisis." In *Decolonization and African Independence: The Transfers of Power, 1960–1980*, edited by Prosser Gifford and William Louis. New Haven: Yale University Press, 1988.

Zald, Mayer N. "Theological Crucibles: Social Movements in and of Religion." *Review of Religious Research* 23, no. 4 (June 1982): 19.

Ziegler, Philip. *Omdurman*. New York: Dorset Press, 1973.

Zulfo, 'Ismat Hasan. *Karari: The Sudanese Account of the Battle of Omdurman*. Translated by Peter Clark. London: Frederick Warne, 1980.

Index

Abdullahi A. Gallab, assistant professor of African and African American studies and religious studies at Arizona State University, is the author of *The First Islamist Republic: Development and Disintegration of Islamism in the Sudan*.

www.ingramcontent.com/pod-product-compliance
Lightning Source LLC
Chambersburg PA
CBHW020529270326
41927CB00006B/497
* 9 7 8 0 8 1 3 0 4 4 4 6 0 *